THE WRISTWATCH HANDBOOK

A Comprehensive Guide to Mechanical Wristwatches

THE WRISTWATCH HANDBOOK

A Comprehensive Guide to Mechanical Wristwatches

Ryan Schmidt

ACC Art Books

CONTENTS

Foreword

One of the most common questions I receive as a watch specialist is, "Where do I start to learn about collecting watches?".

Finally, I have an answer. The book you now have in your hands. As a resource for the new collector, this book is the gateway to informed wristwatch collecting that will open up the world of watches to you in a concise and enjoyable way.

Over the past five years, the growth in scholarship of wristwatch collecting has moved into hyper speed. Wristwatch collecting is a relatively young collecting category, only becoming popular over the last 30 years. In fact, the first auction catalogues primarily dedicated to wristwatches rather than pocket watches were not seen until the mid-1980s.

Since then, tastes and trends have delivered wristwatch collecting to the pinnacle of art collecting circles and now wristwatches, both modern and vintage, are proudly placed next to Warhols and Rothkos at auction exhibitions around the world. With this growth, the scholarship has grown exponentially as more information from the specialist watch community is shared digitally and in print publications.

As more people feel comfortable buying high-end watches at previously unimaginable prices, it has become increasingly clear that people buy watches for incredibly diverse reasons. Some collect for their love of micromechanical beauty, others for the history that lives within many of these timepieces. Some collect out of nostalgia or for investment, and some simply for the thrill of the hunt.

There are as many different places to learn about watches and to build one's watch knowledge as there are reasons for people to collect watches. Blogs, auction catalogues, local retailers, brand websites, factory visits, and fellow collectors are often cited as great ways to get started. Many books have also been written by experts on particular brands and specific wristwatch collecting categories. However few books have been written in recent years that capture the spirit of modern day collecting and educate new buyers in what options there are to buy across both the modern and vintage worlds.

If you own more than one watch, or aspire to own more than one watch, you have the spirit of a collector and need this book as a resource. For the knowledgeable and experienced collector this book opens up the door to other collecting categories that may not have been of interest to you before.

This book brilliantly mixes vintage and modern watches in a visually accessible way with useful and informative reflections on what makes watches unique and special. The diagrams are especially useful and a fun way to educate the reader in how watches work and the correct nomenclature for watch parts.

As one of the first books that mixes the traditional watchmaker with the rise of the modern independent watchmaker, you will be surprised to see the juxtaposition of old and new together. Many surprises await you, and for collectors old and new, it is a reminder that within the world of wristwatch collecting, an educated and informed eye makes all the difference.

On a personal note, when I first saw Ryan attend watch auction exhibitions, it became abundantly clear that his passion and knowledge for watches put him in a class of his own. His countless hours spent closely inspecting all types of watches, from modern Patek Philippes to vintage OMEGAs, made it clear that his appreciation and thirst for knowledge of all types of wristwatches made him a scholar of the highest order hungry to find answers to horological mysteries from the past and present.

John Reardon
International Head of Watches, Christie's

Preface

The journey of the mechanical watch enthusiast is a long and winding one. It might start with a childhood gift, or an inherited timepiece, your first purchase, or a glimpse of something unusual in a magazine or through the window of a boutique. Wherever it starts, there is something in that experience that captures your imagination and instils in you a great sense of wonder. There is something undeniably special about these little machines; something that, even after you have moved further along in your journey and gained a greater understanding of the mechanical principles, still brings you back to that initial sense of wonder.

Watch enthusiasm is a journey of discovery, with each answered question unfolding into new unanswered ones. It is a journey that has no defined end. You will be a rare specimen indeed if you find that your journey has reached its conclusion. The watch industry is a hotbed of creativity, and for every nuance in the superficial look and feel of a watch there is just as much, if not more, innovation pulsing, spinning and ticking from within. From balance spring material, to torque distribution, to enamel firing, there is always something new to point at and ask: "what is *that*?"

So where does this book come in? The Wristwatch Handbook is designed to be a map and compass for your own personal journey. It will provide you with a comprehensive understanding of the mechanical wristwatch. Comprehensive but not *exhaustive*; nothing in horology truly

is. Consider this book as the foundation upon which you can launch yourself further into the unreturnable depths of your passion, or as a gust of wind that blows the dust from the knowledge you have already acquired along your way. The book starts with an exploration of the internal anatomy of the mechanical wristwatch, covering the various elements of the movement from the power source to its regulation. We move on to explore the vast array of mechanical wristwatch "complications", or functions; every conceivable one. We cover the timekeeping complications as well as some of the more esoteric and plain bizarre ones; from the perpetual calendar, to the aneroid barometer, to the watch that doesn't tell the time. Rather than focus on 10 or 20 of the leading brands, the book is brand agnostic, using over 300 illustrations from more than 90 brands. It doesn't matter what price it retails for, what logo it has on the dial, or what holding company owns the logo, if it does a great job of illustrating a given concept, it gets the attention it deserves. By the time you reach the end of the book you will be able to decipher even the most complicated dial and have a fair sense of what is going on beneath it.

Above all I hope that you simply enjoy the book; that it brings you something new and something familiar; that it helps you plot the course for the next stage in your journey and for your next watch. There is *always* the next watch.

Ryan Schmidt

SECTION 1

BASIC WATCH MECHANICS and the WATCH MOVEMENT

On the face of it, two watches might look very much the same. However, behind one dial might exist a world of innovation while behind the other might exist a perfectly decent but uninspired movement. There is more than one way to skin a cat, as they say, and some of the more impressive techniques take many watchmaking years to master, and are lengthy and costly to execute, despite barely improving upon their simpler counterparts. From the multi-axis tourbillon to the fusée and chain, some might argue that these exotic mechanical beasts are redundant technologies, certainly when considering the cost versus the theoretical benefits that they add to the movement. Nevertheless the complexity and subsequent exclusivity of these mechanisms make them desirable to the collector and objects of lust for the enthusiast. This section will distinguish, in detail, the mechanical from the battery-powered quartz movement, and in doing so, how each is achieved will be better appreciated.

The OMEGA De Ville Central Tourbillon Co-Axial Chronometer is impressive in action. Yet in terms of functionality it gives the wearer nothing more than the time. © 2016 OMEGA SA

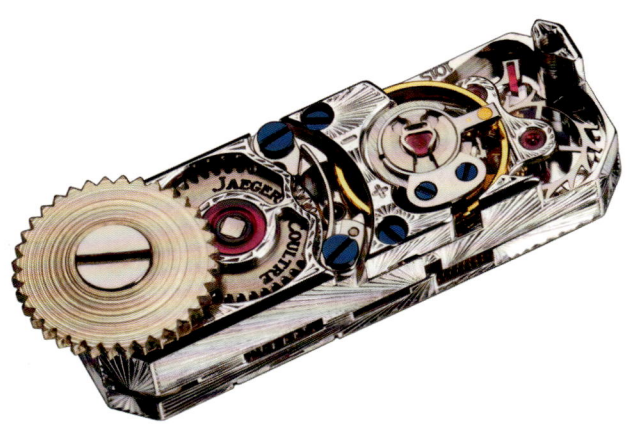

Top: The Jaeger-LeCoultre 101 is the world's smallest mechanical movement and features just 98 parts.　© 2016 Jaeger-LeCoultre

Above: The Calibre 182 as found in the Jaeger-LeCoultre Hybris Mechanica à Grande Sonnerie. Although the movement does little more than tell the time, its 1,503 components allow it to do so both visually and audibly with great innovation and concealed complexity.　© 2016 Jaeger-LeCoultre

Right: A Patek Philippe Calibre R TO 27 QR SID LU C as seen in the Sky Moon Tourbillon ref.6002 comprises 751 immaculately hand-finished parts.　© 2016 Patek Philippe SA

1.1 Overview of a Watch Movement

A true watch enthusiast will naturally want to understand what watches can do. To understand what watches can do one needs to appreciate how they work. You are now entering Mechanical Watch Country. The language is a mix of English, French, German and Latin, and is spoken with a heavy technical dialect.

The Mechanical Movement
A mechanical movement operates without a battery. It varies in complexity and can be constructed from fewer than 100 parts or well in excess of 1,000! A mechanical movement comprises four core elements: the power source, transmission, distribution and regulation. Each of these elements will be covered in detail throughout Section 1.

Despite the busy, almost chaotic appearance of a watch movement, the four core elements are always present. The watch is wound and it charges a coiled mainspring — the power source. The mainspring doesn't instantly release because it is connected to a gear train, which is the transmission element. The gear train is a series of wheels and pinions held together by arbors, the most active of which are pivoted by jewelled bearings to avoid rapid deterioration from friction. Imagine this configuration to be like a tree (arbor is the Latin word for tree) — the pinion surrounds

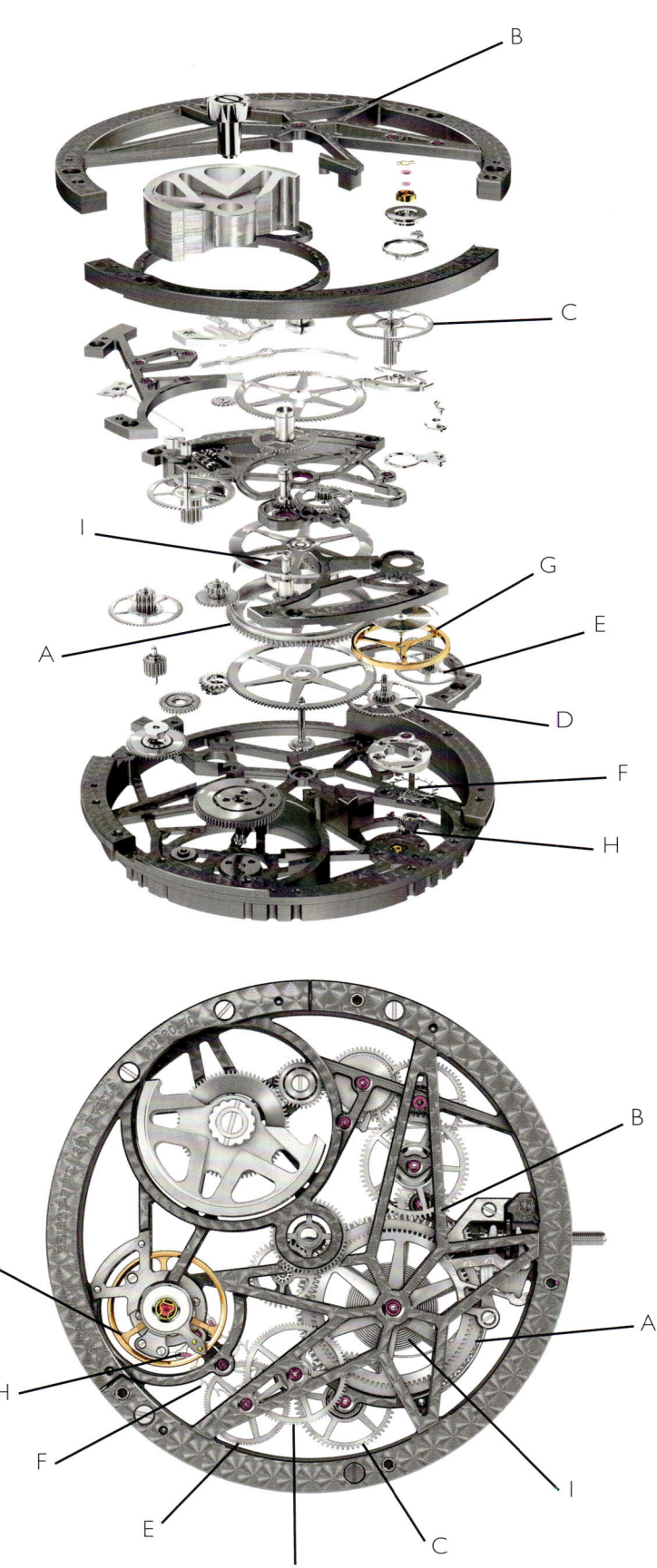

the base of the arbor like bark around the trunk of a tree, the foliage at the top is the wheel. If you want to spin the 'tree' you grip the bark and spin it at the trunk. Now imagine that the wheel at the top of the arbor is attached to the pinion of the next arbor. Spinning the first one would make the second one move as well. The driving wheels are bigger than the pinions that are being driven, therefore the speed of each wheel increases as the motion passes along the gear train. This is the purpose of the transmission; to convert the unwinding of the mainspring into a series of increasing rates (hours / minutes / seconds) using predetermined ratios to increase the gearing in specific proportions. So while the mainspring might take 12 hours to perform one rotation, the escape wheel will do it in less than 10 seconds. The distribution and regulation are responsible for ensuring the accuracy of the various rotations and consist of a lever

Top: While the majority of today's manually wound movements feature an array of independent Lépine-style bridges, the three-quarter plate is commonly found on the bridge-side of many Saxon movements, as beautifully demonstrated by Glashütte Original.
© 2016 Glashütter Uhrenbetrieb GmbH

Right: An exploded and dial-side view of the Roger Dubuis Excalibur Automatic Skeleton movement showing the barrel (A), the main bridge (B), the second to fourth wheels (C-E), the escape wheel (F), the balance wheel (G), the pallet fork (H) and the mainspring (I). This particular movement separates the main train from the motion work at the centre of the dial. It also features an automatic micro-rotor with its own gear train leading to the barrel. © 2016 Roger Dubuis

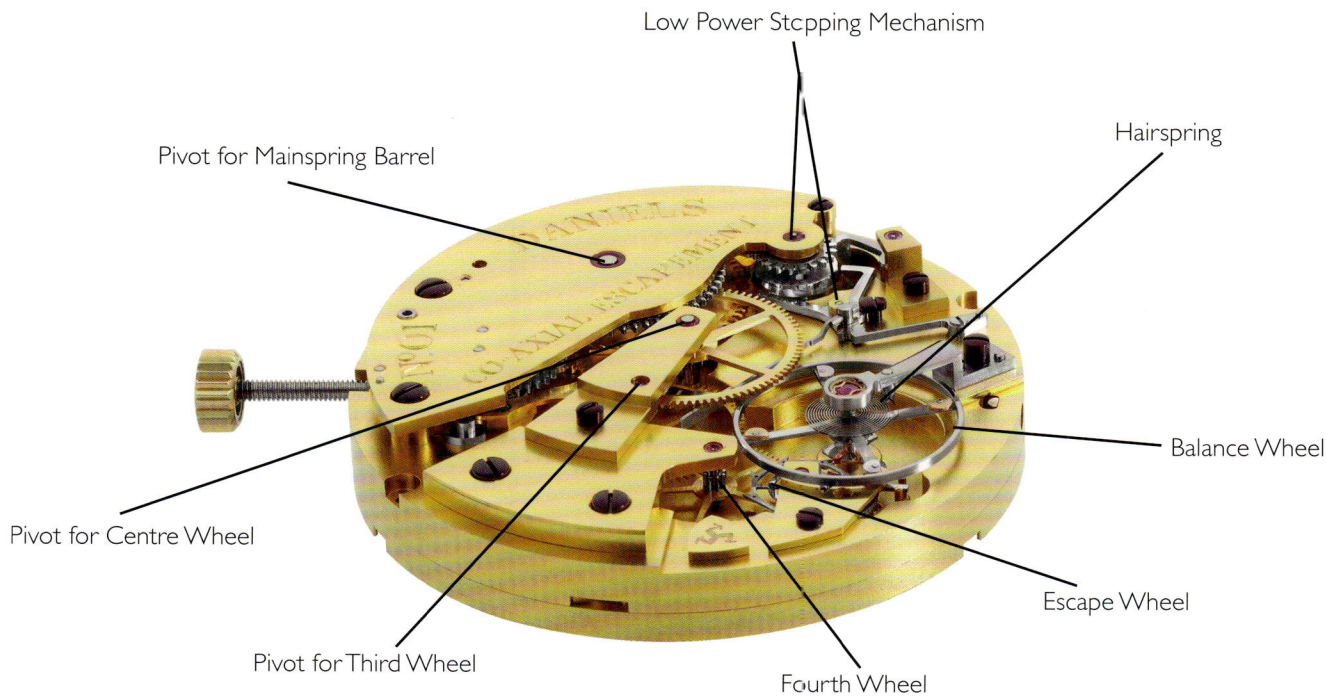

Low Power Stepping Mechanism

Hairspring

Pivot for Mainspring Barrel

Balance Wheel

Pivot for Centre Wheel

Escape Wheel

Pivot for Third Wheel

Fourth Wheel

(usually in the shape of a two-pronged pallet fork) channelling power impulses that cause a balance wheel and hairspring to oscillate. The pallet fork is like a gate latch, which opens and closes, allowing for the escape wheel to release the energy of the mainspring, and in doing so it provides an impulse to the balance wheel so that the oscillating continues. It's a clever

tied loop; so long as the mainspring power is refreshed, it will go on for a very long time (for example, until the lubricant runs dry or the watch is dropped onto a hard floor). The distribution and regulation components: the escape wheel, lever, balance wheel and hairspring — are often referred to collectively as the escapement.

How do the hour, minute and seconds hands on the dial work? The minute and seconds hands can be mounted to the axis of the second and fourth wheels respectively. This is why the wheel ratios are important and why the more traditional

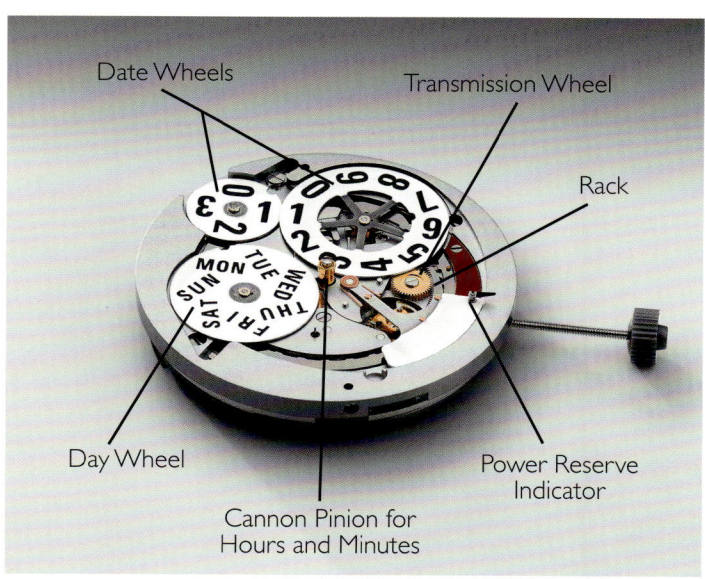

Date Wheels

Transmission Wheel

Rack

Day Wheel

Power Reserve Indicator

Cannon Pinion for Hours and Minutes

Top: The bridge side of the Daniels Anniversary movement. The movement features a co-axial escapement and has a mechanism that halts the movement when the mainspring reaches a level of power that would affect accuracy. © 2012 Roger W Smith

Left: The dial side of the Carl F. Bucherer CFB A1000 movement, showing the two date wheels and the day wheel, which can be seen through apertures on the dial. The rack that runs from the transmission wheel at 3 o'clock can also be seen. The transmission wheel is coupled to the mainspring barrel. As the barrel (and transmission wheel) winds and unwinds the rack causes the white plate to cover the red plate; this is the power reserve indicator, which is visible through an aperture. © 2015 Carl F. Bucherer

mechanical watches have a central minute hand and a subsidiary second dial. Alternative details, such as a central seconds hand, would require the movement to be redesigned.

The hour hand is more complicated and is achieved by a reduction gearing known as the motion work (see Chapter 1.3).

All of these component parts: the wheels, pinions, springs and levers — are sandwiched together between a main plate and a series of bridges. The main plate has a 'dial side' and a 'bridge side' (or movement side). The dial side of a basic movement is fairly featureless, save for some of the keyless work, motion work and perhaps some perlage finishing (overlapping circular patterns, the term perlage comes from the description of bubbles huddling together against the side of a champagne glass). The bridge side is where the party takes place, where the components come together and where the balance wheel often clears the dance floor. It is this view of the movement that is so captivating and convinces us that there is something of a soul somewhere in there.

Manual vs Automatic

A mechanical watch might state 'automatic' on the dial. While this is often used to indicate that the movement is mechanical (and therefore not to be confused with a quartz), it is in fact an *additional* complication compared with a basic manually wound mechanical movement.

With a *manually* wound movement, the mainspring is wound by hand. When dealing with clocks and vintage pocket watches, the winding is often performed with a key, but in the wristwatch the winding is typically via the crown. There are one or two interesting variants on the basic

---

The Ulysse Nardin Freak Blue Phantom. There is no winding crown, instead the bezel is turned to set the time and the caseback is turned to wind the watch. The lip at 6 o'clock acts as a lock mechanism. Confused about the time? It's 10:10; the minute hand is mounted to the entire gear train.

© 2016 Ulysse Nardin SA

The A. Lange & Söhne Lange 31, with a power reserve of 31 days, as tracked on the large 280° reserve indicator at 3 o'clock. The movement reveals a massive double-mainspring barrel which dominates the view. Notice no winding transmission. The barrel is wound with a key rather than via the crown and a winding plate is added to the movement over the vacant space at 9 – 12 o'clock.

© 2015 A. Lange & Söhne

manual wind mechanism worth noting, such as the Ulysse Nardin Freak, which is wound and set by rotating the caseback and bezel; or the A. Lange & Söhne 31, which runs for 31 days and requires a key to be inserted into the caseback in order to wind it.

So how does it work? It is relatively simple; take a manually wound movement and add to it a set of transmission gears that wind the mainspring by way of an oscillating rotor. The rotor is typically anchored concentrically to the movement, however as we shall see in the next chapter, there are some rather exotic alternatives. As the watch is moved, the kinetic energy of the wearer causes the rotor to oscillate, which engages the winding mechanism. Therefore, in addition to being able to wind the watch by hand, which is still the best approach when resetting a stopped automatic, the daily active movement of its wearer ought to be enough to keep an automatic watch powered.

Above: The Unitas manual wind movement as viewed through the caseback of a MeisterSinger No.02. A benefit of the manual wind movement is that the main plate is not obscured by an automatic rotor. © 2015 MeisterSinger GmbH & Co. KG

Left: The Eterna Spherodrive automatic movement with the large oscillating rotor obscuring half of the main plate. On close examination five ball bearings can be seen at the centre; Eterna introduced these back in 1948 and have since incorporated them into their logo. © 2016 Eterna SA

1.2 Power

It has already been established that the power source is the starting point in the mechanical movement, and that the difference between an automatic and a manually wound watch is the way in which the power is charged. In some respects that is all; however, in fine watchmaking even the most simple or fundamental concepts can become complex by virtue of the many different and innovative forms or levels of quality that are available. The mainspring and the power source are no exception.

Although there will be a number of secondary springs (such as the click spring or the centre seconds tension spring) the basic watch will have two primary springs: the mainspring, which releases the power, and the hairspring, which sits at the centre of the balance wheel and causes it to oscillate back and forth. The hairspring is the smaller and more energetic of the two. A passion for watches might begin with, or be accelerated by, observing the seductive dance of the balance wheel and the hairspring. The mainspring on the other hand is more reserved, often unseen. It has the quiet confidence of knowing that without its hard work the watch, including the hairspring, would grind to a halt. Its comparative size and strength are the reasons for it being known as the mainspring. Some of the complications and technical attributes of the mainspring and its supplementary parts are considered below.

The Mainspring

The length and thickness of the mainspring will impact the power of the output as well as the number of turns that it makes in its unwinding. The exact length, width and reserve of the mainspring will be dictated by the size of the barrel, the number of wheels and teeth in the gear train, the speed of the balance wheel oscillations, as well as any additional complications that drain extra power from the mainspring. So a short, thick mainspring can power a complicated watch for a short time, and a long, thin one can power a simple movement for a long time. This is why a complicated watch with a long power reserve is a challenging task and requires multiple barrels. In terms of material, the mainspring was traditionally a basic steel strip. It was later heat-treated to give it a more consistent elastic quality, and more recently a variety of alloys have been used to increase its performance, although the tolerances are less of a concern for this spring compared with the hairspring. It is very unusual for a watch

manufacturer to produce mainsprings or hairsprings, even those boasting the ability to make an 'in-house' movement. It is more common for the springs to be bought from specialist spring manufacturers. Typically an unwound mainspring is spiralled in the shape of an elaborate 'S' to give the spring more resistance and torque towards the end of its reserve. At one end there is a hole that is used to connect it to the barrel arbor, and it is attached in the opposite direction to its resting curve. At the other end the spring looks split. The extra piece of metal enables the spring to be attached to the barrel wall (or to the bridle in the case of a slipping spring mechanism, see opposite).

The Zenith Pilot Type 20 Skeleton, thanks to its massive 60mm diameter and its skeletonised movement, displays the mainspring and barrel clearly at 5:30. The watch includes a power reserve indicator at 3 o'clock and a subsidiary seconds dial at 9 o'clock. A very large balance wheel that one could mistake for an ordinary mainspring sits behind the dial at 11 o'clock.   © 2016 Zenith

Ratchet Wheel and Click

The mainspring is coiled within a barrel and attached to the central barrel arbor. Unless the barrel is skeletonised the spring itself is not visible to the user. The barrel is sealed at the back by a ratchet wheel. Unlike the mainspring, the ratchet wheel is often visible on the caseback and characterised by its large circumference, the large screw that affixes it, and the spiral finishing applied to it. The ratchet wheel is not associated with power release, but with power charging. The crown on the watch is turned by hand, which turns the winding stem. The winding stem has a pinion gear at the end of it which allows the power to be transferred from the vertical stem to the horizontal crown wheel by meshing the teeth at a 90° angle. The crown wheel turns and its teeth engage the ratchet wheel. The crown wheel is smaller with fewer teeth and relies on the power of a finger and thumb to generate the energy required to turn the ratchet wheel. As the ratchet wheel twists the barrel arbor the mainspring is coiled tighter within the barrel. What prevents the mainspring and ratchet wheel from unwinding back through this path of energy? The aptly named 'click' is a pawl that is forced by a spring to engage with the ratchet teeth so that the ratchet wheel does not recoil. Each time a ratchet tooth passes the pawl it clicks into place and it is this sound that is heard when a watch is wound.

The Stop-Work, Slipping Spring and Declutchable Rotor

Anything that connects the movement to the unrestricted force of its owner's fingers needs to have some security measures in place to avoid accidental damage. With a simple hand-wound mechanical movement there will be no security in place. Once the mainspring is fully wound and the force continues, the action of winding the crown will engage with the gear train all the way down to the escape wheel and will likely damage the movement. It is therefore important that the owner of a simple manually wound watch pays attention to the increasing resistance of the mainspring and stops winding when this resistance becomes notable.

To ensure that the movement is not damaged by over-winding the watchmaker can add a stop-work, however this is more of a pocket watch mechanism and is relatively rare in modern watches. The stop-work consists of two wheels, one that is attached to the barrel arbor and is almost a complete circle except for a protruding 'finger'. The other piece is a star wheel, often referred to as a Maltese cross, as it resembles one with a slight defect. The star wheel has five

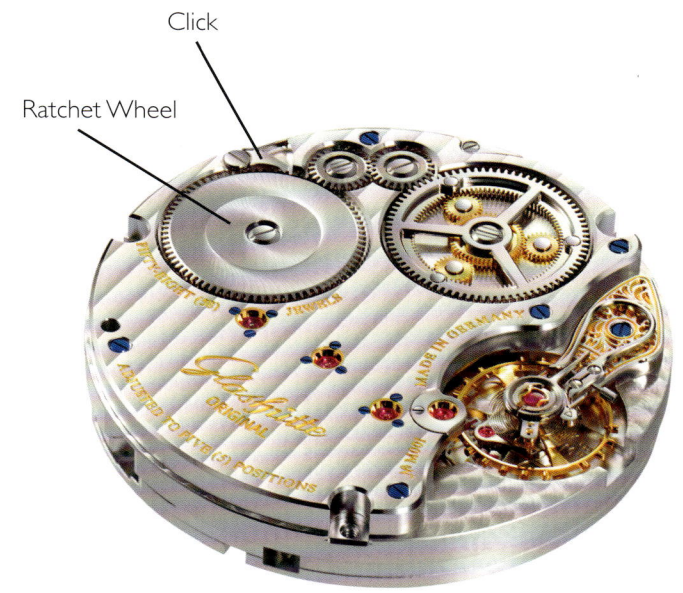

'points', four are concave and one is convex. Every time the ratchet wheel (when winding) or the barrel arbor (when running) completes a full rotation the finger will pass between the points of the star wheel. It will do this four times before it meets the convex star point of the star wheel, at which point the finger cannot pass through and the arbor / ratchet wheel is immobilised. This means that the mainspring can be wound four full rotations and can unwind four rotations, but no more. The number of points on the star wheel can be increased or decreased depending on the optimal number of rotations, but the five-point star is the most common.

The majority of modern watches designed to prevent over-winding will use a slipping spring, which acts as a clutch for the mainspring. The clutch is composed of a bridle within the barrel and is attached to the 'split' end of the mainspring. With a basic movement, the mainspring will be attached to the arbor and the wall of the barrel. When the

The exceptional manual-wound calibre 58-04 of the Glashütte Original Senator Chronometer Regulator gives a fine view of the ratchet wheel and click. Adjacent to it is not another ratchet wheel, but a sophisticated planetary reduction gearing for the power reserve indicator that sits on the dial side of the movement. © 2016 Glashütter Uhrenbetrieb GmbH

Extra Power

Generally speaking a mainspring barrel will perform about 6 rotations during its autonomy (the time it takes to transition from a fully wound state to being exhausted). This period is determined by the sizes of the wheels and the pinions, the requirement for certain wheels to rotate once every 60 minutes and 60 seconds respectively, and the speed of the escapement. With a 4Hz watch (the most common escapement speed), the 6 mainspring rotations take about 48 hours and this is regarded as the most common power reserve of a simple watch movement. Add a complication like a chronograph, or torque-management facility like a slipping spring, and that reserve can shrink further. Why is the length of autonomy important? A person who wears their automatic on a Monday and leaves it unworn on Tuesday and Wednesday will find that it has stopped by Thursday morning. This is fine when the owner has only one watch, a watch winder, or rather likes the experience of resetting their watch. For some, however, the stopped watch is a headache and it is further exaggerated when the watch carries calendar complications that need to be reset by the crown or discreet pushers.

Manufacturers recognised this frustration and developed watches with two or three mainspring barrels, stacked or side-by-side, working in unison. This allowed greater power

spring is attached to a bridle instead of the wall it can disengage with the wall if it is being pulled too hard. This system requires delicate calibration to avoid an overly sensitive bridle preventing the mainspring from winding within its optimal capacity. Unlike the stop-work, the slipping spring is particularly useful in an automatic watch as it allows the rotor to continue to move when stopping it dead can put huge stress on the gears of the rotor.

Although the slipping spring is perfectly effective, in horology there is nothing quite like improving upon perfect. Step forward the Richard Mille RM030 with declutchable rotor, which, instead of restricting winding by way of a slipping spring or stop-work, automatically disengages the winding rotor when the power reserve has reached the top end of its capacity (50 hours) and re-engages when the reserve drops below 40 hours. It's an interesting back-and-forth that can be tracked between the reserve indicator and the rotor clutch indicator, which are both displayed on the dial.

Above and opposite: The Richard Mille RM030 with declutchable rotor. Highly automated and responsive mechanical power management. © 2016 Richard Mille, Horometrie S.A

Right: The Eterna Spherodrive 8 Day Calibre 3510. The exploded image provides a good view of the two barrels and the ratchet wheels above them. © 2015 Eterna SA

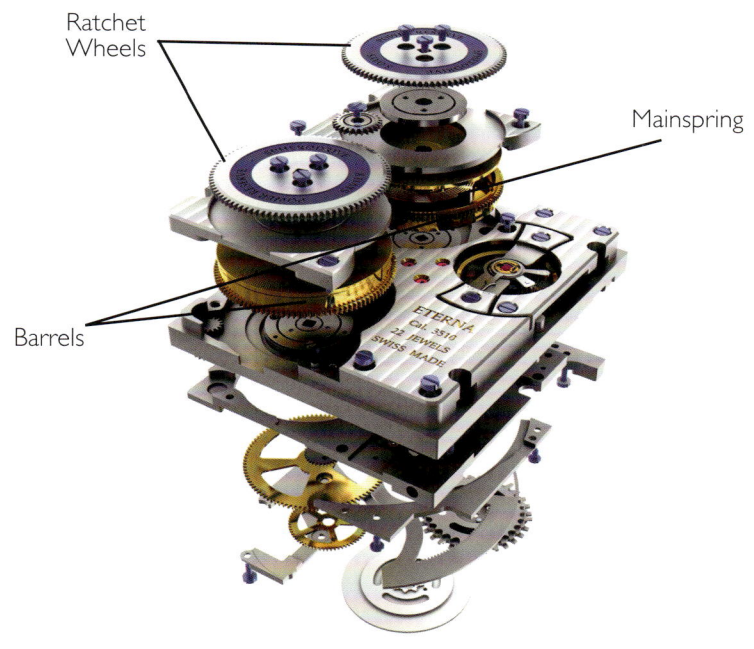

Ratchet Wheels

Mainspring

Barrels

to be distributed across the gear train, which meant fewer barrel rotations and more balance wheel oscillations, resulting in movements that run for as long as 8 days. Such a movement is highly useful; so long as the owner winds it once a week it will continue to run uninterrupted. Today there are many manufacturers offering watches with an 8 day movement; but what happens when the watch has a particularly power-draining complication, or the movement's reserve is used as a unique selling point? There are 10 day movements, such as the Panerai Radiomir 10 Day GMT. There are 14 and 15 day movements, such as the Vacheron Constantin Patrimony Traditionnelle 14-Day Tourbillon and the Jaeger-LeCoultre Master Control Minute Repeater. There are beasts of movements such as the A. Lange & Söhne Lange 31, as mentioned above, that runs for an entire month. Sitting proudly at the top of the pile is The Hublot MP-05 LaFerrari, which amongst its 637 components has 11 barrels, stacked like a roll of coins in order to deliver an outstanding 50 days of autonomy. You can put the watch down in early June and pick it up again in mid-August without needing to reset it.

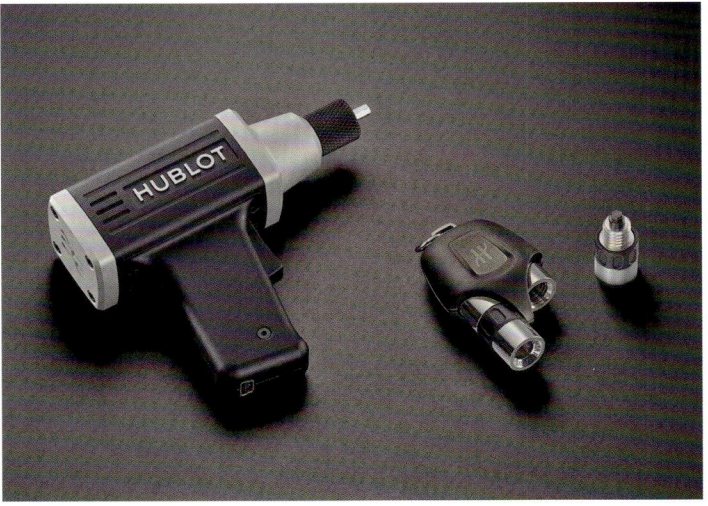

Right, above: The large size and shape of the Hublot MP-05 LaFerrari is less for grabbing your attention than it is for cramming 11 mainspring barrels into it. Still, it certainly does grab your attention.
© 2016 Hublot

Right, below: The MP-05 does not come with a winding key, but instead comes with a small drill!. This particular model sports a sapphire case.
© 2016 Hublot

Opposite: The Jaeger-LeCoultre Master 8 Days Perpetual with an 8-day power reserve courtesy of its two mainspring barrels. This particular model features a stunning skeletonised movement, with calendar, moon phase, power reserve and day / night indicated by hands and rotating crystal discs which pass over a silvered base.
© 2016 Jaeger-LeCoultre

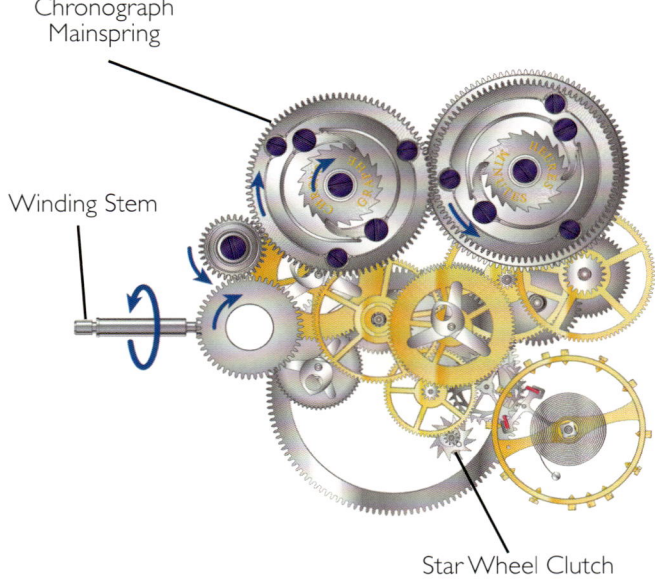

Chronograph Mainspring

Winding Stem

Star Wheel Clutch

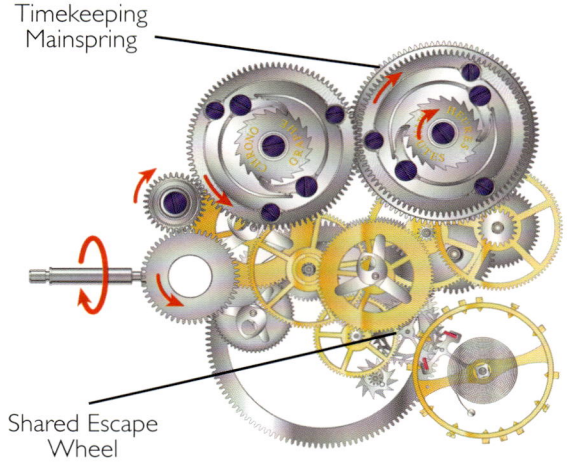

Timekeeping Mainspring

Shared Escape Wheel

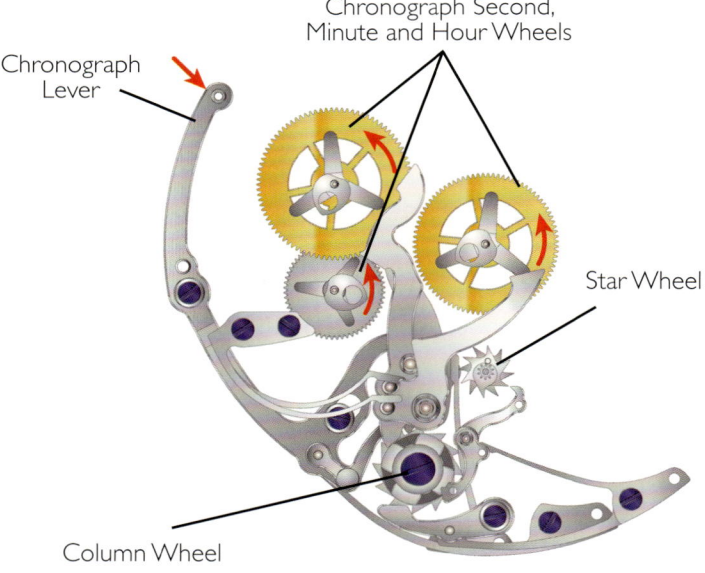

Chronograph Second, Minute and Hour Wheels

Chronograph Lever

Star Wheel

Column Wheel

Independent Power

Extracting a smooth flow of torque from the mainspring is of paramount importance to a mechanical movement. This is particularly important when power is being used unevenly, such as the activating and deactivating of a chronograph. Such disruption is capable of fluctuating the torque, which can impact amplitude, which in turn can affect the rate. As will be covered in Chapter 1.3, there are ways in which a single power source can be managed so that the torque is smoothed. However, there are also watches with additional power sources designed to isolate the complications and prevent them from influencing timekeeping. These alternative sources can share the transmission or the escapement with the regular movement, or they can be entirely independent.

A great example of an escapement-linked independent power source can be found in the Jaeger-LeCoultre Duomètre range, which have 'dual wing' movements designed to isolate one power source for the running time,

Above and left: The Jaeger-LeCoultre dual wing Calibre 380 as featured in the Duomètre à Chronographe. The two mainsprings are hand wound via the crown; winding clockwise powers the timekeeping mainspring, winding anticlockwise powers the chronograph mainspring. The star wheel clutch is activated via the column wheel. © 2016 Jaeger-LeCoultre

Opposite: The Audemars Piguet Millenary Minute Repeater. The sliding switch simultaneously powers and activates the repeater. © 2015 Audemars Piguet, Le Brassus

and another source for the complication. The power for the two functions is generated by their own mainspring and travels along their own gear train before connecting to a shared escapement. In the Duomètre à Chronographe model the regular timekeeping train drives the escape pinion, while the chronograph train directly engages the escape wheel. How does the escape wheel continue to turn when the chronograph is disengaged? It possesses a two-layered star wheel; one is constantly engaged with the escape wheel and the other couples with it only when the chronograph is engaged. It is a clutch as simple as it is small, so small in fact that you could inhale it without noticing.

Some independently powered complications have their own independent regulation but are able to take 'readings' from the regular timekeeping function. The best example of this mechanism is the repeater, which has its own mainspring and regulator (see Chapter 2.8). The mainspring is charged by the action of the sliding switch activator, and the repeater is regulated by a spinning 'governor' rather than an oscillating balance wheel. The mechanism has racks with beaks that come to rest on cams in the timekeeping transmission, with no power interference, in order to obtain an exact reading of the time.

Then there is independent power designed to drive *entirely* independent complications. Take, for example, the Breguet Tradition Chronographe Indépendant 7077, which has a *totally* independent 20 minute chronograph, powered

by a blade mainspring and regulated by a 5Hz escapement, while the regular timekeeping escapement runs at 3Hz. The elevated speed of the chronograph escapement enables the chronograph centre seconds to record a lapse of time to the nearest 1 / 5th of a second. One of the most impressive things about this chronograph is the means by which the power is charged. The blade spring is buckled each time the reset button is activated, storing enough power to run the chronograph for another 20 minutes

when it is next started. It's simple, fun, and allows the chronograph to exist in total isolation from the timekeeping function.

Above and opposite: The Breguet Tradition Chronographe Indépendant 7077. The faster (5Hz) balance wheel for the chronograph is made from titanium. This allows the wheel to retain the proportions of its slower-moving, Glucydur sibling. © 2015 Ian Skellern

The following two movements both have entirely mechanical timekeeping functions, but have an additional, independently powered, electro-mechanical function. First is the HYT H4 Metropolis, which has the trademark HYT approach to time indication by way of a liquid-filled capillary, but also contains two dynamo-powered LEDs that illuminate the dial for around 3 seconds. The AC power of the dynamo comes from an independent mainspring, which is wound by turning the crown (also at 4 o'clock) and released when the button is pressed.

Second, the URWERK EMC (which stands for Electro Mechanical Control) also has an electronic stowaway on board. This beast is equipped with its very own optical sensor that

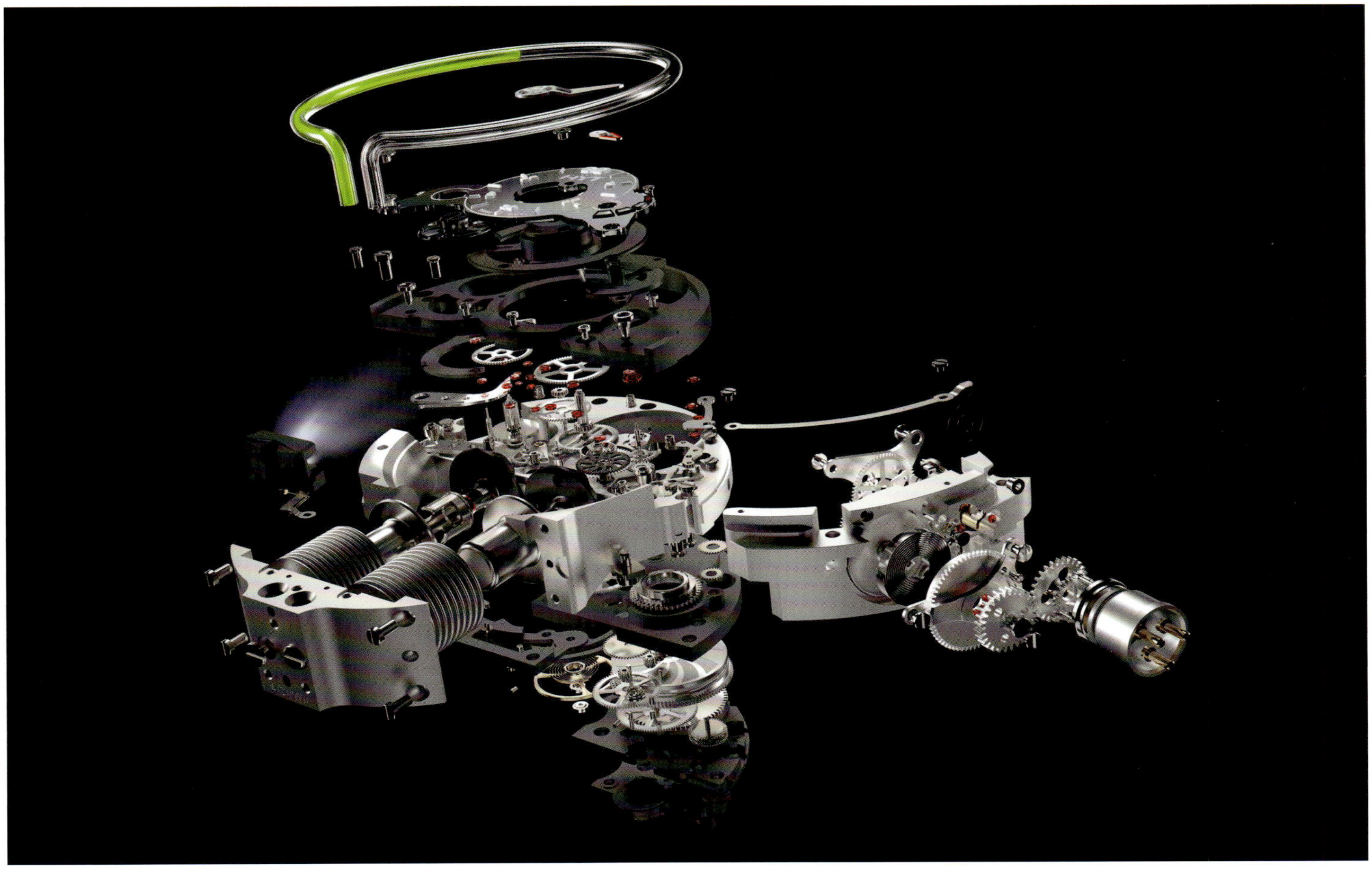

The HYT H4 Metropolis has two discreet LEDs situated underneath the rider at 6 o'clock. Twist the crown at 4 o'clock to power its own mainspring, and press the button located in the crown to release the power to the dynamo for a 3-second light show.   © 2016 HYT S.A

informs a precision indicator. The idea is that even a well-adjusted movement will be subject to unique environmental effects and that these effects may impact the running of the watch. Even if the watch is kept in a neutral environment, time itself will impact the rate as the lubrication on the pallet stones eventually wears thin. The EMC features a fold-away crank on the caseband that generates energy, stores it in a super capacitor, and deploys it to the optical sensor for a rate reading. We will cover this watch in more depth in Chapter 2.3.

Rotors

As already discussed, the winding rotor is designed to transfer the kinetic energy of the wearer into the winding of the mainspring. Its shape and weight, its grooves and (in many new movements) the friction-resistant ball-bearings at its pivot, give

it the freedom to respond to the lightest of nudges. The garden-variety rotor is not particularly pretty, it is concentrically mounted and obstructs the view of much of the movement. It is a utilitarian device. However with the watch enthusiast's growing interest in observing the movement of a watch, and the introduction of the sapphire caseback, the winding rotor has gained something of an elevated aesthetic value.

• **The Decorated / Precious Metal Rotor** — When exposed by a sapphire crystal caseback, the rotor serves as a banner that vies for the attention of the observer and there is simply too much surface area not to embellish it. The rotor is the ideal space upon which the brand name or a fancy motif can be engraved, the shape of the rotor itself can be a design statement, or more precious (and importantly heavy) metals can be used. You will notice that the

Left, above: The Audemars Piguet Royal Oak features a 22k rotor engraved with the company logo and coats of arms for the Audemars and Piguet families. © 2015 Audemars Piguet, Le Brassus

Left, below: A finely hand-finished rotor featuring the logo of Thomas Prescher. © 2016 Thomas Prescher

Above and opposite: The MB&F HM3 Megawind features a giant 22k gold and titanium 'battle axe' winding rotor; a great shape and weight to be swung about the movement with vigour. When it comes to rotor design, the most important rule is to distribute the majority of the weight to a particular segment; creating a rotor with equal weight across 360° will result in the rotor failing to respond to a change in position. © 2016 MB&F

- **Back-to-Front** — Thanks to the sapphire caseback, the dance of the rotor can be observed by simply taking the watch off. But for some this is not enough, and the swing of the rotor is animated onto the dial side of the watch. It can be achieved by retaining the regular rotor and mounting an additional dial-side rotor (which can

Opposite: The Zenith El Primero Tourbillon features a fairly regular-shaped 21k rose gold rotor, made more interesting by its skeletonisation, which incorporates the Zenith star logo.

© 2016 Zenith

Left: The Perrelet Turbine XL. Credited with the 1777 invention of the automatic-winding pocket watch, modern day Perrelets enjoy a playful relationship with the winding rotor. The Turbine aesthetically implements a large 12-blade wheel that sits beneath the dial. The dial can then be given any number of large apertures, allowing the turbine to be seen as it spins underneath. The effect is mesmerising.

© 2016 Perrelet SA

Below: The Cartier Promenade d´une Panthère. Whereas the Perrelet Turbine connects the turbine on the front to the rotor on the back, the Cartier Promenade d´une Panthère inverts the winding mechanism so that the rotor, a white gold and diamond-paved panther, is on the dial. This is a fine example of how a rotor can be decorated so extensively that it no longer resembles its more utilitarian counterpart. The shape of the panther provides the disproportionate weight, causing the rotor to move as the position of the watch changes. Vincent Wulveryck © 2016 Cartier

case of a watch rarely uses gold content over 18k due to the malleability of pure gold, but when it comes to rotors the content increases in order to increase the weight; and as platinum is around 20% heavier than 22k gold, it is regarded as an ideal metal for the entire rotor or its skirting.

be coupled or uncoupled to the regular rotor), or by doing away with the rotor on the back altogether. This is perhaps not the watch of choice for those who suffer from motion sickness, but there is no doubt that a watch becomes highly animated when the movement of the rotor is reflected on the dial.

- **The Micro-Rotor / Eccentric Rotor** — Traditionally the rotor is mounted concentrically and must clear the main plate and bridges of the movement in order to rotate freely. In practice this translates to a thicker movement compared to a manually wound alternative. However, with some redesign, there are ways of retaining the slim profile of a manual wind movement. This can be achieved by using a smaller, off-centre, rotor. In doing so the rotor can be embedded within the body of the movement, and its reduced diameter means that it will not obstruct the larger pinions. As the highest concentration of pinions and wheels is at the centre of the movement, there is more vacant space further out; hence the micro-rotor is often also an eccentric rotor.

    The micro-rotor or eccentric rotor is not exclusively used to reduce the thickness of a movement, but can also serve to satisfy aesthetic or rotor-performance objectives. If the diameter of the rotor is larger than the radius of the movement, or if it passes over the balance wheel and / or mainspring barrel, this is a sign that reducing movement thickness is not the primary goal.

Right, above and below: The Laurent Ferrier Galet Square Boréal and its movement. Despite the beautifully polished bridge above it, the 18k gold micro-rotor does not add to the overall thickness of the movement, instead it rotates underneath the centre wheel, above the third wheel and, importantly, does not cross either arbor. The case of the watch is not significantly thin, at around 11mm, which indicates that the use of this rotor may also be for aesthetic or performance purposes. This is hardly surprising given that the rotor provides greater visibility to some very handsomely finished bridges and wheels. The movement has a 'natural' escapement, which requires less torque from the mainspring, and consequently uses a mainspring that is easier to wind; ideal conditions for the micro-rotor.   © 2016 Laurent Ferrier

Opposite: The Perrelet First Class Double Rotor Skeleton couples the movement-side winding rotor to a dial-side winding rotor.
                    © 2016 Perrelet SA

Above and right: At 2.35mm thick, the Piaget 1208P is the world's thinnest automatic movement (seen here in the Altiplano). The eccentric micro-rotor, eccentric running seconds, and exceptionally thin wheels, contribute to this achievement. © 2016 Piaget

Opposite: The A. Lange & Söhne Calibre L085.1 SAX-O-MAT (as featured in the Saxonia Annual Calendar) has a hand-engraved rotor made of 21k gold with a platinum skirting held in place by five blued screws. Hardly a micro-rotor, notice that it runs over a small portion of the balance wheel. The purpose of its eccentric design is likely to provide unobstructed space above the views of the beautifully hand-engraved balance cock. © 2015 A. Lange & Söhne

- **The Peripheral Rotor** — Originally patented in the 1950s but with first production by Carl F. Bucherer in 2008, the peripheral rotor provides minimal obstruction to views of the movement. The peripheral rotor does not swing on a central crank, instead it travels around the circumference of the movement. The weight of the rotor occupies one section of a 360° ring that has inward facing teeth. The teeth engage with a reduction gear train that leads to the mainspring ratchet wheel.

Above, left: The Panerai P.4000 Calibre features two mainspring barrels, and although the micro-rotor passes over the pinions of the third and fourth wheels, the P.4000 is still only 3.95mm thick. The space-saving is achieved by keeping the rotor away from the barrels and the balance wheel. Note the attractive guilloché finish on the 22k gold rotor.   © 2016 Officine Panerai

Above, right: The Caliber CFB A1002 movement of the Carl F. Bucherer Patravi EvoTec Power Reserve with peripheral rotor. Note the unusual shock absorber on the balance bridge. © 2015 Carl F. Bucherer

Left: The movement of the F.P. Journe Octa Perpetuelle does a great job of demonstrating the difference between a micro-rotor and an eccentric rotor. Despite being eccentric, this large uni-directional rotor covers the majority of the movement, including half the balance wheel, and therefore is not designed with movement thickness in mind; instead the position of the rotor is an intentional attempt to achieve optimal swing from the rotor. Note the 18k rose gold movement.   © 2015 Montres Journe SA

The Vacheron Constantin Harmony Ultra-thin Grande Complication Chronograph. The elegant dial features split chronograph central seconds, tachymeter scale and power reserve indicator at 6 o'clock. The split seconds function is activated by the pusher at 2 o'clock and the integrated crown pusher activates the start / stop / reset. The peripheral rotor as viewed from the caseback delivers automatic winding without obstructing the view of the movement.   © 2015 Vacheron Constantin

- **The Linear Mass** — A rotor rotates, it oscillates; it stands proudly in the movement, swinging its weight around like a medieval flail. It therefore must clear a space in the movement as large as its circumference, and as deep as its thickness. The overbearing effect that a standard rotor has on the movement is overcome by shrinking it or mounting it peripherally. But what if you have a belt-driven transmission with four barrels tilted at a 13° angle? This is no place for a rotating disc, large or small. The TAG Heuer Monaco V4 faced this very problem, and the solution was almost as distracting as the V4's more headline-grabbing concept, the belt-driven transmission. The 4

barrels are charged by a 'linear mass', a rectangular slab of tungsten, which slides up and down a track that runs from 6 o'clock to 12 o'clock, thanks to a series of extremely small ball bearings. The slab has two rods of steel running along either side of its length. The rods are ridged, acting like teeth on a rack, turning the transmission wheel on either side, which in turn belt-charges the barrels.

- **Unidirectional vs Bidirectional Winding** — The majority of automatic movements manufactured today will wind the mainspring whether the rotor swings anticlockwise or clockwise. These are known as bidirectional winding rotors. This is made possible by way of stacked click wheels that will lock and unlock depending on the direction in which the rotor moves. There are alternative technologies such as the Pellaton winding system, named after its IWC-employed creator, and the Seiko Magic Lever system, that deviate from this basic design, but they share the same goal to convert every possible movement into active winding of the mainspring. Conversely, the unidirectional winding rotor is disengaged while swinging with minimal friction in one direction, and only engages the ratchet wheel when it rotates in the opposite direction, which is clockwise in most (but not all) movements.

Which is best? The argument for the bidirectional rotor is that the minor movements of a sedentary watch-wearer will be enough to continue to power the mainspring, and that the extra components of the system make the watch more complex, and effectively more desirable as a complication. The argument for the unidirectional rotor is that the winding efficiency is greater because there is no 'dead angle' caused by the switching of gears when the direction of rotation changes and because the rotor has more momentum behind its wind thanks to the friction-free backswing.

- **The Complicated Rotor** — As the very shape of the rotor can influence its winding efficiency, there exist rotors that can be adjusted to suit the activity levels of their wearers. Richard Mille automatic models use rotors with variable geometry, which are adjusted by the watchmaker to one of six settings before being delivered to the client. The positions increase or decrease the centrifugal force of the rotor, with a particularly active wearer requiring less of such a force than a more sedentary one.

The variable geometry option requires the initial intervention of a watchmaker, and requires the wearer to commit to a standard level of activity. A more interactive rotor complication exists in the URWERK UR-202, which is equipped with a three-option switch on the caseback for 'standard', 'sport', and 'extreme' activity levels. The winding rotor is coupled to two turbines, which force air through small holes into a chamber. When set to 'standard' the holes are open and the turbines operate freely; when set to 'sport' the holes are partially covered, which serves to restrict airflow and increase the pressure against the turbines causing the rotor to operate at around 65% efficiency; when set to 'extreme' the holes are fully covered and this causes the air pressure to act as a brake on the turbines. Whether it would be advisable to do anything extreme while wearing such a precious machine is worth considering; but this complication is as much about interactivity as it is utility.

The Richard Mille RM007 features a small rotor with a skeletonised recess. The recess is PVD coated and filled with more than 100 18k gold micro-balls. The effect is, perhaps primarily, an aesthetic one; however there is a degree of science behind the concept that the balls act as a shock absorber and

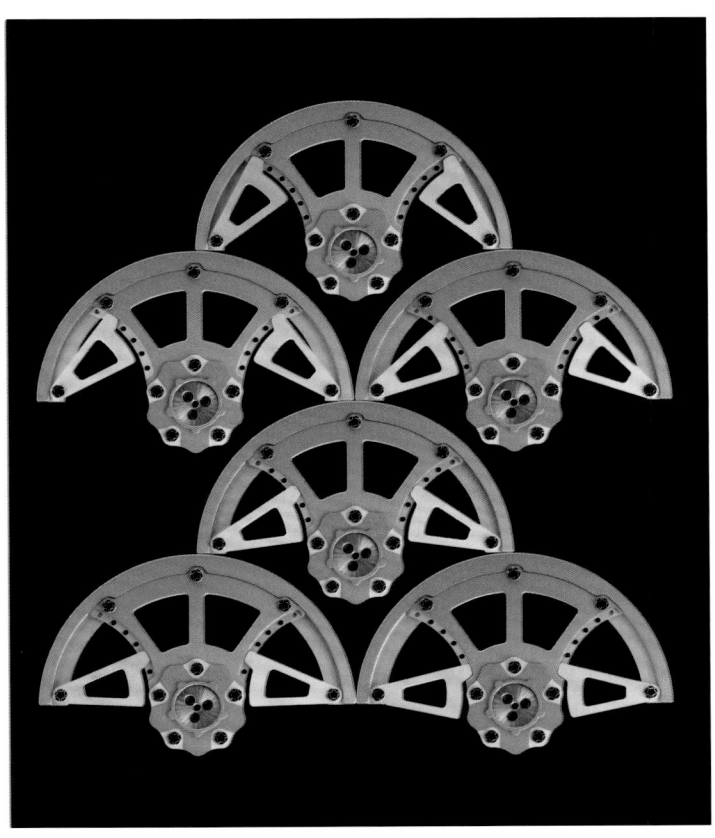

The very attractive and complicated Richard Mille rotor with variable geometry. The shoulders of the rotor can be pivoted so that they are aligned towards each other or towards the skirting of the rotor. When the weight of the rotor is shifted away from the central joint the centrifugal force, and subsequent winding efficiency, is increased.   © 2016 Richard Mille, Horometrie S.A

also serve to increase momentum before the rotor even begins to move — particularly important given that this unidirectional rotor has a very slim dead angle of 7°.

A final comment on rotors. The level to which an eccentric rotor performs in comparison with its concentric and peripheral counterparts, or a unidirectional versus a bidirectional, is almost entirely theoretical. We are talking about performance variables that, even if they are measurable, are simply not going to be perceivable in daily use. So aesthetic appeal is more than sufficient reason for choosing any particular rotor. This is watch enthusiasm in a nutshell — there is ample science to feed the desire, but desire is undisputed king over science when it comes to one's appreciation and love of these obsolete marvels.

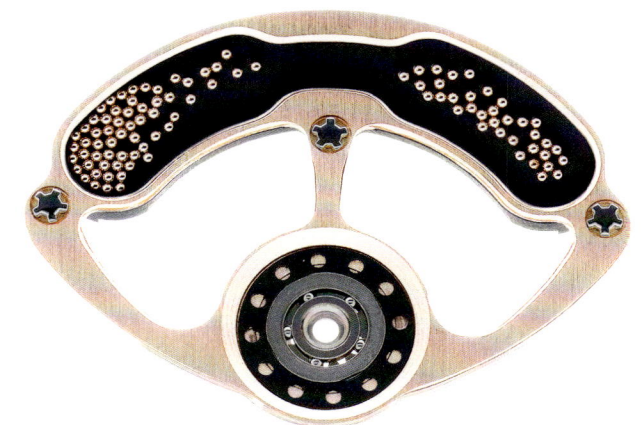

Above and opposite: The caseback of the URWERK UR-202, with its three-option switch for varying levels of user activity. The two turbines can be seen, as well as the small perforations that facilitate the airflow allowing the turbines to rotate.　© 2016 URWERK

Right, top: The small rotor on the Richard Mille RM007 is filled with over 100 18k micro-balls.　© 2016 Richard Mille, Horometrie S.A

Right, bottom: The Thomas Prescher Mysterious Automatic Double Axis Tourbillon places two complications, the date and month, on the winding rotor (at 6 o'clock). Gravity ensures that they remain at a visible angle in all worn positions. Notice also the rotating hour and minute 'barrels', the three-dimensional moon, and the double-axis tourbillon that appears to be cantilevered by an impossibly thin stem. That is exactly what is happening; the movement is partially concealed within the sides of the case and the tourbillon is driven by a lateral gear in the stem.　© 2016 Thomas Prescher

1.3 Transmission

The most impressive mainspring being regulated by the perfect escapement is nothing without its transmission. This is the platform upon which the core functionality of a watch is built, and indeed a good number of broader complications too. This platform does not simply transmit the energy from mainspring to escapement, the transmission determines and facilitates the movement of the hands on the dial and the varying length of time it takes for them to complete a rotation. It increases the rate of each wheel until the escape wheel is able to meet the pace of a rapidly oscillating balance wheel. Transmission largely comes down to teeth and pitch ratios. There is a rigid formulaic relationship between the number of teeth, the sizes of the wheels and pinions, and the rotating speeds of everything from the mainspring to the escape wheel. Theoretically you can add more wheels to a gear train, and this is often necessary to accommodate a particular dial layout, but the reality is that the most efficient gear trains are those with the fewest additional parts. Less is more on a good gear train.

This section will focus on the basic gear train layout, the concept of transmission ratios and two very important, but often unappreciated transmission elements: the keyless work and the motion work.

The Four-Wheel Gear Train

Each of the four wheels on the basic gear train has their own name. The first of these is the centre wheel (or second wheel, as there is already a mainspring barrel), then the third wheel, the fourth wheel, and the escape wheel. The gearing is designed to increase the speed of rotation, the primary goal of the transmission. This progressive advance in wheel speed is achieved by having a larger wheel driving a smaller pinion. Wheels that are used to register the time will have fixed rotation speeds, while the

others are able to be tweaked to suit the design of the gear train. Generally speaking, with a single barrel four-wheel gear train the mainspring barrel will rotate once every 8 hours or so; it rotates the centre pinion once every 60 minutes, the centre wheel rotates the third pinion approximately once every 7.5 minutes, the third wheel rotates the fourth pinion once every 60 seconds, and the fourth wheel rotates the escape pinion approximately once every 6 seconds.

Teeth and Pitch Ratios

The wheels and pinions have teeth and leaves that grip each other. Transmission wheel teeth are curved points, neither sharp like a saw nor flat like a cog; pinion leaves are bulbous at the tip and have thin necks. This is not for aesthetics but serves to maximise the velocity potential of the contact between them. The radius / diameter of any given wheel or pinion is referred to as a pitch radius / diameter, and is measured to the specific part of the tooth that makes contact with the driven / driving tooth, not the end of the tooth, and not the base.

The teeth and pitch ratios dictate the layout of your gear train. It is one of the more notable confines within which the watchmaker must work. First he determines the mainspring length, thickness, the speed at which it will unwind and the anticipated frequency of the escape wheel. With a standard four-wheel gear train the centre wheel and fourth wheels *must* rotate once every hour and minute respectively for timekeeping purposes. The size of the wheels, the number of teeth, and their respective positioning on the main plate are dictated by the ratio; the watchmaker just needs to calculate them. The general principle is as follows: the ratio between the pitch of the driving wheel and the pitch of the driven pinion is the same as the ratio between the number of teeth on the driving wheel and the number of leaves on the driven pinion; which in turn is the same as the ratio between the number of turns the driven pinion makes to every turn of the drive wheel. So if a watchmaker puts 12 leaves on a pinion, the ratio will inform the number of teeth on the wheel that drives it; likewise, if he makes a wheel larger, it will increase the size of the driven pinion too, and therefore it will change the relative positioning of the two components on the main plate.

The Angelus U20 Ultra-Skeleton is a fine demonstration of the four-wheel gear train thanks to the crystal plates and the linear layout of the movement. This particular movement has a fixed fourth wheel; the tourbillon escapement sits within a carriage and it is the pinion of the carriage that is driven by the third wheel. As the carriage rotates, the pinion of the escape wheel rolls along the fixed fourth wheel and delivers impulses to the balance wheel.

© 2016 Angelus

Mainspring
Barrel

Third
Wheel

Centre
Wheel

(Fixed) Fourth
Wheel

Tourbillon
Carriage

Escape
Wheel

The Motion Work

Although it involves a rather clever modulation to the basic gear train, the motion work is not a complication. This is because it delivers part of the primary function of a watch — the rotation of the hours. As mentioned in the overview of the mechanical movement, the minutes of a watch are achieved by simply placing a hand on the arbor of the centre wheel (usually the wheel that immediately follows from the mainspring), which rotates once every 60 minutes. From this point, the gear train ratios will mean that the wheels increase their rotational speed until they reach the rapidly spinning escape wheel. So how can a wheel be made to move *slower* than the centre wheel? This is where the motion work comes in. The motion work consists of a series of gears that are driven by the centre wheel and follow conversely proportioned ratios to the regular gear train. A 'cannon pinion' is placed on the arbor of the centre wheel, this pinion drives a wheel which sits to the side. The extra wheel is also fitted with a pinion that drives the hour wheel, which is positioned on top of the cannon pinion. Note that in both stages it is a pinion driving a wheel; this 'under drive' ratio is the reverse of a regular gear train and has the effect of slowing down the rotations of the driven wheel. The motion work is therefore a tributary of the main gear train with the sole purpose of reducing 12 rotations of the centre wheel into one rotation of the hour wheel.

The Keyless Works, Hacking and Zero Reset

It was explained earlier that turning the crown is the most common means by which the mainspring can be manually charged. In addition, the crown can be used to set the time, and both of these are achieved by way of the keyless works. Named after the method it replaced (a winding / setting key), the keyless works is a series of levers and clutches connected to the stem that enable the crown to perform different operations. When the crown is in its winding position its castle wheel is connected to the crown wheel. Winding the stem will cause the crown wheel to wind a transmission wheel, which in turn winds the ratchet of the mainspring. When the stem is pulled into the setting mode the castle wheel disengages with the crown wheel and instead connects to an intermediate wheel which is in contact with, and can therefore be used to set, the motion work.

Developed to aid the synchronisation of a watch, and often found on pilots' watches, the hacking seconds complication stops the seconds hand whenever the crown is

pulled for time-setting. The keyless work is equipped with a brake lever that makes direct contact with the balance wheel when the crown is pulled, immediately stopping the watch. If you are the type of person that enjoys synchronising your watch to your wall clock, this is the function you are looking for. The hacking function was further developed in 2008 by A. Lange & Söhne to work with a tourbillon. Lange enhanced it again to include a zero-reset mechanism, which simultaneously stops the seconds hand and resets it to zero. The seconds hand has a heart-shaped cam on its arbor and a brake lever drops onto the cam, which is shaped so that the seconds hand snaps to 12 o'clock when the lever comes to rest.

Above: The Roger Smith Series 2 Open Dial gives dial-side views of the beautifully hand-finished movement. Although the motion work sits beneath a bridge, the keyless work is given ample daylight.
© 2016 Roger W Smith Ltd

Opposite: Thanks to the crystal plates of the Angelus U20 Ultra-Skeleton movement, both the motion work and the keyless work are clearly visible.
© 2016 Angelus

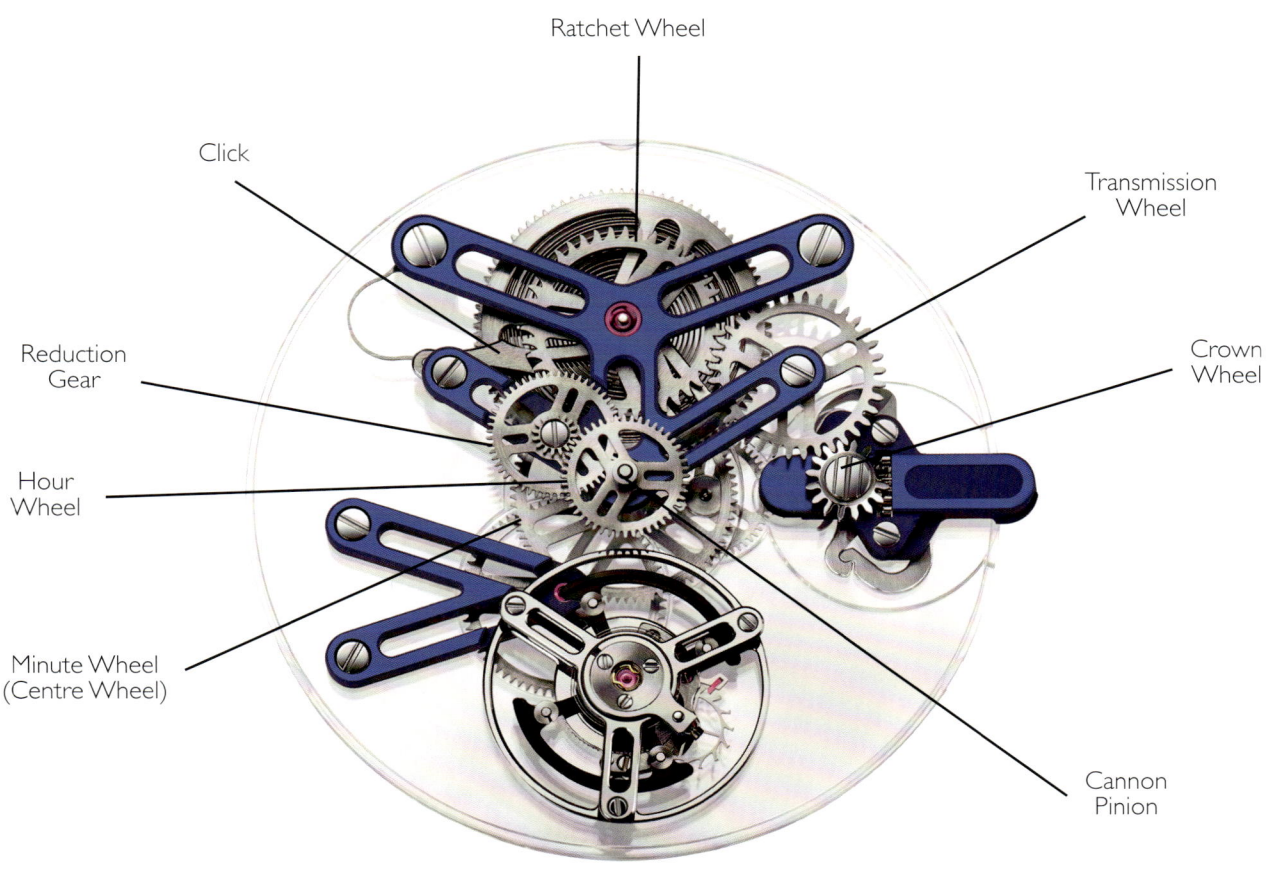

Ratchet Wheel

Click

Transmission Wheel

Reduction Gear

Crown Wheel

Hour Wheel

Minute Wheel (Centre Wheel)

Cannon Pinion

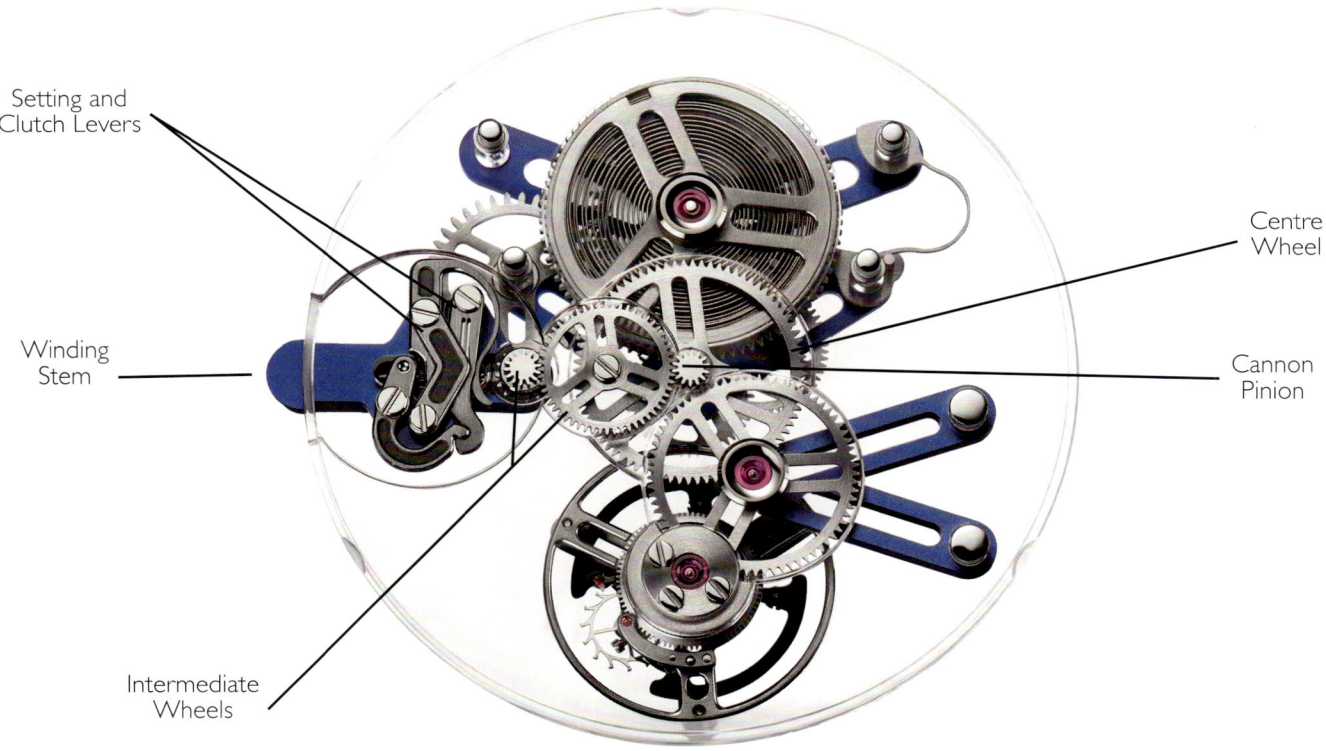

Setting and Clutch Levers

Centre Wheel

Winding Stem

Cannon Pinion

Intermediate Wheels

Constant Force

Watchmaking excellence is proven in a number of areas, some are decorative and others are associated with performance and accuracy. When it comes to the latter, there are few more important areas than achieving a power distribution of constant force. Despite sounding like a *Star Wars* theme, constant force serves to limit the impact that power can have on the amplitude of the balance wheel, which can gradually accumulate into rate errors. Do you remember those practical joke 'electric shock handshake' devices available from old toy stores? They were not actually electric, instead they triggered an explosive unwinding of a

spring. Imagine winding up the spring to only 10% full; not only would it be a very brief shock but it would be noticeably softer than a 100% wound device. Outside of those extremes, there is a 'sweet spot' where the spring can deliver a more regular level of power. This correlation between state of wind and power is replicated in the mainspring of a watch movement. The spikes and troughs at high and low wind are inevitable phenomena, but unacceptable to a watchmaker trying to build a highly accurate timepiece. The simplest controlling technique is to physically limit the state of wind of the mainspring to a range (such as 20–80%) that allows for the torque to be distributed in a smooth linear fashion without experiencing the spikes at either end. A combination of an s-shaped mainspring and slipping spring (both covered in the last chapter) enhance low-end torque and prevent high-end torque respectively.

However, when it comes to managing the level of torque across the operating range of the mainspring, whether it be 1–100% or 20–80%, there are more exotic and complicated techniques. Many of these existed long ago, as the wild deviations of a mainspring were never more of an issue, and some of these methods are presented in watches today by virtue of their old-world charm. These complications can exist right at the beginning of the gear train, further along the transmission, or just before the escape wheel.

Above and opposite: The A. Lange & Söhne 1815 Tourbillon has a running seconds hand mounted on the one-minute tourbillon at 6 o'clock. The zero-reset lever, with its clear pallet stone, can be seen floating above the central point of the tourbillon. The movement features a diamond pivot stone which is visible on the bridge at the back of the movement. Bearing in mind that diamond is 10 / 10 on the Mohs scale of hardness, with corundum (the material that modern pivot stones are made from) at 9 / 10, it is as functional as it is lavish. © 2015 A. Lange & Söhne

Right: The A. Lange & Söhne zero-reset mechanism as featured in the 1815 Tourbillon. The zero-reset hammer is engaged with the heart cam, causing the seconds hand to reset. On the right of the balance wheel the brake has made contact, causing it to halt the movement. © 2015 A. Lange & Söhne

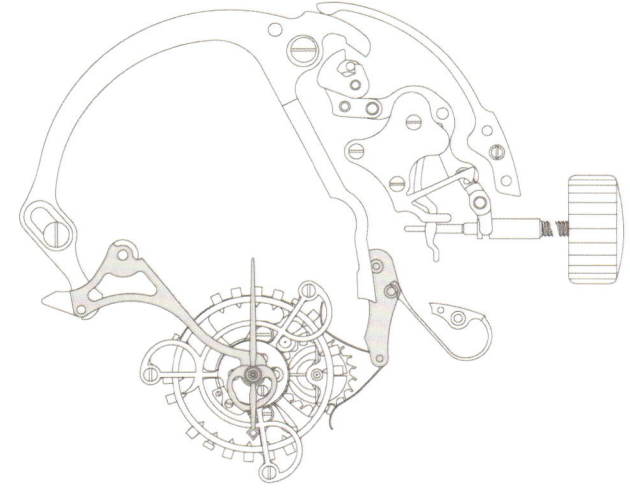

- The **fusée and chain** method dates back to the 15th century. This was a time when movements were regulated, rather poorly, by verge escapements. The early verge escapement had no balance spring and was highly sensitive to changes in power. The fusée and chain was developed to distribute as smooth a level of mainspring torque as possible, from the beginning of the power reserve to the end. This complication is very engaging visually, and can be identified from a distance by what appears to be a tiny bicycle chain wrapped around and connecting two wheels. The similarities are not just visual when we consider the function of the bicycle chain and gears.

Imagine a bicycle being ridden along the road. The bicycle chain connects the pedals to the rear wheel. At the pedal there may be two or three concentric gear wheels and the chain will be driven by one at a time. At the rear wheel you will have an impressive cone of wheels that get smaller as they branch out from the frame. At the start of the journey the rider is filled with energy and grand ideas about how far they are going to travel; legs are fresh and strong. As a result the bike will be set at a high gear, whereby the chain will wrap around the smallest wheel on the cone at the rear wheel end. This is a high gear because there is a greater amount of torque required to turn the rear wheel. Several minutes into the ride a sense of reality sets in: the rider is not as fit as they thought and is going to need to accommodate tiring legs and heaving lungs. The low gear is selected, which shifts the chain along the cone to the largest wheel, reducing the torque required to keep it rotating.

In a watch movement there is no cyclist. The power source, the mainspring, is like a cyclist attempting to maintain exactly the same speed as their energy level moves from 'let's do this' to 'call me a taxi'. The fusée and chain consists of a linked chain that wraps around the barrel of the mainspring and a fusée, a cone which sits on the centre wheel arbor and allows the chain to coil around it from the base to the top. When the mainspring is fully wound the chain is coiled around the smallest ring of the fusée, meaning that the excess power is dissipated by the additional torque required to turn the centre wheel. As the mainspring unwinds and continues to pull the fusée, the chain uncoils and makes its way down the fusée to the largest ring, whereby the diminishing power of the mainspring is able to turn the wheel with greater ease.

Unlike a basic movement, the barrel of a fusée and chain is often wound via the fusée. As the act of winding the fusée would effectively stop the movement, models such as the A. Lange & Söhne Richard Lange Tourbillon 'Pour le Mérite', are fitted with a set of planetary gears that allow power to continue being transmitted while the fusée is being wound. The watch has two additional mechanisms that prevent the mainspring from being wound to full capacity, or from running to a fully unwound state. The first employs a lever, which is triggered when the chain is at the peak of the fusée cone and an arresting tooth engages with the ratchet of the fusée. The second employs a lever via the power reserve wheel; the finger at the end of the lever blocks the fourth wheel (the running seconds wheel) when the reserve is at its lowest tolerable point. This means that the watch will stop dead before it begins to run below acceptable levels of performance.

Left: The A. Lange & Söhne Richard Lange Tourbillon Pour le Mérite with its intelligent fusée and chain constant power. The dial has a regulator format and the portion of the hour dial that overlaps with the tourbillon aperture snaps in place only between the hours of 6 and 12.   © 2015 A. Lange & Söhne

Below: The A. Lange & Söhne fusée and chain mechanism.
          © 2015 A. Lange & Söhne

Opposite: The Romain Gauthier Logical One delivers an interesting twist on the concept of the fusée and chain. The fusée at 10 o'clock is not a cone, but a flat snail cam. The cam is connected to an intermediary wheel at 8 o'clock by way of a short chain with a synthetic ruby on each link in order to reduce friction. The mainspring is located on the back of the movement, behind the balance wheel. There is no winding crown. Instead the mainspring is wound by depressing the button at 9 o'clock. Each push of the button simultaneously winds the barrel, turns the snail cam and temporarily gives energy to the movement to maintain the timekeeping precision during winding. As the barrel unwinds the torque required to turn the snail cam decreases. The time is set via the crown at 2 o'clock.

          © 2016 Manufacture Romain Gauthier SA

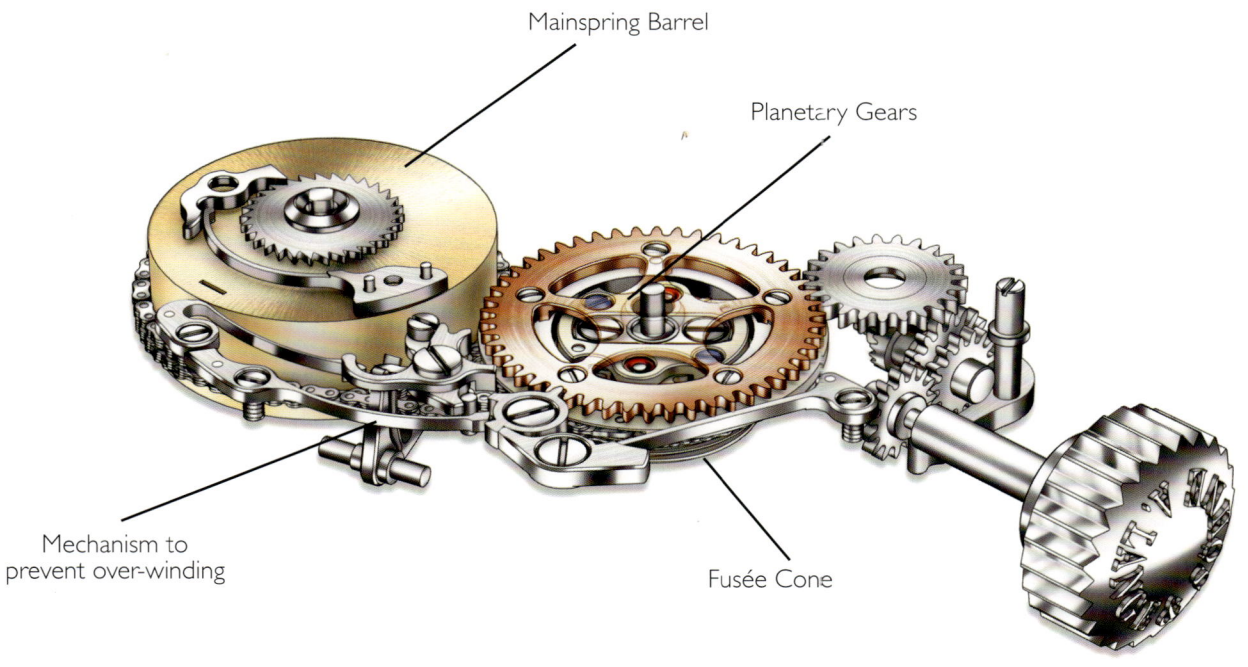

Mainspring Barrel

Planetary Gears

Mechanism to prevent over-winding

Fusée Cone

- **Remontoir d'Egalité** — Even if the power in early clock movements emanated from the mainspring smoothly, as it continued to flow through the gear train, power would be lost to poorly meshed gear teeth, recoil, gravity and pivot friction. This meant that even a fusée and chain movement would experience power deviations as it ran from the fusée to the escapement. The remontoire dates as far back as the 15th century and was designed to prevent such interference from disrupting the rate of unwind and the accuracy of the movement. Today, with contemporary materials, design and production techniques, there is less impact on power; and so the remontoire exists both as a nod to the past and as an alternative distributer of mainspring torque to that of the fusée.

The remontoire is a mechanism that causes energy to build up further down the gear train. The power of the mainspring is then released in periodic bursts of power. Each time it is released it charges a

Above: The movement of the A. Lange & Söhne Zeitwerk Minute Repeater. Note the additional gears used to gain leverage on the ratchet wheel of the extra-strong mainspring (centre-left from 8 o'clock); the blue spring of the remontoire assembly can be seen near the centre-right of the movement at 3 o'clock. The pivoted apparatus above it not only facilitates the charge and release of the remontoire but it also prevents the minute disc from changing time or the crown being pulled out while the repeater is in action.
© 2015 A. Lange & Söhne

Right and opposite: The F.P. Journe Chronomètre Optimum has a double escape wheel escapement fed by the constant force of a remontoir d'égalité. The remontoire would traditionally be charged at 15 second intervals (or more), but this remontoire charges every second and is mounted with an additional seconds hand on the reverse of the movement, which beats at the dead seconds pace anticlockwise. The blade spring remontoire operates under the same principles as the Tourbillon Souverain model.
© 2015 Montres Journe SA

spring, which delivers uninterrupted constant power to the remainder of the gear train. The burst of power is unlocked by a finger or pallet lever downstream in the gear train. Traditionally, remontoires have been calibrated to release energy from the mainspring once every few seconds. While there are examples of this principle being condensed to a single second (for a dead second complication), the A. Lange & Söhne Zeitwerk has a remontoire that releases once every 60 seconds and governs the relatively massive power required to move the hour and minute discs. The watch relies on a mainspring that is far stronger than regular mainsprings, with a notable resistance when winding, and runs on a reserve of 36 hours. Seeing the turn of an hour is rarely more entertaining.

Above and opposite: The Grönefeld 1941 Remontoire Constant Force employs an 8-second remontoire. The caseback reveals a three-pronged pallet fork pivoted at 4 o'clock. The remontoire is attached to the transmission wheel at 5 o'clock and its teeth cause the pallet lever to unlock the mainspring power by way of a snail cam at 3 o'clock. The pivot for the governor is to the left and can be seen bursting into life every 8 seconds on the dial side. © 2016 Grönefeld

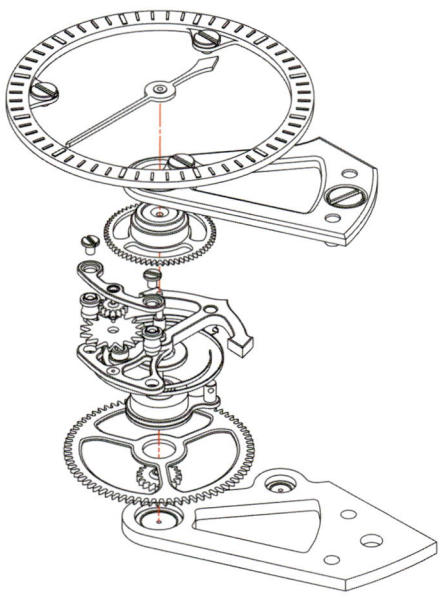

The Arnold & Son Constant Force Tourbillon. The mainspring barrel at 2 o'clock is connected by an intermediary gear to the barrel at 10 o'clock, powering the motion work, the one-second remontoire (at 7:30), and the tourbillon (at 4:30). Unlike the Tourbillon Souverain this remontoire features a stacked set of gears that power a spiral spring.

Dead Second / Independent Second

Despite being hugely common today, the sweeping seconds hand is not inherent to a mechanical movement. Pendulum clocks, for example, were typically regulated by an anchor or deadbeat escapement in conjunction with the swinging pendulum. The generous proportions of such a clock allowed the oscillations of the pendulum to run at 0.5Hz, or 1 beat per second. The seconds hand could therefore be mounted directly onto a 60-tooth escape wheel. In doing so, a pendulum clock displayed the passing of the seconds in single-second intervals. But the smaller and faster balance wheel of the watch movement forced a departure from the precise display of the seconds hand. No doubt the increased

The Jaeger-LeCoultre Geophysic True Second houses an inconspicuous spiral spring-powered dead second mechanism It is not stacked, but tightly packed near the centre of the movement. The arbor of the escape wheel is also armed with a star wheel, whose teeth unlock an intermediary wheel via a thin blade. This causes a burst of energy that charges the remontoire spring, and causes the seconds hand to progress, before the blade locks with the next tooth of the star wheel.   © 2016 Jaeger-LeCoultre

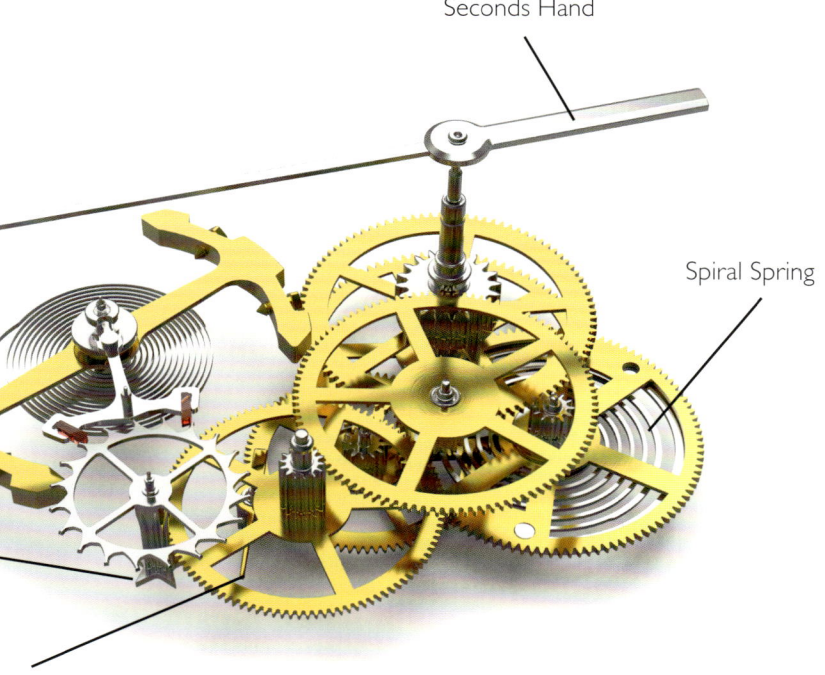

Seconds Hand

Spiral Spring

Star Wheel

Blade

visual pace unnerved some and, during the 18th century, watchmakers revived the dead second.

The most common dead second complication is effectively a one-second remontoire, whereby the periodic release of mainspring energy powers the jump of the seconds hand. However there are also alternatives that rely on a dramatically reduced escapement frequency. The original dead second complication was further tweaked about 20 years after its initial invention with the creation of the independent second.

Here, the seconds hand was driven by an additional gear train, with a motion work autonomous to the minute and hour hands. This allowed the hand to be stopped at will, without it affecting the timekeeping function. The seconds hand woud not reset, it would just start or stop — a stopwatch, and arguably the earliest form of chronograph.

The F.P. Journe Tourbillon Souverain uses a blade spring one-second remontoire. The mechanism features an intermediary wheel that drives the escapement and is driven by the fourth pinion (the seconds hand). The intermediary wheel is mounted on a pivoted lever that is held under tension by the blade spring. The lever has a pallet which locks and unlocks the fourth wheel, causing the seconds hand to beat. When the power of the Tourbillon Souverain is healthy, the blade spring and the lever cause the intermediate wheel to roll along the locked fourth pinion

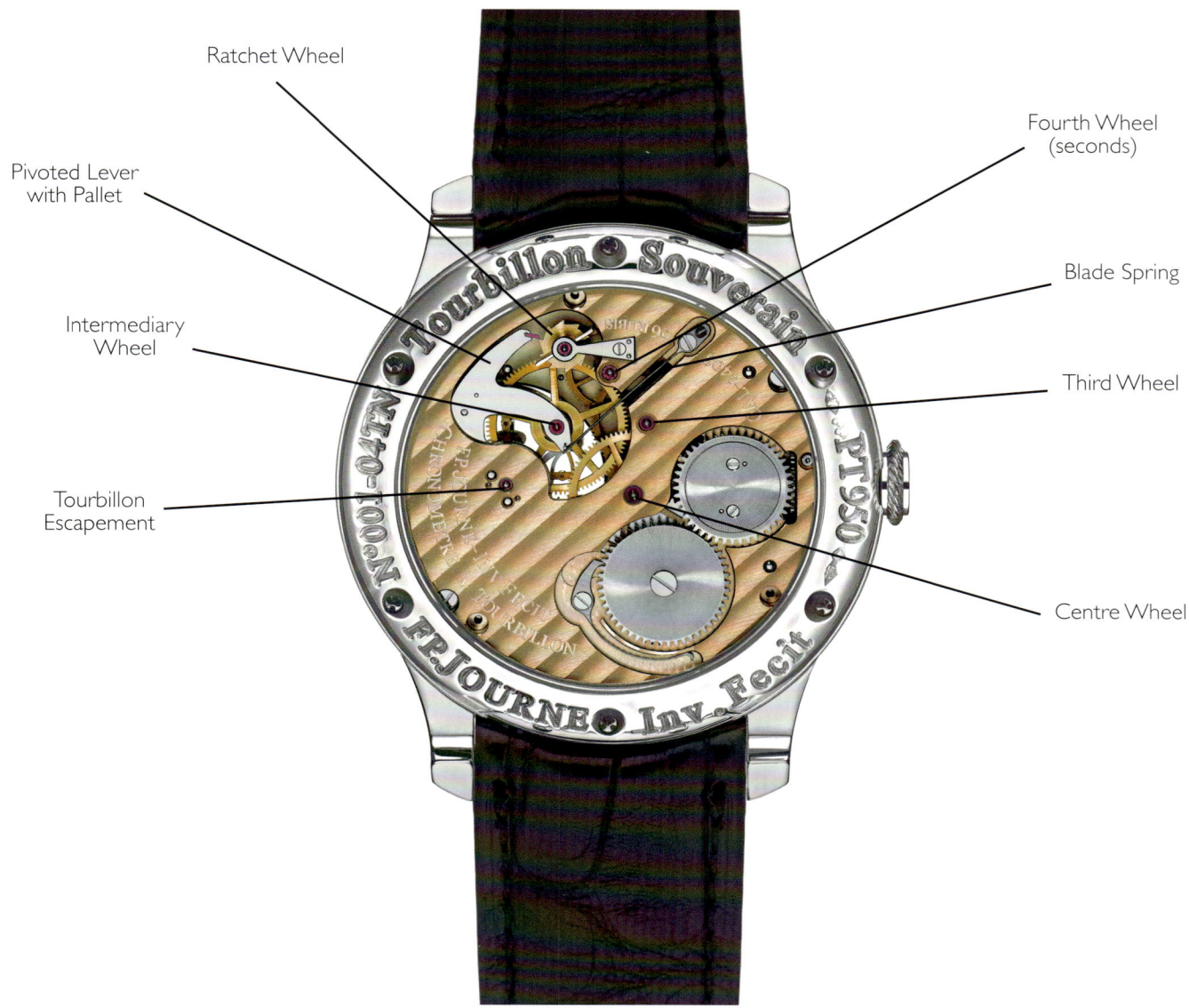

Ratchet Wheel

Pivoted Lever
with Pallet

Intermediary
Wheel

Tourbillon
Escapement

Fourth Wheel
(seconds)

Blade Spring

Third Wheel

Centre Wheel

and drive the escapement. As the blade spring forces the intermediate wheel along, the pallet unlocks the fourth wheel, causing a release of mainspring power. This animates the seconds hand, before locking the fourth wheel once more and recharging the blade spring. The process repeats

itself every second and ensures that the tourbillon is powered by the constant force of the blade spring.

One further point to note: when the power of the mainspring is no longer strong enough to reset the mechanism, the pallet fails to lock the fourth wheel. This means that the fourth pinion takes over from the blade spring in driving the intermediate wheel. As a result, for the last few hours of the power reserve, the seconds hand changes from deadbeat to the six-times-per-second trot of its 3Hz escapement.

Above and opposite: The F.P. Journe Tourbillon Souverain.
© 2015 Montres Journe SA

Pivot for Dead Seconds
Unlocking Lever

Primary Mainspring

Centre Wheel

Third Wheel

Fourth Wheel

Secondary
(Independent Seconds)
Mainspring

Escape Wheel

Alternative Transmission

Because of the rigid principles of transmission, the wheels
and pinions of the gear train are among the most
undisturbed elements of the mechanical watch in terms of
radical innovation. The primary focus is upon continuously
reducing play through greater meshing of teeth and leaves. In
2004 TAG Heuer introduced the Monaco V4, a watch that
showcased a new approach to transmission. Initially a
concept watch but later put into commercial production, the
V4 possesses a belt-driven transmission. Its five-wheel gear
train is connected by 'notched micro-drive belts'. These tiny
belts are, at their thinnest, only 0.07mm thick. The system
allows the wheels to sit independently without the
traditional meshing and with the additional wheel in the
train between the fourth and escape wheels it is one of the few
watches with a transmission that outshines the escapement.

Above: The Grönefeld One Hertz Techniek is a fine example of a
watch that combines both the dead second and the independent
second complications. The two mainsprings are wound together,
but not meshed in their release of energy. The barrel at 12 o'clock
drives the gear train that runs clockwise down the movement to
the balance wheel at 5 o'clock. It also runs the timekeeping at 11
o'clock. The second barrel at 7 o'clock is entirely devoted to
powering the dead second hand. How is it regulated? The fourth
wheel of the regular gear train has a second wheel on its axis. The
wheel has large obtuse-angled teeth that unlock a pivoted pallet
lever to unlock a ratchet wheel on the dead second train. It is not
unlike a lever escapement, except the regulator is continuous
instead of oscillating. © 2016 Grönefeld

Opposite: TAG Heuer Monaco V4 with its extremely cool belt-
driven transmission. © 2016 TAG Heuer

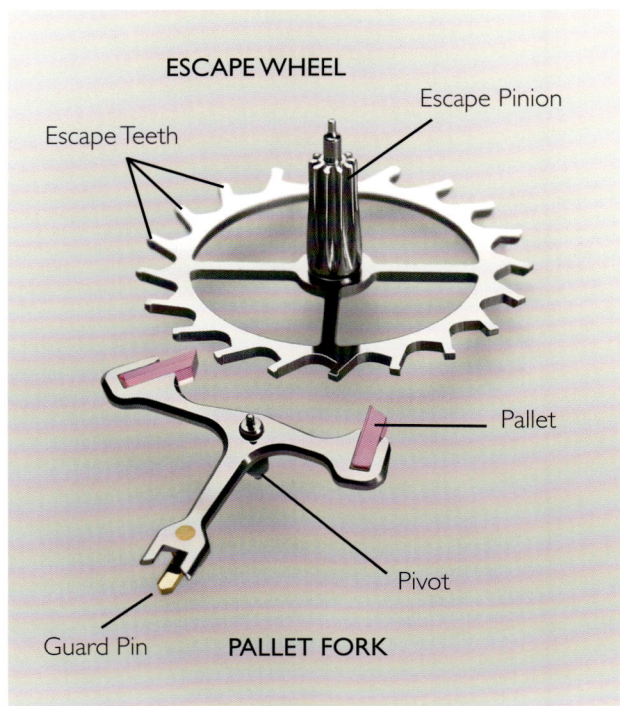

ESCAPE WHEEL

Escape Pinion

Escape Teeth

Pallet

Pivot

Guard Pin

PALLET FORK

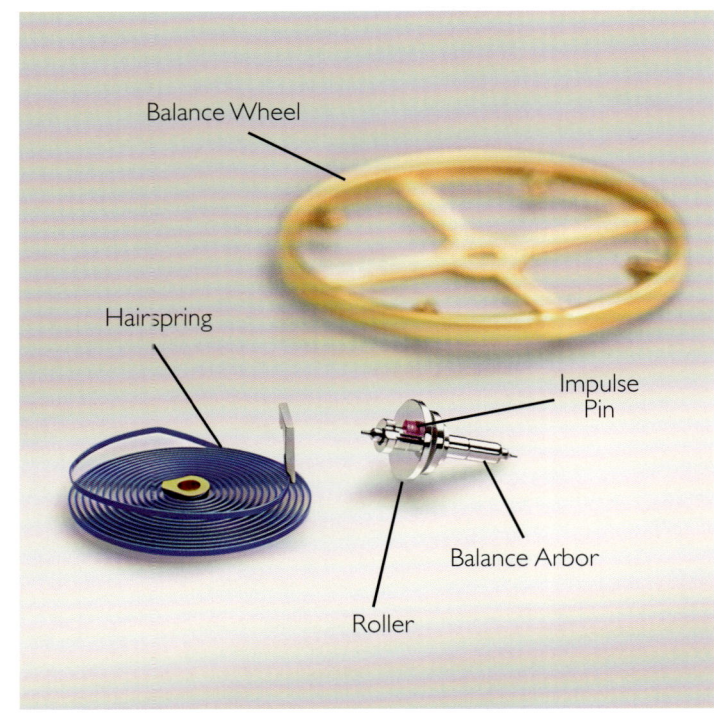

Balance Wheel

Hairspring

Impulse Pin

Balance Arbor

Roller

1.4 Distribution and Regulation

The power source is wound, and the transmission gears have been finely calibrated to deliver a series of specific readings, but with only an open-ended train the mainspring would cause the wheels to turn at an unacceptable pace and fluctuation. The watch would be useless as a precision instrument. In order for the transmission to flow at a steady, predetermined rate, the power needs to be distributed in a regulated manner, and this takes place in the escapement.

The Escapement

The most common mechanical escapement is known as the Lever Escapement, and its principles were developed by a number of watchmaking greats, including Thomas Mudge and Abraham-Louis Breguet. It comprises a balance wheel, with a balance spring connecting it to its arbor, a forked lever (also known as a pallet fork) with synthetic ruby pallets at the end of each fork, and an escape wheel, which delivers impulses to the pallets.

The lever is forked, pivoted, and lies between two banking pins. While one pallet is unlocking the escape wheel, the other is receiving an impulse and locking it. When an impulse is received from the escape wheel, the other end of the

lever (which has horns) passes the impulse to the balance wheel. The horn pushes a synthetic ruby impulse pin on a roller table, which sits at the bottom of the balance arbor. The impulse received by the roller causes the balance wheel to rocket in one direction before its hairspring tightens, stopping the motion, and sending it rocketing back in the opposite direction. This is known as a vibration, but is only half of the full action of the escapement.

As the roller reaches the location of the original impulse, the pallet fork is once again shifted, but this time it is the

Above: The component pieces of a Rolex lever escapement.

© 2016 Rolex

Opposite: The MB&F Legacy Machine No.1 puts the lever escapement, literally, above all things. It is suspended by a wishbone bridge well above the dial thanks to the domed sapphire glass. The watch gives an excellent view of the balance wheel, hairspring, escape wheel and the frantically moving pallet lever. Notice the two lacquered dials which are managed by independent trains and crowns, and the three-dimensional power reserve indicator at 6 o'clock.

© 2016 MB&F

impulse pin feeding back to the lever. The lever is able to pivot across the roller only when its safety pin is aligned to a recess in the safety roller. This brief moment of alignment allows the lever to pivot and the pallet to unlock the escape wheel. As the pallet is unlocking the escape wheel, and the safety pin is passing through the safety roller, the pallet receives another impulse.

This new impulse ends when the other pallet locks the escape wheel, the lever hits the banking pin, and the horn sends the roller pin on its way. The balance wheel flies back until the balance hairspring tightens, stopping the motion, and sending it flying forwards again. This repeating cycle is called an oscillation.

A single oscillation of a lever escapement consists of two vibrations and two impulses from a traditional lever escapement. This takes place about four times every second. This concept alone is sufficient reason for periodically servicing a watch. Lubricant is key with the lever escapement. Although the use of synthetic rubies at certain high-friction points of contact will limit the effects of sliding friction, the watch will still rely on lubrication and this lubrication will eventually age and develop inconsistencies. Imagine leaving a car running permanently and never changing the oil; eventually the oil would run dry and you would have metal grinding on metal until the whole thing seized up. The movement of a watch is no different.

It is worth noting that the lever escapement is a detached impulse escapement as opposed to a frictional rest escapement (the latter are common in earlier escapements). This means that the impulse is not delivered directly to the balance axis, but by way of an intermediary, the lever, which secures the escape wheel during the period that an impulse is not being received so that the balance can move without friction from the gear train. There are several examples of both types of escapement covered in this chapter.

The frequency of an escapement is measured by the number of oscillations per second (Hz) or the number of vibrations per hour (vph). For example, a standard escapement, described as running at a frequency of 4Hz or 28,800 vph, indicates that a 4Hz escapement is performing 4 oscillations every second, 8 vibrations per second, 480 vibrations per minute, and 28,800 vibrations per hour. The most common frequency today is 4Hz (28,800 vph), however there are popular movements that run at 5Hz (36,000 vph), 3Hz (21,600 vph), and a few at 3.5Hz (25,200 vph) and 2.5Hz (18,000 vph). Generally speaking the low-Hz movements are characterised by larger balance wheels and

The Glashütte Original PanoInverse XL places the escapement proudly on the dial side of the exposed movement, beneath a hand-engraved bridge. The balance wheel features poise screws and not one but two 'swan-neck' regulators. The regulator on the right adjusts the effective hairspring length and the one on the left adjusts for 'beat error'. Beat error arises when the impulse pin of the balance roller does not sit in line with the pivots of the escape wheel and lever; the asymmetry causes the two vibrations of an oscillation to be uneven. © 2016 Glashütter Uhrenbetrieb GmbH

are often manual wind and classical in nature. This is often because they are inspired by historic pocket watch movement design. High-Hz movements are often associated with chronograph movements or movements that profess high precision. Despite these associations, all of these frequencies are capable of delivering great accuracy and reliability so long as they are well built, and expertly adjusted.

Rate, Amplitude and Isochronism

The ultimate goal of an escapement is to achieve isochronism. Isochronism is a consistent rate, independent of fluctuations in amplitude. It is measured by the delta (δ), which is the difference between the fastest and slowest rate fluctuation when testing in multiple positions.

The rate of a movement is its accuracy. It is expressed in terms of + / - seconds per day and is usually the average rate across several tested positions. So a watch with an average rate of +3 seconds per day will run solidly for 20 days before it ends up a minute ahead of the *actual* time. There is not a single mechanical movement capable of producing a more accurate rate than a good Quartz movement. Generally speaking a Quartz rate will deviate by a second per day or less, whereas a mechanical movement or mechanical chronometer movement might deviate by 5 or 3 seconds respectively per day. Mathematically speaking there is very little difference between the two in terms of perfect accuracy; just consider that the COSC certification (earned by any watch bearing the name 'chronometer') ensures 99.994% mechanical accuracy. But if improving on every 0.001% is paramount then a high quality Quartz watch is the most suitable. The mechanical watch enthusiast has a certain tolerance for the barely perceptible lower accuracy, favouring aesthetics, soul and craftsmanship over cold and calculated absolute precision.

The amplitude of a balance wheel is its arc of oscillation (approximately 280°). A significantly high amplitude (anything over 320°) will risk the impulse pin impacting the back of the lever horn. A significantly low amplitude will cause the watch to run unacceptably fast or slow and / or may not generate the necessary momentum to unlock the next impulse.

The rate and amplitude of the watch can theoretically be stabilised by perfecting the mainspring torque, transmission and distribution, but the two will fluctuate depending on environmental effects or the accumulation of minute internal effects. To achieve perfect isochronism is watchmaking nirvana. Much like a fine painting, the watchmaker needs to know when to put down the brush.

Adjustments

The practical goal of the watchmaker is to ensure as minimal a rate fluctuation as possible across different stages of winding, the different positions and the shocks that a watch receives. The back of a movement will often state that it has been 'adjusted in X positions'. This indicates that the assembled movement has been adjusted to deliver the best rate across these varying conditions.

An adjusted movement is usually tested in three to six positions. The three core positions are: vertical with the winding stem at 12 o'clock, vertical with the winding stem at

A Rolex balance wheel with four Microstella nuts on the inside of the rim. By re-positioning the screws the moment of inertia can be altered, thereby increasing or decreasing the speed of the wheel.

6 o'clock, and vertical with the winding stem at 9 o'clock. A five-position adjustment will include the two horizontal positions, and the sixth position is vertical with the winding stem at 3 o'clock. Taking into consideration the many positions that a watch is in throughout a full run of power it is clear how important it is to ensure that the rate doesn't dramatically fluctuate in any particular position.

How are the adjustments made? Aside from changing the mainspring or replacing other components, there are two kinds of manual adjustment that the watchmaker will make on a finished movement. The first is to adjust the effective length of the hairspring, which can be increased (to slow the rate) or shortened (to speed up the rate). This adjustment is only possible on a movement with a regulated balance, which is often identified by a needle on the balance cock with a + / - indicator. If the hairspring is not adjustable, there will be no regulator and this is referred to as a free-sprung balance.

The second adjustment can be made to the inertia of the balance wheel itself. This adjustment is possible when the

An unusually-shaped Arnold & Son tourbillon balance wheel with inertia weights. It might be hard to imagine at this scale but the direction of the 'notches' on the weights will serve to adjust the moment of inertia.   © 2015 Arnold & Son

movement has variable inertia screws. These are tiny screws (or small weights) positioned along the outside rim of the wheel. When they are screwed down (or rotated) the weight is distributed inward, which speeds up the rate (imagine an ice-skater pulling in during a spin) and vice versa. Every screw / weight has an identical screw / weight at the opposite end of the balance wheel because an adjustment to one side must be repeated on the other side so as to maintain poise. A quarter-rotation of one screw without repeating on the other end is the watchmaker's equivalent to spilling your coffee on your laptop.

Important Escapements of the Past, Present and Future
Although the lever escapement was largely perfected in the mid-to-late 18th century, and is employed in the vast majority of mechanical wristwatch movements, there exist to this day a number of variants to the basic lever escapement. Some have important historical roots, and exist today as meditations on the early days of horology rather than delivering the most efficient functionality. Others sit at the frontier of technological development, seeking to edge ever closer to the ideal of isochronism.

The earliest timekeeping devices (with the exception of the gnomon and the sundial) relied upon a constant flow, rather than an oscillating regulator, to indicate the passing of time. Ancient water clocks, hourglasses, and hour lamps / candles fall into this category, but have no application in mechanical escapements. Mechanical clock and watch movements all require some sort of oscillatory escapement to regulate timekeeping. This was arguably the most competitive and technologically innovative area of watchmaking for the several hundred years preceding the invention and perfection of the Swiss lever escapement. There are scores of historical escapement designs that failed to make it into serious production, or that were immediately beaten to the finish line by others with superior designs.

Similarly, important clock escapements such as the anchor, or early pocket watch escapements such as the verge and the cylinder, had no place in the wristwatch movement. This might have been due to the proportional impracticality of the escapement or the unacceptable level of friction that the balance wheel experienced outside of the brief moment when it received its impulses. They might also have been conducive to recoil or overly sensitive to torque fluctuations.

Modern escapements are detached in such a way that the balance wheel can oscillate with only the smallest moment of friction during impulse, or they avoid a conventional balance wheel altogether. Some still deliver impulses that cause sliding friction between the escape wheel teeth and the pallets, but this issue is somewhat mitigated by modern lubricant technology. Others can deliver their impulses with radial friction, or deliver directly to the balance, reducing or eliminating the need for lubricant. As might be guessed, reducing friction is key, and goes some way to explain the recent introduction of silicon into the mix, as pioneered by the likes of Ulysse Nardin and Patek Philippe.

The following are some of the more important escapements:

- **The Detent (or Chronometer) Escapement** — Invented by John Arnold and Thomas Earnshaw at the end of the 18th century, the detent is a truly impressive detached escapement. The balance wheel swings with only occasional instances of contact with the escape wheel, which is locked by a pallet connected to the detent. The detent itself is a spring-mounted rod, often pivoted, with a semicircular locking pallet at its midpoint (locking the escape wheel) and a claw at the end. The claw runs to the roller of the balance wheel and is accompanied by a blade spring that stretches just beyond it. When the discharging pallet on the roller passes the spring in one direction it moves the claw and the locking pallet on the detent causing the escape wheel to unlock and deliver a radial impulse to the impulse pallet on the roller before being promptly locked again. As the discharging pallet passes in the other direction it only agitates the blade spring which does not push against the detent. The detent therefore gives only one radial impulse (as opposed to two sliding friction impulses) to the balance wheel per oscillation and the resting friction of the escape wheel is isolated from the balance for all but that moment. As a result the detent is highly accurate and the escape wheel teeth require no lubrication. The detent was a key contributor to the life-saving accuracy of the marine chronometer.

  Despite all of this good news, it has some major drawbacks. First, it is not a reliably self-starting escapement. Imagine that the watch stops shortly after receiving an impulse; the detent receives only one impulse per oscillation, therefore in order to restart

The Bvlgari L'Ammiraglio Del Tempo Minute Repeater features a traditional detent escapement. The detent is pivoted with a spiral spring and has a semicircular locking pallet and a claw at the end. The pallet locks with the escape wheel and the claw delivers impulses to the balance roller. This particular escapement also features a cylindrical balance spring and a constant force spiral-spring remontoire on the fourth wheel.   © 2016 Bulgari S.P.A

following a wind, the balance wheel needs to generate its own momentum in order to pass back through the blade spring to receive an impulse. Second, it is prone to stopping when it receives a shock. This is because the locking pin is in place by spring, so a sudden jolt may cause the spring to move and unlock the escape wheel out of sequence, which is likely to cause the balance wheel to arrest due to an insufficient impulse. This was less of an issue with marine chronometers, which sat in gimbals and being on a boat were not subject to sudden shock, but was not ideal for pocket watches. Consequently there are very few detent escapements in modern wristwatches as they require even more customisation to an already highly specialised escapement. Nevertheless there still exist watchmakers capable of such feats.

The Urban Jürgensen & Sønner 1142 CS. The P8 movement not only sports a detent escapement, but one with an enhanced safety roller and detent shape, designed to improve stability. As a consequence a shock will not unlock this escape wheel as it would a traditional detent. The self-starting issue is solved by a less scientific method; the wearer needs to give the watch a shake. © 2016 Urban Jürgensen & Sønner

- **The Natural Escapement and Independent Double-Wheel Escapement** — The lever escapement was more suitable in a pocket watch than a detent, but Abraham-Louis Breguet was not satisfied with the 18th century lubrication required to accommodate the sliding friction of the lever escapement. So he set out to design an escapement that was similar to the lever but eliminated sliding friction. The *'échappement naturel'* features two coupled escape wheels, with one being driven by the gear train; they are locked in place by a single locking pallet. Two direct radial impulses are delivered to the balance axis, each escape wheel alternating with every vibration. The concept was excellent, and the visual effect of two alternating escape wheels a delight, but the escapement simply wasn't as effective as the detent. The friction was transferred from the pallets to the pinion of the escape wheel and any play between the two wheels would impact accuracy. Breguet abandoned it and moved on. However, master watchmakers have in

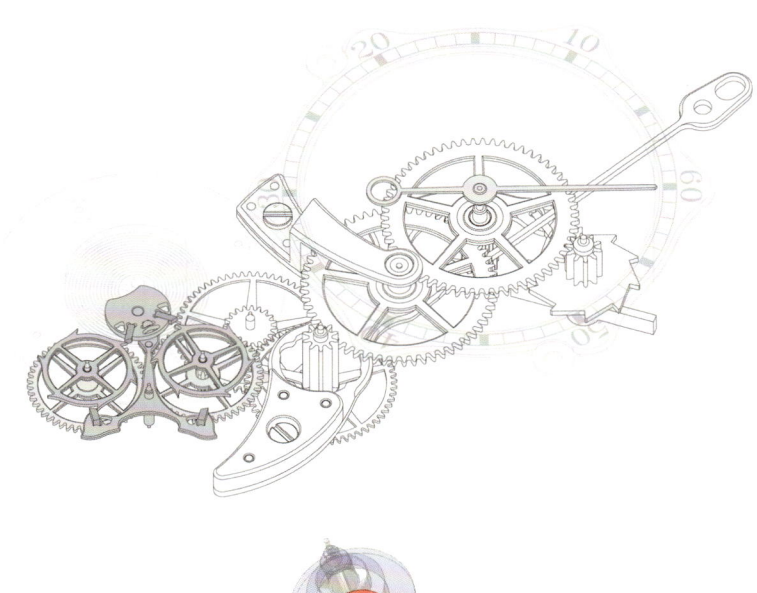

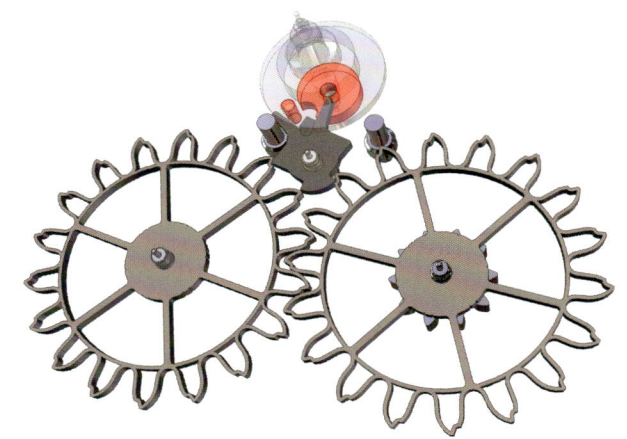

Right, top: The lubricant-free 'High-Performance Bi-Axial Escapement' (EBHP) of the F.P. Journe Chronomètre Optimum (as seen from the movement side). Whereas a common lever escapement is set out in a linear fashion, often without overlap of escape and balance wheel diameters, the EBHP places the escape wheels very closely to the balance. This allows the teeth of the wheels to deliver direct impulses to the pallets on the balance roller, while the lever unlocks the wheels on the opposing side. Being that each of the two wheels delivers one impulse per oscillation (i.e. two impulses) this is one of the few direct impulse escapements that is easily restarted. Think of an impulse as an opportunity to kick the balance wheel into life. The more impulses that occur within an oscillation, the more likely it will restart when the wheel moves only a few degrees from a nudge.

© 2015 Montres Journe SA

Right, middle and below: The Ulysse Nardin 'Dual Ulysse' escapement is perhaps the most advanced interpretation of the natural escapement and it has grown up within several iterations of the unforgettable Freak range. The two escape wheels mesh together (directly, not via the coupling wheels) with one being driven by the gear train. The 'lever' is extremely short, almost circular, and the impulse pin of the balance wheel causes both wheels to unlock. It receives an instantaneous impulse from one wheel, before locking both again. The process is mirrored in each oscillation. © 2016 Ulysse Nardin SA

recent years set out to piece together and realise the dream of an accurate watch-sized natural escapement.

In some pocket watches the original design of the natural escapement was altered so that the two escape wheels were independently powered, rather than meshed; this is known as the independent double-wheel escapement and is beautifully executed in George Daniels' Space Travellers' Watch (see Chapter 2.7).

Today the natural escapement, and independent double-wheel escapement, have been successfully executed in a small number of watches thanks to a combination of modern lubricant, the equalising effect that a remontoire has on the play between the wheels, and the marked improvements that have occurred in wheel-cutting precision today.

The Kari Voutilainen GMT-6. The dial is an exercise in fine engine-turning. Note the thick gold hour indices, and the trademark Voutilainen hands, which are like modern exaggerated Breguet hands. Turning over the watch one is struck by the large diameter of the leisurely 2.5Hz balance wheel, beneath which a glimpse can be caught of the two direct impulse escape wheels.

© 2015 Voutilainen, Horlogerie d'Art

- **The Co-Axial Escapement** — The detent was fragile and only delivered one radial impulse per oscillation, and the natural escapement sacrificed the relative simplicity of the basic lever escapement. Deep into the 20th century, while many settled into the basic lever format there were watchmakers still committed to finding a detached double-radial-impulse escapement. George Daniels, a master watchmaker in the fullest sense of the word, patented the modern co-axial escapement in 1980. What sets the co-axial apart from a regular lever escapement is the unusual shape of the lever and the escape wheel. The lever has three arms instead of two and in most cases is horned at the end of an arm rather than at the shank. The escape wheel has two concentric sets of teeth that sit on different levels. The outer teeth deliver impulses directly to the balance roller and the inner teeth deliver them to the lever. The short radial impulses reduce (but do not remove) the need for lubrication and deliver a strong consistency across longer service intervals. The design was adapted by OMEGA in 1999 and exists in a large number of their modern movements, with a particularly flamboyant 'ninja star' of an escape wheel and a silicon balance in their automatic calibre 9300 / 01.

- **The Constant Force Escapement** — This should not be confused with the constant force mechanisms of the fusée and chain or the remontoire, which exist on the power and transmission elements of a movement. They are all trying to achieve the same thing, but are differentiated by the location along the movement that they are deployed. The constant force escapement is the last line of defence against amplitude-effecting fluctuations in power, delivering a uniform impulse to the balance wheel regardless of the level of power that flows from the mainspring to the escape wheel.

  Produced in 2012, the Girard-Perregaux Constant Escapement features two parallel escape wheels with three peculiar 'teeth'. There is a multi-part lever sitting between the wheels with a horn at its base where the impulse pin on the balance roller traverses. The entire escapement is framed within a single silicon brace, which has an exceptionally thin blade running from one side to the other, passing through two arms and the central point of the lever.

The OMEGA co-axial escapement. When nothing less than a double-radial-impulse per vibration will do.   © 2016 OMEGA SA

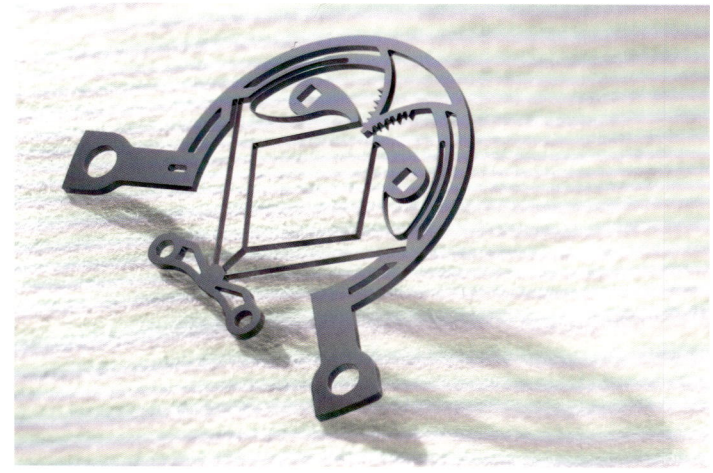

The configuration is structured so that the blade is in permanent tension, buckled in such a way that it forms a shallow wave across the escapement. As the impulse pin on the roller passes through the horn it unlocks the escape wheels, causes the buckled blade to deliver an impulse, and channels that impulse directly to the balance axis. The escape wheels recharge the blade before locking with the lever. This happens in each direction and with every vibration. The energy from the escape wheels is stored at a uniform level in the blade. So long as the escape wheel manages to buckle the blade, a fluctuating level of power from the mainspring will have no impact on the amplitude of the balance wheel because the impulse is delivered by the blade.

In 2014 Ulysse Nardin released the Ulysse Anchor Escapement, which shares similar qualities with the Girard-Perregaux escapement. It features a silicon framework that suspends the lever in place. Instead of a pivot, there are two buckled blades of silicon running from both sides of the framework that converge at the pivot point of the lever. The teeth of the silicon escape wheel and the pallets of the silicon lever require no lubrication.

Above: The Ulysse Nardin Anchor Tourbillon featuring the Ulysse Anchor Escapement.   © 2016 Ulysse Nardin SA

Opposite: The Girard-Perregaux Constant Escapement LM features the very first silicon constant force escapement.   © 2015 Girard-Perregaux

The Tourbillon and Other Gravity-Defying Escapements

Perhaps the most lauded achievement of Abraham-Louis Breguet was his invention of the tourbillon, patented in 1801. The 18th century pocket watch, despite its many developments, was highly susceptible to errors in rate. These errors were predominantly caused by temperature change, magnetism, shock and friction, as well as the effect of gravity on a watch that spent much of its operating life vertical in a waistcoat pocket. The first four issues were able to be adequately mitigated through a broad range of progressive innovations in materials and production methods, but the gravity effect needed some out-of-the-box thinking. If one considers that even a reliable modern movement needs to be adjusted in a number of vertical positions, one can infer that the prolonged effects of gravity on the poise of an escapement are still a threat. But as the poise of a balance wheel is unaffected by gravity when in a horizontal position, this is less of an issue for a wristwatch (which is more commonly oriented in a horizontal position).

Breguet came up with the idea of mounting a lever escapement within a carriage (or cage) that shares the same axis as the balance wheel and is held in place by a bridge. The carriage rotates in the same way that a traditional fourth wheel might, allowing it to be mounted with a seconds hand. The carriage rotates at this rate because the entire escapement is mounted to and rotates around a fixed fourth wheel. The third wheel drives the carriage pinion and as the carriage rotates the leaves of the escape pinion mesh with the teeth of the fixed fourth wheel. So the power is transferred from the third wheel to the carriage and from the carriage to the escape wheel, and the fixed fourth wheel provides the grip for the transfer of power to take place. As the tourbillon rotates, the effect of gravity is somewhat neutralised while the watch is held in a vertical position. The watchmaker is now presented with one accumulated average vertical error to adjust to rather than several independent ones. It was a beautiful solution to a genuine problem. So beautiful in fact, that it survived its own redundancy. As production methods and materials improved, but most importantly as the watch moved from a static position in a pocket to a dynamic position on the wrist, there was no longer as much of a problem for the technology to solve. The wristwatch is attached to a multi-axis human arm, meaning that the cumulative effects of gravity are smoothed out, not just across a vertical axis, but a horizontal one too. Despite this, the tourbillon has proven too beautiful and too compelling for the watchmaker to confine it to history; and so it exists in the wristwatch, where it has continued to be reborn and to evolve into a number of fascinating variations.

Above: The Breguet 3757. A fine example of a one-minute tourbillon. As the carriage doubles as the fourth wheel, a hand can be mounted to the arbor to read the seconds. In this particular layout the dial has a double-ended hand to give the 60 second reading across its 180° chapter ring.   © 2015 Christie's Images Limited

Opposite: The tourbillon carriage on the Vacheron Constantin Tour de l'Ile is shaped like a Maltese cross, which is the logo of the company as well as the wheel used in the stop-work of the watch.
© 2015 Vacheron Constantin

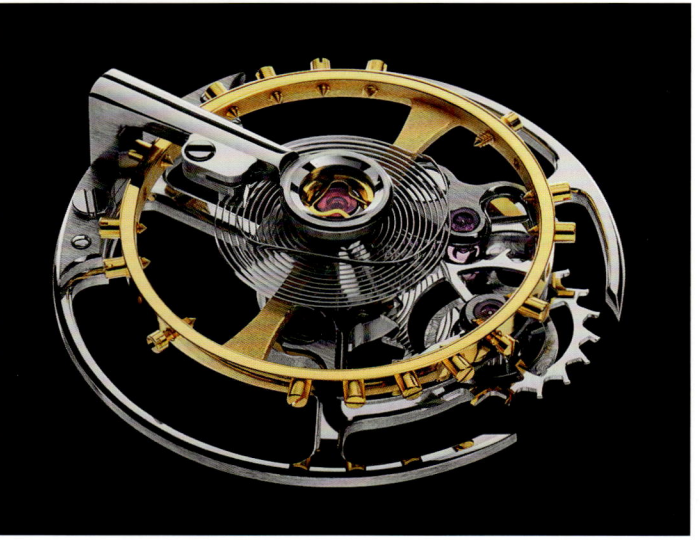

- **The Flying Tourbillon** — The flying tourbillon is a regular tourbillon with its bridge removed for aesthetic purposes. Instead of being attached to the main plate at its axis by the bridge it is cantilevered at its base, giving the impression that it is unfixed, perhaps even flying. Although there is much to be admired in a well-polished tourbillon bridge it is probably more impressive to have unobstructed views of the full carriage. The carriage itself has become something of an opportunity for branding and design flamboyance as demonstrated by many of the modern iterations.

Above: The Cartier Rotonde de Cartier Flying Tourbillon features a tourbillon cage in the shape of a 'C'.
Vincent Wulveryck © 2016 Cartier

Right, above: The Bell & Ross BR01 Tourbillon features a flying tourbillon with the brand's logo on the carriage. © 2016 Bell & Ross

Right, below and opposite: The Grönefeld Parallax Tourbillon features a flying tourbillon with cage that extends a single arm over the top of the balance wheel. In doing so it doubles as a seconds register and moves in perfect parallel to the central seconds hand. The chapter ring of the central seconds is elevated so that the hand is almost flush with it, meaning that it makes a precise reading from any angle (so no parallax error). © 2016 Grönefeld

The Karussel / Carrousel —The karussel was originally created as a cheaper-to-build and slower-moving alternative to the tourbillon. Whereas the tourbillon is an escapement mounted onto the fourth wheel, the karussel is mounted on an additional wheel, which is turned by the pinion of the third wheel. This means that the rate of rotation for the typical karussel is slower, measured in minutes rather than seconds, compared with the typical tourbillon, which rotates once each minute. The karussel is not used on a wristwatch in its purest form. Instead, on the rare

Above: The Blancpain L'Evolution Tourbillon Carrousel helps to clarify the confusion between the karussel and the carrousel. The 'tourbillon' at 11 o'clock is pivoted at its lever. This is a flying tourbillon, but it also fits the description of a carrousel. The escapement at 5 o'clock is very much a modern high-speed karussel, with an intermediate gear train driven by the third pinion. © 2015 Ian Skellern

Opposite: The Jaeger-LeCoultre Master Grande Tradition Grande Complication features a 72-part orbital tourbillon in a titanium cage. The dial is a sandwich of discs and the tourbillon sits on the sky chart disc which rotates once every 23 hours, 56 minutes and 4 seconds. The tourbillon is designed to resemble a star and acts as the indicator for a sidereal day. © 2016 Jaeger-LeCoultre

occasions it is used, it has additional gearing to speed up the rotations of the carriage so that it looks very much like a tourbillon to the viewer. Then there is the carrousel, which according to some is a flying tourbillon with an axis of rotation at the lever rather than the balance wheel. This allows for a simpler carriage design and gives greater access to the components of the escapement, it is therefore more commonly found on the more affordable tourbillons. According to others, the carrousel is simply a modern high-speed karussel. If the balance wheel is eccentric and it rotates rapidly, it suggests that it is a flying tourbillon, if it takes more than a minute to rotate it suggests the latter.

The Orbital Tourbillon —The orbital tourbillon not only spins around its own axis, it orbits the centre of the dial. Easily confused with the flying tourbillon, it is something extra special for the eyes, although arguably not for greater accuracy than the regular tourbillon. The effect is achieved by mounting the mechanism to a wheel earlier in the gear train, or on the motion work, such as the hour wheel. The orbital tourbillon can therefore be used to indicate a particular cycle, such as an hour, or a more abstract period of time.

The Cartier Rotonde de Cartier Astrotourbillon skeleton is not quite an orbital tourbillon, but an escapement that turns around the centre of the dial. The escape pinion engages with a fixed wheel around the centre of the dial and the long cage acts as a crank arm for a central fourth wheel. Because the escapement rotates once a minute it is something between an orbital tourbillon and an eccentrically pivoted tourbillon.

Vincent Wulveryck © 2016 Cartier

The Cartier Rotonde de Cartier Astromystérieux takes the concept of the Astrotourbillon and puts the entire movement into orbit. This is achieved by fixing the movement to a crystal plate that rotates on its own centre wheel once every hour. The minute hand is therefore fixed to the bridge of the movement. The movement is wound and set by two additional sapphire discs that access the ratchet wheel and the motion work via the central axis.

Photo 2000 © 2016 Cartier

The Jean Dunand Tourbillon Orbital contains a Christophe Claret movement with a fascinating take on the orbital tourbillon. The mainspring rotates an entire portion of the movement, including the dial and tourbillon. The side of the movement provides a linear power reserve indicator and the back plate contains a moon phase as well as the keyless works.

- **The Inclined Tourbillon** — A reasonable argument against the need for a tourbillon on a wristwatch is that it does not sit in a vertical position long enough for any gravitational rate fluctuations to accumulate. Of course the balance in a permanent horizontal position may still suffer errors in rate, but the benefits of a tourbillon are likely being wasted when it is mounted horizontally on such a watch. The inclined tourbillon is an interesting response to this issue. By positioning the tourbillon at a tilt the idea is that it will almost never be on an absolutely horizontal plane for any significant period of time. A regular tourbillon, however, can spend its entire reserve in a horizontal position if it is sitting in a watch box. It is an interesting thought that the incline is actually seeking out the potential for more significant gravitational errors in order to provide their smooth average.

- **The Double-Axis, Triple-Axis and 'Gyro' Tourbillon** — A multi-axis tourbillon enables the mechanism to rotate across more than one axis simultaneously. Because of the gearing, the internal axis runs at the

Opposite: The Greubel Forsey Tourbillon 24 Seconds Contemporain. Its inclined tourbillon rotates once in 24 seconds. The entire dial is designed to create vast amounts of space and depth which can be flooded with light so that every polished detail can shine. Note the crystal disc for the hour markers, and the crystal tourbillon bridge. The dial has three levels: the chapter ring, the dial from 11 to 5 o'clock, and the recess for the tourbillon. The depth is best expressed by the tall cannon pinion of the hour and minute hands, which is supported by its own bridge. The plate is blued titanium.　© Greubel Forsey, Art of Invention

Right: The Thomas Prescher Triple Axis Tourbillon is a wonder, as one might expect from the watchmaker who invented the first wearable triple-axis tourbillon wristwatch. The tourbillon is cantilevered on such a dainty bridge that it appears to float in space. More impressive is the fact that the bridge is concealing an incredibly thin lateral gear linking this marvellous regulator to its power source. Even more impressive is the tiny constant force mechanism, as small as a match head, placed on the carriage of the tourbillon. The two axes of this mechanism are suspended in the large aperture, the third axis is the bridge rotating around the circumference of the aperture. With each new axis, the space that a movement requires to execute it grows; to deliver a triple-axis tourbillon without housing it in a clock-sized case, deserves respect.　© 2016 Thomas Prescher

highest speed and the external axis runs at a slower speed. This mix of rotational speeds and axes greatly increases the variety of positions experienced by the escapement. As with the inclined tourbillon, the idea here is to rotate the escapement in such a way that it does not occupy a single plane long enough to exaggerate the error of that plane. This is because the error will be the average of all the positions, which in turn can be adjusted by the watchmaker to be as minimal as possible.

The issue with adding additional axes is one of complexity, weight and size. The gear train needs torque from the mainspring and the multi-axis tourbillon demands huge additional torque. You can only channel so much of it to the end of the train without compromising stability, so the answer lies in

building something as small as technology will allow using the lightest materials possible. A successfully executed multi-axis tourbillon is therefore a tour de force for a watchmaker, an exercise in highly complex design and assembly within the confines of a very small group of exotic materials.

The Jaeger-LeCoultre Gyrotourbillon range executes and displays the multi-axis tourbillon with tremendous skill and style. All three models feature double-axis tourbillons. What sets them apart from other double-axis tourbillons, even triple-axis tourbillons, are their fascinating three-dimensional cages. They are made from aluminium to preserve weight and simply could not have been designed without modern technology. The Gyrotourbillon 1, 2 and 3 use a flat spiral, cylindrical and spherical hairspring, respectively. The spherical spring in the Gyrotourbillon 3 is thought to be the optimal hairspring shape for isochronism, but is hard to construct. The 3 has no visible bridge; instead it is pivoted to the movement at an angle, making it a tilted double-axis tourbillon.

Above and opposite: *From left to right, the Jaeger-LeCoultre Gyrotourbillon 1, Reverso Gyrotourbillon 2, and Master Grande Tradition Gyrotourbillon 3.* © 2016 Jaeger-LeCoultre

Above, left: The Cabestan Triple Axis Tourbillon is among the fastest triple-axis tourbillons around. Its inner tourbillon rotates once every 17 seconds, the second axis once every 19 seconds, and the third axis once every 60 seconds. Their master watchmaker, Eric Coudray, was the brains behind the Jaeger-LeCoultre Gyrotourbillon, which goes some way to explain the confidence with which this mechanism has been executed.

© 2016 Cabestan C.P. Luxe Sàrl

Above, right and opposite: The Vianney Halter Deep Space Tourbillon is a three-dimensional dome built around an extravagant triple-axis tourbillon designed to imitate the *Star Trek: Deep Space Nine* space station. The tourbillon cage rotates once every 40 seconds on a crossbar that rotates once every 6 minutes within a larger cradle that rotates once every 30 minutes. The jumping hour and minute hands claw their way around the outside of the dial and make full use of the exceptional headroom afforded by the sapphire crystal. © 2016 Vianney Halter

Left: The Greubel Forsey Double Tourbillon 30° Technique possesses an inclined tourbillon that rotates on two axes. The first tourbillon is tilted on a 30° axis and rotates once every 60 seconds. The second cage is not tilted and rotates once every four minutes; it is mounted with four crystal hands, each taking turns to indicate the passing minute on the arced register at 6 o'clock.

© Greubel Forsey, Art of Invention

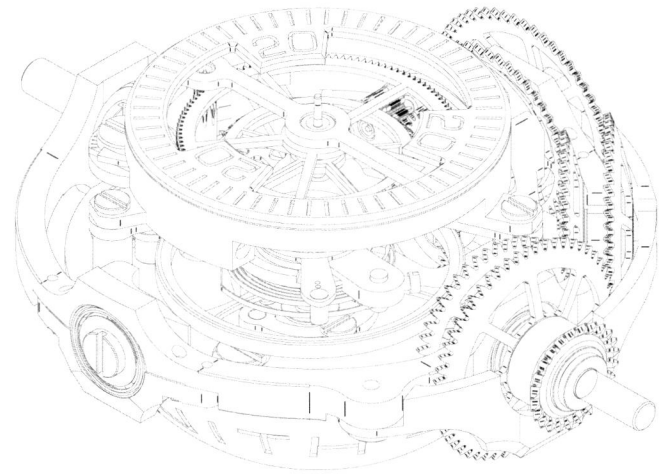

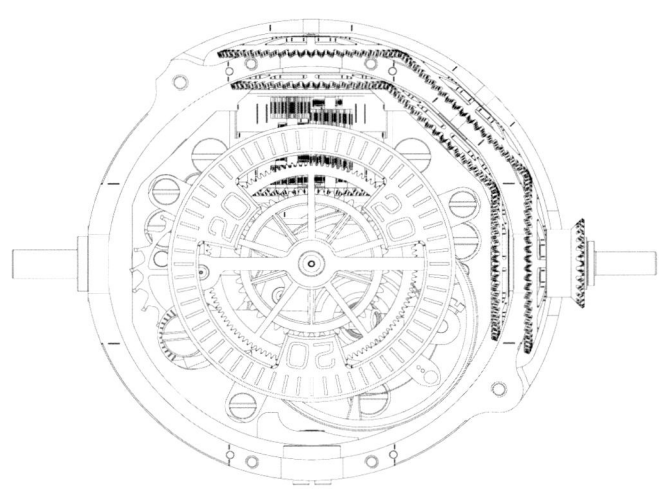

balance wheel escapement, on a weighted gyroscope that moves in such a way as to keep the escapement horizontal regardless of the position that the watch is in. This is essentially a move away from the tourbillon-powered pocket watch and further back to the gimbal-mounted marine chronometer, which was a precision instrument at sea designed to remain steady regardless of its ever-moving surroundings. However, with the marine chronometer the entire clock was suspended in the gimbal, with the gimbal escapement it is only the escapement which sits in the gimbal. The biggest technical issue therefore is how to maintain contact with the transmission of the gear train while almost entirely detaching from the movement. The escapement uses a combination of lateral and curved gears that arc within the framework of the cage to allow the escapement to remain coupled with the gear train (on the left intersection of its axes) no matter what position it is in. It has more parts than some entire movements.

Multiple Escapements

There are three occasions when more than one escapement might be functionally useful, even more than one tourbillon, and if the watchmaker can pull it off without making the watch too unwieldy it can also provide a visual treat.

- **Separate Movements** — First, a watch may be designed to give two totally independent readings, and in doing so might devote entire gear trains and escapements to each complication. For example a high precision chronograph might benefit from using a high frequency escapement and independent train for the chronograph, but a more sedentary one for the timekeeping (see the Breguet 7077, Chapter 1.2). This way the chronograph activation doesn't disturb the rate of the running time and the high frequency, which is a drain on power, can be isolated to be used only when needed.

- **The Gimbal Escapement** — This escapement is easily mistaken for one, but it is not actually a tourbillon. The gimbal escapement shares similarities with the tourbillon in the sense that it sets out to eliminate gravitational rate errors, however its balance wheel does not rotate around its own axis. Instead, it overcomes gravity by rolling with it. The goal of the gimbal escapement is to operate in a gravity-controlled environment so that it can benefit from the specifically-tuned regulation of a single position.

    Zenith, in their Academy Christophe Colomb (and earlier Defy Xtreme Zero-G) range of watches, have created a movement with a 'Gravity Control Gyroscopic Module'. It features a regular oscillating

- **The Differential** — Second, a movement might be designed to have more than one escapement in order to mechanically average-out their errors in rate. Here, the two escapements serve a single gear train and their average rate is channelled via a

Left and below: The Philippe Dufour Duality runs two escapements through a single gear train via an incredibly small differential on the fourth wheel. Extra accuracy is achieved by having two escapements whereby one will compensate for any errors that the other is producing.   © 2015 Gary Getz

Opposite: The MB&F Legacy Machine No.2. Whereas its older brother has a single escapement regulating independent gear trains, the LM2 has two escapements regulating one. Part of the differential is displayed beautifully on the dial, the exposed wheel driving the pinion to its right. The pinion on the left is driven by a wheel on the other side of the stacked differential and the wheels of these two pinions can be viewed on the caseback.   © 2016 MB&F

differential. The differential works according to similar principles of a car transmission. With a car, it is important to feed different wheel speeds when the car is turning (as the wheels on the outside bend will need to rotate faster to cover the greater ground), and a differential is needed to do this. With a watch the differential is usually in planetary format (stacked as opposed to in a train), and is an intermediary in the gear train between the power and the escapements. The single power source delivers impulses to both balance wheels and the differential apportions approximately 50% of the rate from either escapement to the rest of the gear train. The purpose of the differential is to deliver an effective rate that is a little worse than the better performing escapement and a little better than the worse performing escapement. Consider it as an insurance policy against a single escapement misbehaving. However the visual effect, and the fact that there are several multi-tourbillon models that use this method, suggests that function might follow form with the differential.

Left: The Roger Dubuis Excalibur Quatuor resembles a regular watch viewed through a kaleidoscope. It features four escapements, each occupying its own unique axis. The two escapements at the top share a differential, the two at the bottom share a differential, and the two differentials are powered by a third differential. © 2016 Roger Dubuis

Opposite: The Antoine Preziuso Tourbillon of Tourbillons places three 60-second tourbillons on a revolving plate with a planetary differential. The tourbillons orbit the dial once every 10 minutes, the three combined act as one large tourbillon.
© 2015 Antoine Preziuso Genève

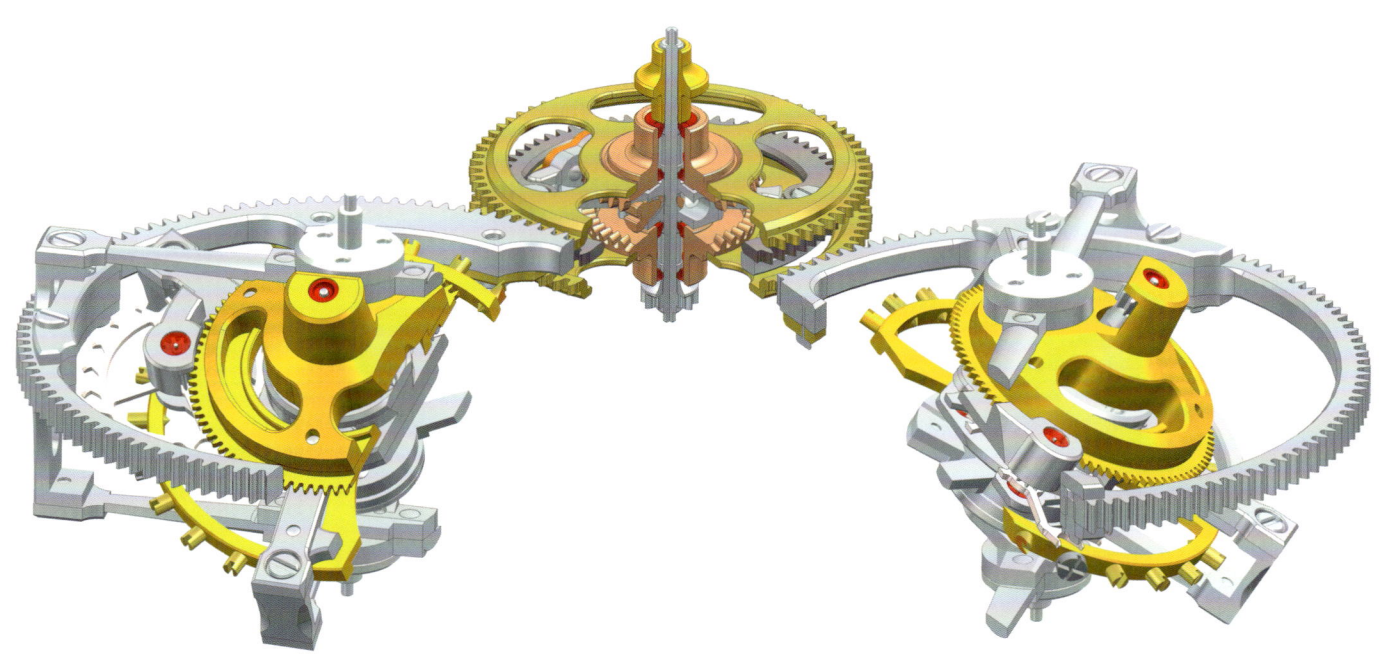

Right and above: The Greubel Forsey Quadruple Tourbillon GF03 Asymmetrical features two double tourbillons and a spherical differential, which can be seen coupled to them via the caseback. The double tourbillons are positioned concentrically although their rotational axes are different; the inner tourbillon rotates once every minute on a 30° tilt, and the outer wheel rotates at a slower rate of 240 seconds and without a tilt.

© 2016 Greubel Forsey, Art of Invention

Opposite: The Speake-Marin Magister Vertical Double Tourbillon is housed in the distinct 'Piccadilly' case, which consists of long straight lugs and a large crown. Other Speake-Marin trademarks include the two tourbillon cages that are designed to emulate an old topping-tool (used to cut wheel teeth), and the 'Foundation' poire-shaped hands. The hands are blued steel on an eccentric dial with day / night and power reserve apertures at 12 and 6 o'clock. Each tourbillon is powered by its own mainspring and coupled to a 'limited-slip spring clutch' differential.   © 2016 Speake-Marin

The Resonance Watch — Third, and far less common, is the resonance watch. There are several areas of mechanical watch theory that venture into near-witchcraft territory, certainly for those of us without a comprehensive knowledge of physics; this is one of

them. The resonance theory states that two linked or closely positioned balance wheels will influence each other's oscillations and that this will have an averaging effect on the rates of the two. Resonance through two *linked* escapements was demonstrably proven in a number of clocks during the 19th century; the two pendulums would eventually settle into a synchronised sympathetic frequency.

But what if the escapements were uncoupled? Could they resonate through the bridges, the plate, or

The F.P. Journe Chronomètre à Résonance.

through thin air? Breguet considered this in a series of tests on pocket watches, and the results surprisingly suggested that they were able to beat sympathetically even with a screen placed between the two wheels (ruling out the influence of air friction). However the two escapements needed to be within just a few seconds per day of each other in the first instance.

Two watchmakers have explored these two different paths in developing resonant wristwatches. Beat Haldimann, with his H2 Flying Resonance, places two balance wheels opposite each other, both with spring remontoire escape wheels. The escape wheels are powered by the same mainspring. The hairsprings do not connect to a pin on the wheel, instead they connect to a coupling spring that links the two. This is a coupled resonance watch and the sight of it alone is spectacular, regardless of the science.

Conversely, the Chronomètre à Résonance, by F.P. Journe, features two totally independent movements, from mainspring to balance wheel, one telling the time with concentric 24-hour and 60-minute discs. Both barrels are wound by the crown at 12 o'clock. The

crown at 4 o'clock enables the adjacent seconds hand to be reset so that it can be synchronised with the other. The two balance wheels sit almost flush against each other. The screw at the centre of the movement is adjusted by the watchmaker and allows the bridge of the balance wheel on the right to be edged closer to or farther away from the bridge on the left. The bridge moves concentrically on the same axis as the escape wheel so the balance wheel and lever maintain the same distance from the escape wheel.

This is an uncoupled resonance watch, each movement telling its own time to the second so that their connection may be tracked on the dial.

The coupled resonance theory is put into animated practice by the Haldimann H2 Flying Resonance. It is easy to forget that this amazing device also tells the time. The hour and minute hands are attached to concentric discs so that they do not interfere with the central escapement.   © 2016 Haldimann Horology

escapement is that it delivers 10 impulses per second, which means that the watch can be calibrated to record time to the nearest 0.1 second.

Beyond 5Hz things become more problematic. The friction caused by the excessive oscillating and the effect of the additional torque required to run across the gear train ceases to deliver the results that a higher frequency movement seeks to achieve. But this hasn't stopped manufacturers from redeveloping the escapement in order to unlock higher frequencies. There has been something of a revolution in recent years with regard to high frequency escapements, and these inventions are worthy of specific mention. Here is a list of notable high-frequency (>5Hz) movements:

- **8Hz** — In an attempt to find the intersection of high frequency, stability and accuracy, Chopard developed an 8Hz escapement for their chronometer-grade LUC 8HF. The movement uses a lever escapement and the risk of heightened friction is mitigated by the use of a silicon escape wheel and lever.

Beyond 5Hz

As we have previously touched upon, the higher the Hz, the more vibrations per second, which tends to mean more frequent impulses and rotations of the escape wheel and gear train. In theory, the higher the Hz the more accurate the timepiece, but a balance must be kept between stability and potential accuracy. A good mechanical watch can run with acceptable accuracy using escapement frequencies between 2Hz and 4Hz. Movements associated with fraction-of-a-second accuracy, such as precision chronographs, tend to run at 4Hz to 5Hz. The specific benefit of a 5Hz frequency on a dual-impulse

Above The Grand Seiko Hi-Beat has a 5Hz escapement running beneath its calm exterior. It is a good example of a high Hz movement without a chronograph application.
© 2016 Seiko Watch Corporation

Right and opposite: The Chopard LUC 8HF has a titanium case, monobloc lugs, and a rapid 8Hz escapement, viewed through a porthole in the caseback.
© 2016 Le Petit Fils de L.U. Chopard & Cie SA

30Hz, recording lapses of time to the nearest 1 / 60th of a second. This was not a pocket watch, but a stop-watch designed for precision astronomical readings. The movement used a sapphire-coated cylinder escapement and a hairspring balance with two adjustable platinum weights as well as a regulator for fine adjustments. This abundance of technology, and the fact that it took another century for anything of this frequency to be developed, suggests that Moinet may well have also invented a time machine.

- **50Hz** — The TAG Heuer Carrera Mikrograph has a 50Hz chronograph escapement enabling 1 / 100th of a second precision. There is no traditional balance wheel, instead the naked spring is attached to the pin and the staff, which has an anchor sitting at its base. This keeps a tight centre of gravity in order to enable such a violent oscillation. We will cover this watch more closely in Chapter 2.1. Of equal merit is the MikrotourbillonS from TAG Heuer. The typical tourbillon rotates once every minute, but there are high-speed alternatives, most notably multi-axis tourbillons with the fastest axis rotating once every 17 seconds. The MikrotourbillonS has a 50Hz chronograph regulator that rotates once every 5 seconds; that is a monstrously fast tourbillon. In order to achieve this frequency, TAG removed the carriage and used a significantly smaller wheel and spring than a conventional tourbillon. Coupled with a central lightning seconds hand, the two spin around like two sugar-addled children vying for attention.

- **10Hz** — The Breguet Classique Chronométrie 7727 runs a 10Hz movement for regular timekeeping and animates the dial with a small subsidiary hand that rockets around its axis once every two seconds. The stability of the rapidly oscillating balance wheel is maintained by placing magnets behind the pivot stones. The dial-side magnet is the stronger of the two, meaning that the balance staff does not actually make contact with the movement-side pivot, and is instead suspended by the magnetic field. This arrangement dramatically reduces the friction at one of the most frantic parts of the escapement and also serves as a shock absorber, allowing the balance to move out of place for a brief moment before being magnetically drawn back to the central point.

- **30Hz** — In 1816 Louis Moinet created the first chronograph and did so with an astonishingly advanced movement running at a frequency of

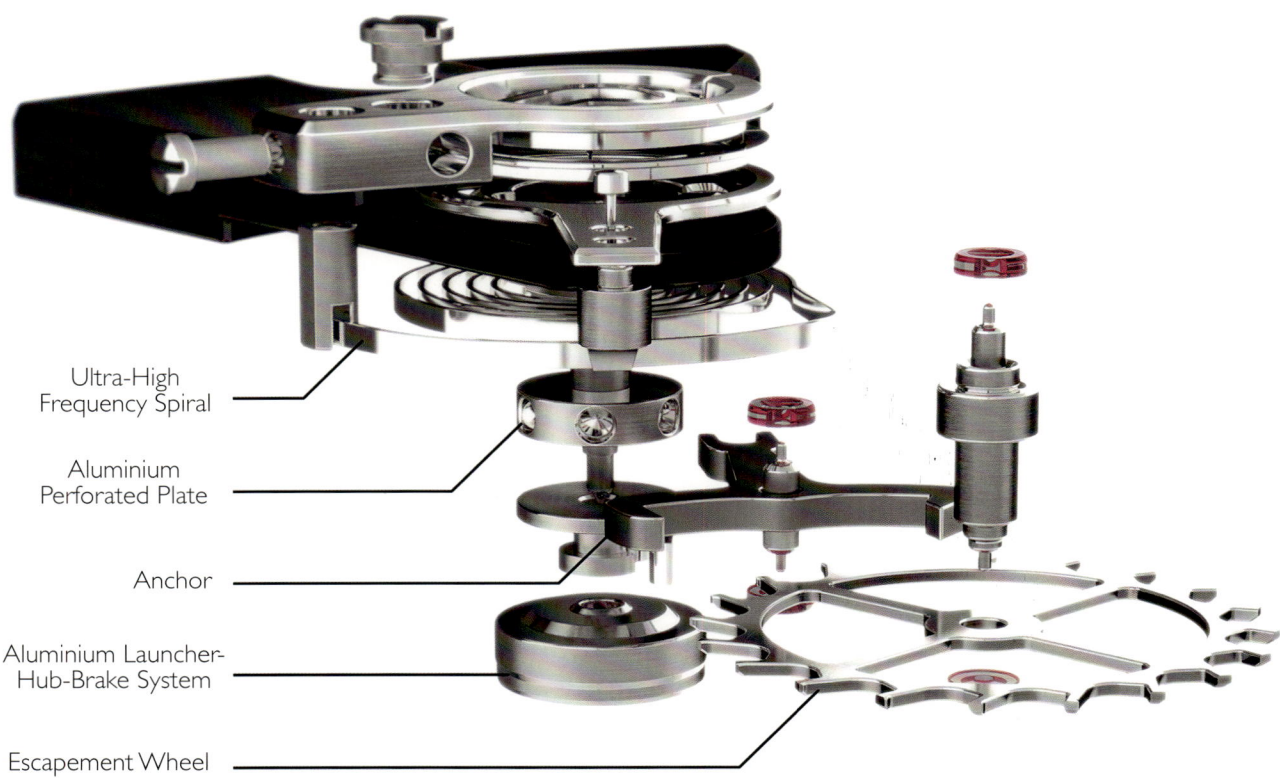

Ultra-High
Frequency Spiral

Aluminium
Perforated Plate

Anchor

Aluminium Launcher-
Hub-Brake System

Escapement Wheel

- **500Hz** — The TAG Heuer Carrera Mikrotimer
  Flying 1000 gives precision to the nearest 1 / 1,000th
  of a second. As with the Mikrograph there is no
  balance wheel and the ultra-high frequency spiral
  spring is attached to an anchored staff. When you
  activate the chronograph, the central hand becomes
  a blur. With a regulator of this frequency, the hand
  performs ten rotations per second.

- **926Hz** — In 2011, the R&D lab of De Bethune
  presented an acoustic resonator and magnetic
  escapement rotor capable of achieving a frequency of

Above: The TAG Heuer Carrera Mikrotimer Flying 1000
escapement.   © 2015 TAG Heuer

Left: The De Bethune Résonique Oscillator is at the very frontier
of mechanical high frequency technology.   © 2016 De Bethune SA

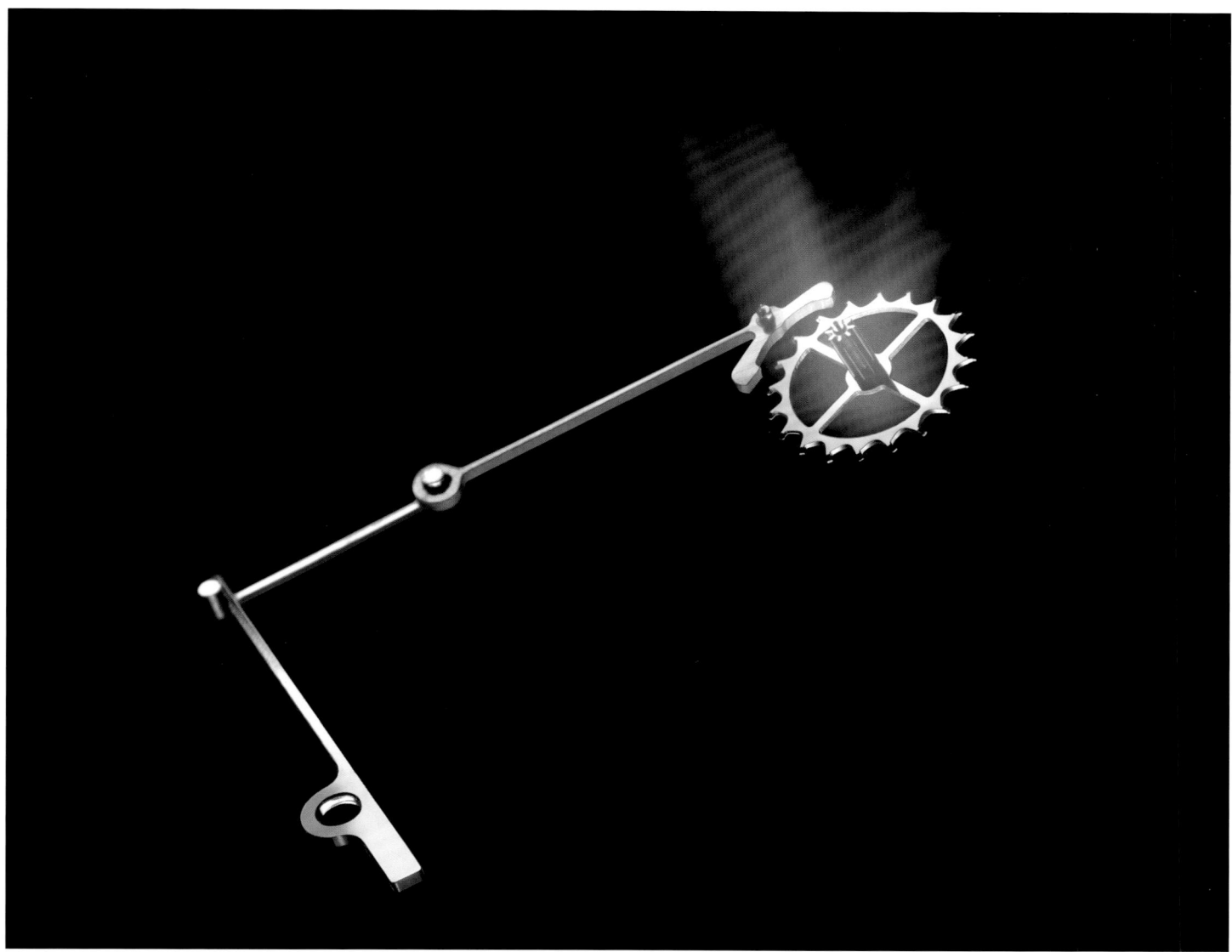

926 Hz. The escapement rotor is magnetic, as are the miniscule bars on the acoustic resonator. Each escape tooth operates as a magnetic pole and their near contact with the magnetic bars causes the resonator to contract for an instant before returning to its original form. During this contraction the escape tooth is able to pass. De Bethune put 926Hz into practical application, but the theory has charted a course that could find frequencies as astronomical as 20,000Hz.

- **1,000Hz** — Instead of an oscillating balance spring and wheel, the TAG Heuer Carrera Mikrogirder uses the tension between two spring blades (or girders)

and a tiny pivoted lever to regulate the escape wheel. When the chronograph start button is pressed the central chronograph hand disappears. Were it not for the buzzing and vibrations emanating from the watch you would not be aware that the hand was still there and performing 20 rotations of the dial every second.

The 'microblade regulator' of the TAG Heuer Carrera Mikrogirder. When achieving 1,000Hz even the most advanced balance wheel and spiral spring would require monumental power and would fall to pieces in seconds.   © 2015 TAG Heuer

1.5 Alternative Movements

Many are aware of the 'Quartz Crisis' during the 1970s and 1980s, when the mechanical watch industry was turned on its head by the rapid introduction of cheaper and more accurate quartz-regulated electronic watches. Several decades later, with the continued availability of cheaper and more accurate technology, you would think that quartz would have well and truly buried mechanical watch production. It very nearly did, and certainly in terms of volume the numbers today are vastly in favour of the integrated circuit. But perhaps it is a testament to the power

of the hairspring that today's global industry is around 80% mechanical in terms of value.

For many watch enthusiasts, hearing the word 'quartz' tends to have an adverse effect on their nervous system. It is easier to associate soul, humanity, and craft with the wheel and the spring, not so much with the integrated circuit. But to discredit the quartz movement is a shame, because there truly exist some remarkable alternatives to the 100% mechanical movement. This chapter outlines some of these alternative movements.

The Tuning Fork Movement

The most radical predecessor / competitor to quartz was the tuning fork movement. Pioneered by Bulova with their Accutron watch, the tuning fork movement set the balance wheel aside and in doing so was able to achieve far higher frequencies by harnessing the acoustic resonance of two fork tines. The fork was large, occupying the diameter of the movement, with two large cups at the end of each tine to house the coils. To one of the tines was attached a miniscule arm with an even smaller pallet stone that delivered its frequency to a 300-toothed wheel. Note that the tuning fork not only regulated the movement, but it also distributed the battery's power to the gear train, and ran in reverse to the power flow of a mechanical movement. The Accutron's tuning fork movement ran at 360Hz, and later models, such as OMEGA's MegaSonic, were developed to achieve up to 720Hz. The resonance of these marvels was perceivable to the human ear and they became known as 'humming' watches.

The Quartz Movement

The first thing to know is that 'quartz' does in fact refer to a crystal and this crystal is key to the *regulation* of the watch (not the power). A quartz movement is typically powered by a disposable lithium battery, although you can power a quartz watch with a lithium-ion battery that is recharged by mechanical rotor or the crown, as with Seiko's Kinetic Direct Drive; or by solar power, as with the Citizen Eco-Drive.

Consider the basic battery-powered quartz movement. The battery translates chemical energy into electrical energy and is the power element of the movement. The transmission element is split between the integrated circuit and the motion work. The integrated circuit is a microchip responsible for 'reading' the feedback from the quartz oscillator and determining the right level of electricity to

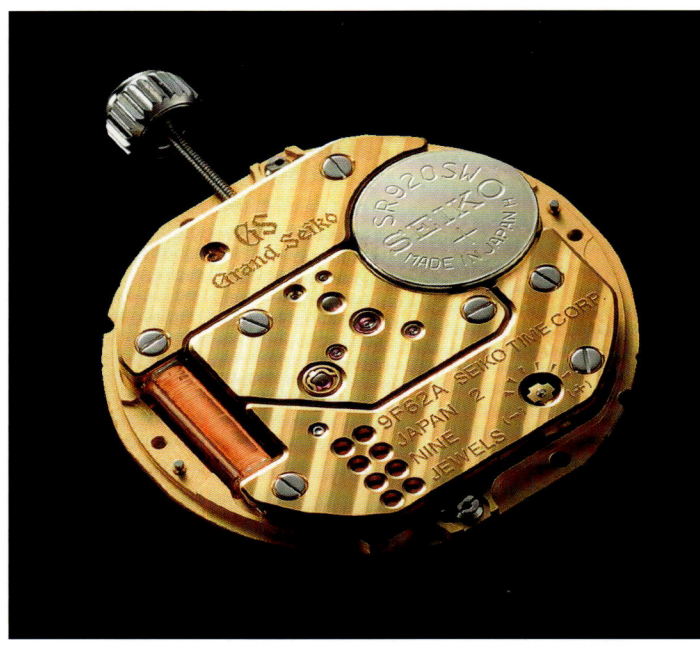

circuit the feedback that allows it to send out its instructions to the motor. Quartz has what is known as piezoelectric properties, which means that it vibrates when an electrical impulse is passed through it. The size and cut of the crystal will determine the frequency at which it vibrates; the most common frequency being a superfast 32,768Hz. Quartz is usually housed within a vacuum-sealed shell, within which it is set out in a tuning fork arrangement. The microchip is responsible for counting the quartz vibrations before issuing a signal to the stepper motor; after each 32,768th vibration the motor can advance the second wheel one increment.

Advanced Quartz-Regulated Movements and the Soul of a Watch

Even though the quartz-regulated movement is far from simple and highly accurate, it does very little to flutter the hearts of watch enthusiasts. This is largely due to a combination of the automated high-volume production of which they are born, and the subsequent low cost of production that allows them to be deployed into some staggeringly cheap and unimpressive watches. Many of us need to see the beating heart, the signs of hand finishing, the meshing of teeth and leaves. These things combine to give us a glimpse of the soul of the watch, or perhaps the soul of the craftsman reflected in the product of their craft. After all, surely there is only so much elegance, beauty and soul with which you can teach a robot to paint?

For those prepared to look, perhaps there do exist some movements that, despite there being a copper coil here and an integrated circuit there, deliver enough soul to steal a watch-enthusiast's heart.

Exhibit A is the Seiko Spring Drive movement. The movement is powered by a mainspring and charged by a high-performance 'magic lever' winding rotor. It has a regular wheel / pinion gear train transmission right up to the escapement. But instead of an oscillating balance wheel unlocking the escape wheel several times per second, there is a constantly and smoothly rotating 'glide wheel'. The speed of the glide wheel's movement is managed by an integrated circuit and electromagnetic brake. The integrated circuit draws its power from the gear transmission, it uses some of this energy to power a quartz oscillator, and it uses the quartz 32KHz feedback as a baseline frequency against which it can regulate the glide wheel (using the electromagnetic brakes). The concept is excellent and the execution delivers a staggering + / - 15 second deviation in accuracy per *month*. What gets enthusiasts excited is the smoothness

power the stepper motor. It sends and receives its messages via a broader electrical circuit board. The motion work, as with the mechanical movement, transmits the power into uniform rotations of the hour, minute and second wheels. With a digital / LED / LCD watch, the motion work is replaced by the digital display and the microchip is responsible for choreographing the digits.

The distribution element of the movement is the stepper motor, which features a copper coil (sometimes two, and often the most visible component aside from the battery) and a magnetised rotor that sits within a bridge called a stator, connected to the coil. When an electrical current passes through the coil it magnetises the stator, causing the rotor to rotate into one position. The rotor is able to rotate because the coil delivers negative and positive magnetic impulses in alternating bursts. The quartz crystal is responsible for regulating this process, giving the integrated

A quartz movement, as with this Grand Seiko 9F62A, is most easily identified by the battery and the copper coil of the stepper motor. While the quartz movement can be executed in a very basic manner, this particular movement is not. It features polished bridges, jewelled bearings for the motion work, and is adjustable to compensate for thermal variations.

of the glide wheel. Whereas the mechanical escapement subjects the fourth wheel to its jittery frequency, with the seconds hand sweeping the dial at a handful of ticks per second, the glide wheel glides. The seconds hand on the spring drive movement sweeps more smoothly than the highest frequency pure-mechanical movement.

Exhibit B is the sleeping quartz movement of the F.P. Journe Elégante. The calibre 1210 is in some respects just a quartz movement; it has an integrated circuit, stepper motor, quartz oscillator and a battery. But the movement also has heart and soul. There are two stepper motors and a mechanical motion detector in the 1210; if the motion detector is dormant for 30 minutes, then the watch goes into hibernation, the hands freeze on the dial. When the watch is moved again one of the two motors rotates the hands in whichever direction will reach the correct time first. This process is managed by the integrated circuit and means that the watch-battery life can be extended by up to 15 years for the most sedentary or infrequent wearer. A quartz motion-based clean energy movement had already been introduced by Seiko in 2005 with their Kinetic Perpetual, however this technical feat is only part of the soul of the timepiece, the rest comes through its presentation. The dial side is as attractive as any mechanical counterpart, and the aperture at 4:30 reveals the rotations of the motion detector. When the caseback is turned over the viewer is presented with arguably the most visually attractive quartz

Above, left: The Seiko Spring Drive Calibre 9R65A could easily be mistaken for a regular automatic movement. However close inspection of what at first appears to be the balance wheel reveals a wheel without a hairspring. Observing the movement in action, with the wheel endlessly gliding, rather than oscillating, would confirm that something unusual is going on under the bridge.
© 2016 Seiko Watch Corporation

Above, right: The SBGA125, or the 'Snowflake' as it is also known. Named after the snow drift effect applied to its dial, the Snowflake is a beautiful watch housing a fascinating movement. The smooth sweeping seconds hand is mesmerising. Put one of these alongside a mechanical watch with a dead second complication and you will baffle all but the most seasoned watch enthusiast.
© 2016 Seiko Watch Corporation

movement to date. A large 18k rose gold plate with Geneva stripes encloses the motion work and battery, artistically laid conductive tracks lead to and from the integrated circuit that sits beneath a rose gold heart. Surely this watch has captured more of the soul of its creator than the beating heart of a run-of-the-mill balance wheel in a mass-produced movement?

The F.P. Journe Elégante. Viewed from the front you have the unmistakeable aesthetic of F.P. Journe. The dial is entirely photoluminescent and the mechanical motion detector is visible through the aperture at 4:30. The back of the watch reveals 18k rose gold Geneva stripes and a heart! © 2015 Montres Journe SA

Atomic Movements

It is widely acknowledged that the final word in accuracy is the atomic clock, but it is a lesser-known fact that this technology has been harnessed in a wristwatch. The Hoptroff No.16 is a dual-dial beast of a watch, capable of retaining accuracy to the nearest second for a thousand years. This is achieved by way of Caesium 133, a stable non-radioactive isotope, which is harmless in its sealed vessel inside the movement. The isotope is heated to 130°C in a miniature oven, before being blasted with a laser to stimulate its resonant frequency. Whereas a quartz oscillator delivers a frequency of 32.8 KHz to its integrated circuit for counting, the atomic movement delivers 4,596 MHz, which is a cool 4.6 billion Hz.

The Hoptroff No.16 with atomic movement. The right dial provides sidereal time, mean solar time, and the equation of time. The left dial runs a perpetual calendar, moon phase, times of sunrise and sunset, and power reserve indication. Whether it be mean solar or sidereal time, if every second counts, this watch will not miss a single one. © 2016 Hoptroff London Limited

SECTION 2

COMPLICATIONS

Watches are inherently complicated, even when displaying their functionality in a sober and pragmatic fashion. Peering through the crystal of a caseback is enough to mesmerise and baffle — certainly for those unfamiliar with watch mechanics. This wonder is something many of us may still experience despite having seen a thousand watches. Who could forget the first time their eyes fell upon an active tourbillon — how can this seemingly autonomous dance possibly have anything to do with the running of a watch?

Watches are indeed complicated, and yes, the industry uses the term 'complication' in reference to the additional parts, assembly time, and sheer innovation on display; but in horology it is principally used to identify the many additional functions that a watch may have over-and-above the display of hours, minutes and seconds. One could be forgiven for considering the term 'complication' to be a poor alternative to 'function', but there is good reason for keeping some distance from the idea of pure functionality, as there are occasions when a complication will cross the thin line between the functional and the whimsical and the downright superfluous.

Other complications provide a technical solution to an issue within the movement. These have less to do with the user deriving a reading from a dial and more to do with improved performance. The tourbillon for example, is often described as a complication, but there are many who would argue against this: the tourbillon is an escapement and adds nothing to the basic readings that the watch delivers. Some may reject them as complications, some might call them 'technical complications' but all would agree that they are a means by which a watch can be differentiated, embellished and complicated.

A watch manufacturer views complications as individual pigments on an artist's palate; choosing which to use and how to apply them is where it all comes together or falls apart. There is also a kind of code behind certain combinations of complications. It is generally appreciated that to be a manufacturer of 'high horology' you must master six core complications: the minute repeater, the moon phase, the split-second chronograph, the perpetual calendar, the ultra-thin and the tourbillon (notice that the last two are technical complications). Design six watches that can deliver these functions with reliable finesse and you are a very serious player. Alternatively a manufacturer who can combine a timing complication with an astronomical complication and a chiming complication in one watch is among the few capable of producing a Grand Complication.

As they venture across the landscape of haute horology (the art of fine watchmaking) most watch enthusiasts will establish a preference for, or an aversion to, certain complications. Some enthusiasts will take a very pragmatic view, shunning any watch with functions that are superfluous or rendered obsolete by its wearer. If you have no need to record the passage of time, much less one's average speed, a chronograph becomes less of an attractive addition to the case and dial and more of a burden to maintenance and wrist real estate. Other enthusiasts will pursue complications that will specifically map to their lifestyle or to the heritage it honours — the regatta chronograph for the boat-owner, the GMT for the aeronautical enthusiast, the dual time for the business traveller. Others might prefer complications that reflect the pinnacle of watchmaking skill, or might simply prefer a busy dial.

The Montblanc Nicolas Rieussec Monopusher Chronograph, a wonderful watch and an homage to the inventor of the 'time writer' and the world's *second* chronograph. Note the 60-second and 30-minute chronograph hands are fixed and it is the sub-dials themselves that rotate. The apertures at 3 and 9 o'clock display the date and the day / night indicator (for the time zone shown by the additional hour hand).   © 2016 Montblanc

2.1 Recording Lapses of Time

When it comes to recording lapses of time there is one dominant complication – the chronograph. The common chronograph features its own seconds hand, minute hand (often) and hour hand (occasionally). The counter is started, stopped and reset by pressing pushers on the caseband.

This chapter looks at the functional and technical variations of the chronograph, each designed to offer enhanced precision or additional readings. Many of these complications were developed as solutions to legitimate problems, providing pioneers and professionals with the ability to monitor their activities on land, sea and air with refreshing mobility. Today, with the availability of more accurate timing devices, they are of less use. Furthermore, when one considers that human reaction time is around

0.25 seconds, one can see how high performance chronographs are something of an oxymoron. Nevertheless, they still have their place in the hearts of watch enthusiasts.

Above and opposite: The Louis Moinet Compteur de Tierces. A staggering feat of timekeeping technology from 1816, with a balance wheel that ran at 30Hz, ten times faster than the majority of precision mechanical watches today. The start button is integrated with the crown at 12 o'clock. At 11 o'clock is the zero-reset. Elapsed seconds and minutes are recorded on the 1 o'clock and 11 o'clock sub-dials. The sub-dial at 6 o'clock is a 24-hour register, split into roman numerals and pips. The view of the back reveals the hairspring, the two platinum weights beneath it, and the large central escape wheel. © 2016 Les Ateliers Louis Moinet S.A

The First Chronograph

A chronograph is essentially a stopwatch, a means by which the wearer can measure the passage of time without disrupting the primary hours / minutes / seconds display of the watch. The word 'chronograph' translates as 'time writer'. Some of the earliest models were developed on watches and clocks with enamel dials and the seconds hand marked the dial with ink. After the time was 'written', the dial could be wiped clean and prepared for a new reading. The earliest of these chronographs was created in 1821 by Nicolas Rieussec, leading to homage models like those of the Montblanc Nicolas Rieussec watch collection. It was Rieussec whom the world of horology credited with inventing the chronograph; however in 2003 the history books were re-written when experts concurred that it was in fact a contemporary of Rieussec, Louis Moinet, who created an incredibly advanced high-frequency stopwatch, the first chronograph, as early as 1816.

The Tachymeter / Telemeter / Pulsometer / Asthmometer

Some chronograph watches include an additional scale, divided into increasing increments, along the circumference of the main dial or etched onto the bezel. These additional scales rely on a central chronograph seconds hand and are referred to as tachymeters (measuring average speeds over a base distance), telemeters (measuring the distance of an object or event by the time it takes for the sound to be heard), pulsometers (measuring the heart rate over a base of 30 pulsations), and asthmometers (measuring the breath rate over a base of five breaths and often included as a secondary scale to the pulsometer).

Each scale has a 'base' reference, however it is perfectly possible to use several base volumes and units. The operator activates the chronograph for the period of time it takes to achieve that base figure. When the vehicle has reached the 1km mark, or the 30th heartbeat has been counted, the chronograph is stopped. The seconds hand is no longer used to refer to the elapsed seconds, but instead is read against the scale to give the average speed / distance / heart rate / breath rate.

Above, left: The Patek Philippe 1518 somehow crams a tachymeter, chronograph and perpetual calendar into a beautiful 35mm case without making a mess.   © 2015 Christie's Images Limited

Above, right: The 175th Anniversary Ulysse Nardin Pulsometer is a fine example of a monopusher pulsometer chronograph.
                    © 2015 Christie's Images Limited

Opposite: The Rolex Daytona has a tachymeter scale etched into the fixed bezel. It does not specify the base unit of distance, allowing the user to use their own native units (km or miles, or any other unit that can be travelled in less than a minute). Imagine you are in a car. Start the chronograph and drive one mile before stopping the chronograph. Read the chronograph hand against the tachymeter scale and you have your average speed. © 2016 Rolex

Why would anyone need a telemeter? As canons are no longer used in battle (the telemeter was a key tool for calculating firing range), perhaps the best modern application is in calculating the distance of a storm based on the elapsed time between lightning and thunder.

The Speedometer

Although not directly concerned with recording a lapse of time, a speedometer makes use of the same technology to record actual speed. The Breva Génie 03 has an in-built speedometer that instantly and mechanically measures airspeed. With their wrist exposed to the open air, the user presses the screw-down pusher at 2 o'clock and the speedometer module emerges from the case to expose a miniature Robinson cup (anemometer) device, which spins while a red hand indicates the speed. The back of the watch is inscribed with a kilometres-to-miles conversion scale.

Above: The Montblanc Villeret Vintage Chronographe with its monopusher on the crown, telemeter scale and spiralled tachymeter.   © 2016 Montblanc

Right: The Breva Génie 03 with built-in speedometer. When the mechanism is activated, the three cups of the anemometer can be seen in action.   © 2015 Breva Geneve SA

Opposite: The Longines Asthmometer Pulsometer Chronograph does exactly what it says and is one of *very* few watches with such a scale.   © 2016 Compagnie des Montres Longines, Francillon S.A

Above: The Richard Mille RM 011-FM flyback chronograph. Note the start / stop and reset / fly-back labels on the pushers at 2 and 4 o'clock, respectively. The watch has central chronograph seconds and chronograph minutes and hours at 6 o'clock. The sub-dial at 9 o'clock is a 60-minute countdown timer that is essentially another chronograph minutes dial with a reverse scale. There is a small month indicator in-between the 4 and 5 o'clock numerals and a large date window at 12.

© 2016 Richard Mille, Horometrie S.A

Opposite: The pilot-inspired Bell & Ross BR 126 Blackbird flyback chronograph. The flyback seconds hand and chronograph minute hand are central on the dial. Chronograph hours, running seconds, and 24-hour dial are positioned at 6, 3 and 9, respectively.

© 2016 Bell & Ross

The Flyback Chronograph

The flyback function enables the operator to reset the chronograph and initiate a new timing sequence with one push of a button, whereas the basic chronograph would perform this with three separate depressions. The seconds hand 'flies back' to zero and continues its journey along the chapter ring with an almost imperceptible speed. This complication was particularly useful to pilots as they calculated their consecutive average speeds. As they were travelling at such a velocity a three-step sequence would be materially wasteful. Doctors also benefited from the efficiency of the flyback function when used in conjunction with a pulsometer.

The Rattrapante / Split-Seconds Chronograph

The word 'rattrapante' comes from the French 'rattraper', which means 'to catch up with'. Whereas a flyback enables a quick reading of two consecutive events, or an immediate fresh attempt at the original event, the rattrapante enables the operator to register two concurrent events. Also referred to as the double chronograph, the rattrapante has the ability to track two cars in the same race. Typically the chronograph's seconds hand conceals an additional, but alternatively coloured or counter-weighted hand. When the rattrapante button is activated the seconds hands will 'split' and the operator will see both the fixed reading of the moment of the split (car 1), and the ongoing chronograph seconds as they continue to march forward (car 2). For a fine example of a split-seconds chronograph see the A. Lange & Söhne Double Split, which not only executes the split seconds with great finesse, but has the addition of a split minute hand on the register located at 4 o'clock.

The Regatta Chronograph

Whereas the flyback and the rattrapante are additional functions that can be added to a standard chronograph layout, the regatta will often require a redesign of the dial if not the movement. To understand the regatta we must take ourselves to a boat race. It is not hard to understand why a large number of boats cannot simply take their marks, get set, and go. Whether it be a group of yachts or rowing boats, the race will require that the participants have enough time to prepare and gather, before they commence the race. This is managed by way of intervals. There are often three flags used to signal a 10-minute warning, a 5-minute warning, and start. These 10 minutes can be frantic to say the least as the team wrestles with the vessel to maintain a fixed position on the rolling waves; the passing of each second must feel painfully slow.

The regatta chronograph is quite simply a countdown timer, often fixed at 5 or 10 minutes, sometimes enabling the wearer to reduce the recording period in 1-minute increments. In some cases this countdown replaces the traditional chronograph function entirely, reducing the minutes dial to a 0 – 10 retrograde scale and doing without an hours register. In some models the minute countdown is displayed via five apertures that turn from blue to red (as per the flag colours) as the chronograph seconds move around the central dial; and in others the central-hand chronograph layout is retained but enhanced to allow the

user to step back the starting point of the minute hand so that it commences timing at -5 minutes. This adjustment is made by way of an additional pusher, which sets back the timer in 1-minute increments. The benefit of the latter is that it will roll past the 0 mark, the point at which the race commences, and will enable the wearer to continue timing the actual race.

Above: The Panerai Luminor 1950 Regatta 3 Days Chrono Flyback Automatic Titanio. The central blue hand for chronograph seconds and the central orange hand for chronograph minutes. The orange hand is moved backward by pressing the orange-tipped pusher at 4 o'clock once for each minute.   © 2016 Officine Panerai

Opposite: The A. Lange & Söhne Double Split. The beauty of the *double* versus the *single* split is that the two events can be tracked even when they differ by more than a minute.
          © 2015 A. Lange & Söhne

Other Specialised Timers

Aside from the regatta, there also exist other chronograph mechanisms designed for recording very specific events. The Hublot Big Bang Unico Bi-Retrograde Chrono King Gold Carbon, for example was developed for the 2014 FIFA World Cup to record the passage of two 45-minute halves of football, including extra time, by way of a two-levelled retrograde display for minutes and seconds. Then there is the Audemars Piguet Royal Oak Concept Laptimer that Michael Schumacher developed in consultation with the brand to operate as a laptimer for multiple successive laps on a Formula 1 track. The watch works as a flyback – rattrapante hybrid. The chronograph seconds are initiated and when the first lap is completed the laptimer button is pressed which simultaneously stops one of the split seconds hands and causes the other to fly back. Unlike a regular flyback or rattrapante the laptimer indicates the last lap time while the current lap continues to be timed. The process can be repeated indefinitely.

Right, above: The Hublot Big Bang Unico Bi-retrograde Chrono King Gold Carbon displays the chronograph minutes and seconds in a retrograde arc designed for the 45 minutes of a football half. There is an additional area marked out for injury time as well as a register for extra time. The pusher at 2 o'clock starts and stops the timer, while also progressing the 1, ½, 2 and END display in the aperture at 12 o'clock to signal the stage of the match.

© 2016 Hublot

Right, below: The Audemars Piguet Royal Oak Concept Laptimer Michael Schumacher. Push the start button at 2 o'clock and the chronograph seconds commence (there are two split second hands). After the first lap is complete the laptimer button at 9 o'clock is pressed, causing one of the seconds hands to stop and the other to fly back for an immediate recording of lap 2.

© 2015 Audemars Piguet, Le Brassus

Opposite: The Rolex Yacht-Master II is a 10-minute countdown timer with red central chronograph seconds and red triangle retrograde minute counter. While the countdown is running, the seconds and minutes can fly back, or fly *forward* to the nearest minute on the countdown by pressing the 2 o'clock pusher. The countdown can be 'reprogrammed' to run at a less-than-10-minute cycle, by a delightfully complicated combination of rotating the bezel, depressing the 4 o'clock pusher, and turning the crown.

© 2016 Rolex

The Foudroyante: the Lightning / Jumping / Flashing / Flying Second

Although the chronograph is limited by its operator's reaction time, not to mention the nanoseconds it takes for the energy to transfer from the fingertip, through the pushers, levers, cams and column wheels, this has not deterred manufacturers from developing mechanical chronographs capable of measuring smaller and smaller intervals *between* seconds.

The foudroyante, which translates as 'lightning', is designed to animate and record fractions of a second with a hand that rockets around the dial making a series of impossibly brief stops along the way. The foudroyante register is usually located on a sub-dial, although some alternatives use the central dial, with the chapter ring running the outer circumference of the dial. The register might run from 0 to 8, recording a lapse of time to the nearest 1 / 8th of a second. There are some variations with 0 – 6 registers and for the decimally-minded, with 0 – 10 registers. This is dictated by 4Hz, 3Hz and 5Hz movements, respectively. A movement is not capable of recording events that occur more quickly than the pace of its impulses. Therefore a 5Hz movement, which oscillates 5 times per second and delivers 2 impulses per oscillation, can record a maximum of 10 increments of 'time' per second (in other words 1 / 10th of a second). The higher the Hz, the smaller the fractions of a second that can be recorded.

The foudroyante is not exclusive to the chronograph. As testament to the importance of aesthetics, there are watches that leave the foudroyante permanently in charge of the running seconds (as with the Jaeger-LeCoultre Duomètre à Quantième Lunaire).

Although precision can generally be improved by increasing the oscillating frequency, as considered in Section 1, there is no complication more benefited by high frequency escapements than the chronograph.

When it comes to pushing the boundaries of high frequency mechanical chronographs, there are few brands that have pushed as hard in recent years as TAG Heuer with their 'Mikro' range. These watches were initially 'concept' models, although several have since made it onto the market. Each variation in the range is essentially a dual movement watch, meaning there is no need for a clutch system to couple the two trains. The regular running gear train has its own 4Hz escapement, with a monster of an escapement reserved for the regulation of the chronograph.

The Mikrograph boasts a separate chronograph escapement oscillating at a highly rapid 50Hz, and measures to 1 / 100th of

Above: The Jaeger-LeCoultre Duomètre à Chronographe. The chronograph is controlled by the monopusher at 2 o'clock and displays the chronograph seconds and hours via the sub-dial at 2 o'clock, and the minutes via a widened aperture at 6 o'clock on the same sub-dial. The foudroyante steams around the sub-dial at 6 o'clock.   © 2016 Jaeger-LeCoultre

Opposite: The Zenith El Primero Striking 10th has a 60-minute chronograph with seconds and minutes at 3 and 6 o'clock, respectively. The foudroyante is centrally mounted and races across the dial once every 10 seconds, with 100 momentary pit-stops.
                        © 2016 Zenith

a second. The foudroyante hand truly is a lightning bolt, flying around the main dial every second with an imperceptible 100 stops along the way. Naturally this is a power-eater, so the chronograph has a power reserve of only 90 minutes.

The Carrera Mikrotimer Flying 1000, as the name suggests, raises the frequency to a terrifying 500Hz. The foudroyante hand rockets around the centre dial a staggering 10 times per second. A full reading of the elapsed time is made by adding the seconds of the central white hand (which rotates once in 150 seconds) to the 1 / 10th and 1 / 100th indication on the sub-dial at 6 o'clock and the 1 / 100th and 1 / 1,000th indication from the yellow central hand. The power is drained from the chronograph after just 150 seconds; not good for timing eggs but ample time for a Formula 1 lap.

Finally, the Tag Heuer Carrera Mikrogirder watches (2,000 and 10,000 model variants) are both capable of measuring up to 5 / 10,000th of a second. It is something of a marketing term to talk about 5 / 10,000th of a second, as the simpler fraction would be 1 / 2,000th of a second. Regardless, these are truly impressive inventions, the foudroyante rotating twice as fast around the dial as the Mikrotimer (i.e. 20 times per second) at a nosebleed-inducing 1,000Hz; it's 250 times swifter than the El Primero. To achieve such pace the balance spring and lever are replaced by two blade springs (seen in Chapter 1.4). It takes a little bit of mathematics to derive the full reading from

the dials of these two models which, as with the Mikrotimer, requires that you add the data from multiple registers; and there is the minor detail of human reaction time clearly being the overriding factor when dealing with 1 / 2,000th of a second! Nevertheless, these are great examples of a brand pushing beyond concept and beyond the everyday remit of their core business in order to deliver genuine technological innovation.

Chronograph Dial Layout

As the chronograph is one of the most popular complications, some watch designers go to great efforts to accompany the function with a unique display. They might use retrograde dials or jumping numerals; they might run all dials concentrically, with five hands sprouting from the same central arbor. But these are the exceptions to the rule. Many brands have built their reputations on the consistent layout of their chronograph model (the Daytona, the Speedmaster, the Navitimer), and some of these have served as design templates for other brands. Additionally, and perhaps more

Above: The De Bethune DB29 Maxichrono Tourbillon is an unusually designed monopusher chronograph. It has three concentric dials, with scales from 1 to 24, 1 to 12, and 1 to 60. Moving from the centre to the periphery, the triangular chronograph hour hand indicates 1 to 24 hours; the Breguet-style running hour hand uses the 1 to 12 Arabic numeral ring; the inner 1 to 60 chapter ring is for the Breguet-style running minute hand and the rose gold chronograph minute hand. The outer 1 to 60 chapter ring is for the long thin hand of the chronograph seconds.
© 2016 De Bethune SA

Opposite: The TAG Heuer Carrera Mikrogirder 5 / 10,000th. As it rotates 20 times per second, each rotation of the central chronograph hand represents 0.05 seconds. But if you look at the register it is divided into five repeating scales of 20 increments. Therefore each scale reads 0.01 of a second (0.05 / 5) and any single increment on the scale will be 0.0005 of a second, otherwise known as 5 / 10,000th or 1 / 2,000th of a second. To read the chronograph, start with the sub-dial at 12 o'clock for the whole seconds, the dial at 3 for the 0.XX seconds, and the central dial for the 0.00X0 or 0.00X5 seconds.
© 2015 TAG Heuer

significantly, mechanical chronograph movements since the mid-20th century (such as those manufactured by Universal and Zenith) were sold to and incorporated into the chronograph models of other brands, and so the layout was determined as much by the outsourced movement design as it was by the in-house dial design.

• **Compax / Bi-Compax / Tri-Compax / Valjoux** — Watches with chronographs are most commonly presented with three sub-dials, one for chronograph minutes (often to 30, sometimes 45 or 60), one for chronograph hours (often to 12, sometimes 24), and one for the running seconds. The chronograph

Above, left: The iconic Universal Genève Compax with registers at 3, 6 and 9 o'clock. © 2015 Christie's Images Limited

Above, right: The Breitling Chronomat sporting the Valjoux 7750. © 2015 Christie's Images Limited

Opposite: The Breitling Chronomat 44, which has a new layout courtesy of the in-house 801 movement. © 2015 Breitling SA

seconds tend to be centrally mounted for maximum legibility. When the sub-dials are located at 3, 6 and 9 o'clock it is often referred to as the Compax layout (after the Universal movement). When they are located at 6, 9 and 12 o'clock it might be referred to as a Valjoux layout (after the ETA-owned Valjoux 7750 movement). Occasionally a chronograph will have a Compax layout as well as an additional fourth dial to register another complication (moon phase, for example). This is referred to as a Tri-Compax layout.

When the chronograph has only two sub-dials, it is typically at the expense of the regular seconds or the chronograph hours. If the subsidiary dials are at 3 and 9 o'clock, it is referred to as Compur, Uni-Compax or Bi-Compax, the latter two also being used to describe a 6 and 12 o'clock layout.

Bi-Compax appears to have been added by watch enthusiasts and was likely a misunderstanding of the 'uni' and 'tri' prefixes, which denote the number of complication sub-dials *in excess* of the running seconds. Nevertheless the term has stuck.

Above, left: The Patek Philippe Nautilus 5980 with clock-face register for the minutes and hours of the chronograph.
© 2016 Patek Philippe SA

Above, right: An OMEGA Speedmaster Automatic with Calibre 1045 movement, based on the Lemania 5100. © 2016 OMEGA SA

Opposite, left: Universal Genève's Tri-Compax model layout.
© 2015 Christie's Images Limited

Opposite, right: There are variants of the OMEGA Speedmaster, such as the '57, that sport the Bi-Compax layout but that avoid having to lose the chronograph hour register by using clock-face hours / minutes. © 2016 OMEGA SA

- **Central Chronograph Seconds and Minutes** — With the chronograph seconds and minutes mounted centrally the user is able to draw accurate readings of both units from the primary chapter ring. To some this is more useful than a 30-minute sub-dial, which requires that the user refers to the hour register to know which of two cycles it is running. Incidentally these chronographs can also be referred to as Compax, Bi-Compax, etc., as they are typically laid out with two sub-dials for regular seconds and chronograph hours, at 3 and 9 o'clock, or at 6 and 9 o'clock, and the occasional third dial at 12 o'clock for a 24-hour indication of the running time.

- **Clock-Face Chronograph Minutes / Hours** — For the more inconspicuous chronograph, a single sub-dial with two hands, mimicking the layout of a regular watch face, will do a perfectly good job of registering the 60 chronograph minutes and 12 hours. The clock-face chronograph can be featured on a watch with a single sub-dial, or can be found on Bi-Compax dials in conjunction with other displays, such as the running seconds.

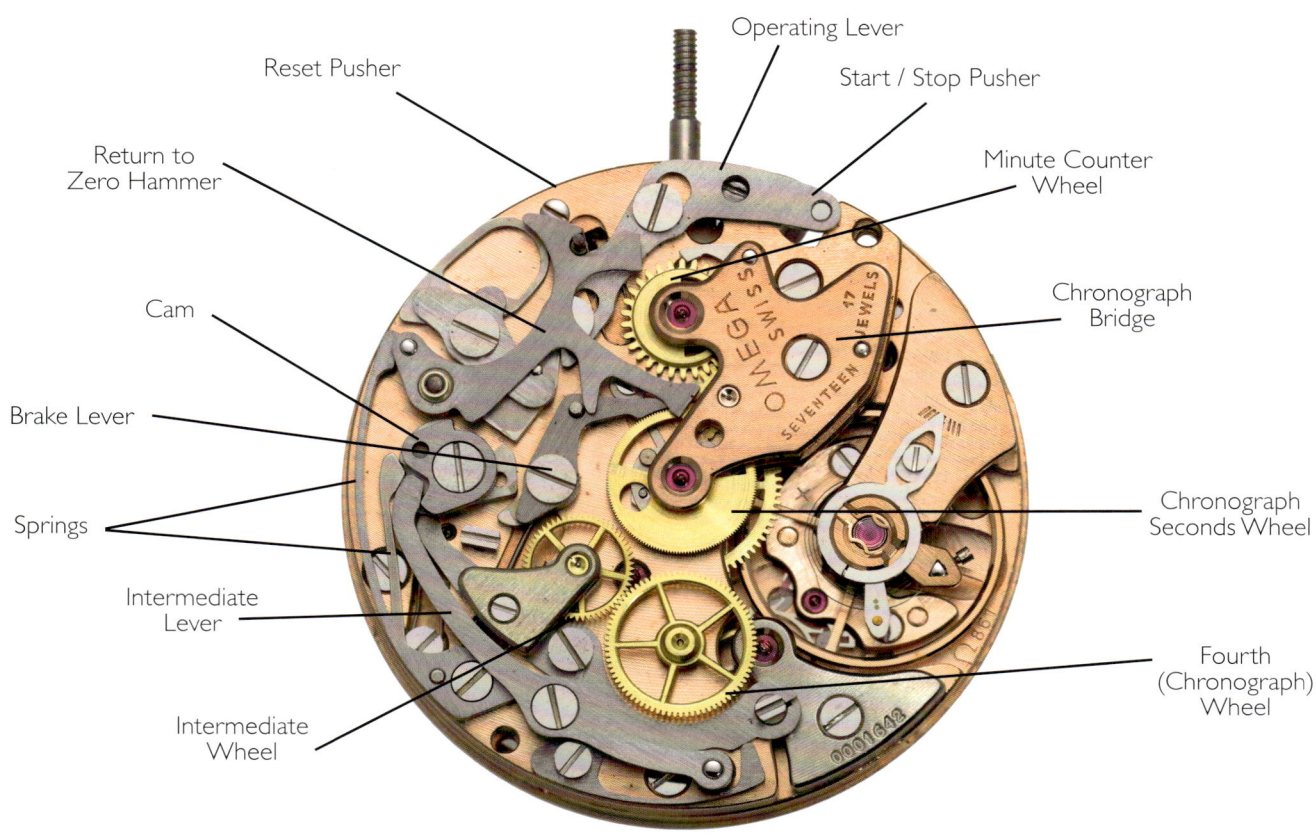

Reset Pusher

Operating Lever

Start / Stop Pusher

Return to
Zero Hammer

Minute Counter
Wheel

Cam

Chronograph
Bridge

Brake Lever

Springs

Chronograph
Seconds Wheel

Intermediate
Lever

Intermediate
Wheel

Fourth
(Chronograph)
Wheel

The Actuator and the Clutch

A hard-core chronograph enthusiast is certainly interested in layout and design, but they will have a particular combination of requirements when it comes to what lies beneath the dial. This is because there are different ways in which chronographs can be mechanically executed, both in terms of how the pushers actuate the mechanism, and in terms of how the gear train of the chronograph and the main movement are coupled.

- **Column Wheel or Cam / Lever Actuated Chronograph** — When you push your chronograph start / stop / reset button, the action will be relayed via a set of cams and levers, or a column wheel system. The latter uses a more three-dimensional wheel that resembles a rook on a chessboard. The former can be identified by the many flattened levers that occupy the movement, as well as the clear absence of the column wheel.

The column wheel features a set of ratchet teeth along its base, and perpendicular columns protruding upward. It is held in place by a jumper. The start / stop push button causes a large pivoting lever to rotate the column wheel tooth by tooth. There are three levers with beaks or teeth that press against the wall of the column wheel, and with

Above: A cam / lever movement with horizontal clutch as sported by the OMEGA Calibre 1861, and housed in the Speedmaster Professional (the watch initially featured the 321, then the 861, and more recently the 1861). Based on an original movement by Lemania (which was subsequently acquired by Breguet, OMEGA's Swatch Group sibling), the 861 is an iconic hand-wound workhorse.

Opposite: The IWC Da Vinci Chronograph with clock-face chronograph registers in a tonneau-shaped case.

each turn of the wheel they drop into the wall or are forced back out. The first is the intermediate lever, which engages and disengages the clutch when the start / stop button is pressed. The second is the braking lever, which stops the chronograph second wheel when the stop button is pressed. The third lever is referred to as the return to zero hammer. The hammer is 'charged' by the column wheel when the start button is pressed, and directly released by the reset button. This causes the hammer to impact with heart cams on the chronograph wheels so that their hands snap back to zero on the dial.

The cam system puts a two-tiered cam in the place of the column wheel. It is held by a jumper

and is snapped into one of two alternating positions when the start / stop pusher drives an operating lever into the lower tier of the cam. This causes the higher tier of the cam to shift into one of two positions, causing an intermediary lever to engage and disengage the clutch. The higher tier of the cam also charges the return to zero hammer when the start button is pressed. Finally, the brake lever, which stops the chronograph hands, is operated via the lower tier of the cam.

Although the two offer similar functionality, the column wheel is often found in today's higher-end timepieces and often marketed as being a complication in and of itself, as well as a superior system. But this is not entirely true. Both systems are equally effective in actuating the function as well as reducing the risk of damage caused by pressing the reset and stop / start buttons in the wrong order or pressing them with too much enthusiasm. The column wheel is considered superior because it has a much smoother feel when activated and because it is more labour-intensive to produce. In addition, the cam / lever system requires a bit more pressure be placed on the pusher, as well as a deeper depression to account for play in the system.

Above: The Valjoux Calibre 72 movement of the Universal Genève Compax features a column wheel and horizontal clutch.
© 2015 Christie's Images Limited

Opposite: A column wheel movement with horizontal clutch as sported, dial side, by the Louis Moinet Memoris. The fourth wheel can be seen behind the running seconds hand at 9 o'clock. A smaller intermediary wheel sits towards the top of the wheel and horizontally couples with the central wheel of the chronograph seconds when activated. The column wheel sits proudly at 12 o'clock.
© 2016 Les Ateliers Louis Moinet S.A

- **Vertical or Horizontal Clutch** — One of the benefits of the column wheel system is its ability to couple the chronograph wheels with the going train via a vertical clutch (although it can also employ a horizontal one). This means that the wheels are already joined by the same arbor and the clutch simply drops the chronograph wheel onto the running wheel in order for the chronograph to start. The vertical clutch experiences more friction when the chronograph is disengaged than when it is engaged. In terms of components and operation the vertical clutch mechanism is significantly more complex than the horizontal clutch.

  Conversely the cam / lever system is limited to a horizontal clutch whereby an intermediary wheel is kept in constant contact with the fourth wheel of the movement. The intermediary lever rolls this wheel laterally until it meshes with the chronograph seconds wheel, causing it to burst into

life. This not only causes an initial stress manifesting itself in temporary loss of amplitude, but it can also result in a visible 'jump' of the chronograph seconds hand as the teeth of the wheels fight to connect. Despite this, the horizontal clutch remains popular and can still be found in the majority of the most iconic column wheel chronographs. It is also worth noting that the horizontal clutch has been refined over the years and certain movements (such as the very popular ETA / Valjoux 7750) run an 'oscillating pinion' horizontal clutch which has less of an aggressive impact on the going train when engaged and results in a less visible jump.

The cam-actuated horizontal clutch system is easy to maintain and is long-lived; it appeals to those who like the snap of the jump. Its parts are easy to replace and an infrequently used function will have a longer life. The column wheel vertical clutch offers a feel of luxury; the functions withstand frequent and prolonged use, and the transition from the seconds hand is seamless. The column-wheel-actuated horizontal clutch is a fine pairing of smooth operation with animated activation.

Above and opposite: The Piaget Calibre 883P is a particularly impressive vertical clutch chronograph as the stacked clutch does not impact the overall world-record thinness of the Altiplano Chronograph that it powers. The clutch, which is always partly engaged with the transmission, can be seen at the centre of the movement. The column wheel is adjacent at 1 o'clock. © 2016 Piaget

Above, left: The 1913 Longines 13.33Z Calibre featured a monopusher for the chronograph and was used in a number of handsome models, including this one from 1918.
© 2016 Compagnie des Montres Longines, Francillon S.A

Above, right: The 1915 Breitling Chronograph, another fine example of an early 20th century monopusher style reborn for the modern age. © 2015 Breitling SA

The Monopusher Chronograph

The earliest chronograph wristwatches were operated via a single pusher at 2 o'clock or integrated with the winding crown. This simple layout meant that the start / stop / reset functions were performed in sequence, but the desire to instantly restart and measure a new lapse of time led to the development of the flyback function in the mid-1930s which necessitated a second pusher. This two-pusher layout soon dominated the movement and case design of the chronograph, flyback or no flyback, during the mid-20th century. Today the monopusher has experienced something of a revival, with some vintage-inspired models opting for the crown-positioned or 2 o'clock pushers. More modern imaginings do without the pusher altogether, operating the chronograph by pressing on the crystal or twisting the crown.

Above, left: The Habring² Chrono ZM is a monopusher with central chronograph seconds and minutes.   © 2016 Habring²

Above, right: The Habring² Chrono CO5 has a central chronograph seconds and a 30-minute sub-dial; its start / stop / reset is managed by twisting the crown.   © 2016 Habring²

The Bell & Ross WWI Monopusher Chronograph Heritage is a very handsome two-register layout monopusher in the style of a pocket watch converted to a wristwatch. It was the urgency of battle that prompted the watch to migrate from the pocket to the wrist. © 2016 Bell & Ross

The Jaeger-LeCoultre AMVOX7 Chronograph. Earlier iterations of the AMVOX range feature a transponder for remotely locking / unlocking an electronically-paired Aston Martin. The AMVOX7 features a power reserve indicator that arcs across the top of the dial, and a vertically-triggered chronograph. The chronograph is started and stopped by pushing on the crystal at the top and reset by pressing the bottom. The switch on the left allows the user to lock and unlock the chronograph function.

© 2016 Jaeger-LeCoultre

2.2 Diving and Nautical Complications

One of the most popular styles of wristwatch is the diving watch, despite few people actually taking one to the dark and murky depths of the ocean. Nevertheless the diving watch is in abundance, with its excessive waterproofing, rotating bezel, clearly marked dial and vibrant luminescence.

Although many may borrow from its styling, a wristwatch marketed as a diving watch will have to comply with the ISO 6425 standard so as not to be discredited. The standard marks out the minimum requirements that the watch must meet in order to perform its functions. Those watches that choose to formalise their compliance with the standard will feature the word 'Diver's' on the dial or caseback. To meet the requirements of the standard, the watch must be totally waterproof to a minimum depth of 10 bar / atmospheres (the equivalent of 100m or 330ft depth). The watch must also be fitted with a unidirectional bezel on which there are clear minute markers and 5-minute increments. The watch must be legible at a distance of 25cm in darkness (thus requiring luminous materials to be applied to the markers and hands). The diver must be able to verify that the watch is continuing to run as indicated by the running seconds hand, and if it is a quartz movement there must be a display for the battery life. Finally, the watch must also be anti-magnetic, resistant to corrosion, and the case and strap must have shock and stress-resistant qualities.

Diving Bezels

The mechanical diving watch is an instrument of simplicity and functionality. The instrument needs to be able to track lapses of time, like the chronograph. However, chronograph pushers, certainly in the early days of diving watches, were the enemy of serious water resistance not to mention heavily gloved hands. So brands like Blancpain and Rolex (with their Fifty Fathoms and Submariner, respectively) came up with a far easier way to time a sequence of minutes while underwater – the rotating bezel. The user simply rotates the bezel so that the zero marker aligns with the minute hand. As the minute hand tracks across the circumference of the dial it also indicates the elapsed time on the bezel.

Left, above: The Oris Divers Sixty Five is a vintage-inspired example of a diver's watch that meets the criteria for carrying the name 'diver'. © 2016 Oris

Left, below: The Blancpain Fifty Fathoms. A handsome diver with unidirectional bezel, and solid heritage. © 2014 Christie's Images Limited

The Rolex Submariner. An extremely popular and enduring design.   © 2016 Rolex

Internal and Locking Bezels

Rotating bezels are often unidirectional for safety. A unidirectional bezel ensures that if the bezel is knocked, it can only be knocked anticlockwise. It will no longer be possible to know exactly how much time there remains to dive, but it will serve to accelerate the recording, meaning that the diver will not think there is more time than they actually have.

It is interesting to note that the rotating bezel is rarely used for its designed purpose. Those serious divers in possession of a mechanical dive watch will wear one as back-up to an exceptionally reliable wrist-bound dive computer. Nevertheless the rotating bezel is considered to be one of the ultimate 'tool-watch' complications. In fact it is barely complex, and it is ambitious to call it a complication as it has no relation to the movement. For many, the value is almost entirely in the sound and the feel of it as it is moved – the pronounced 'click' delivered with a smooth and precise operation.

For those who need more than a unidirectional bezel there are two solutions to ensuring that the bezel stays put. Option 1 is to use an internal rotating bezel, which is commonly operated by an additional crown that sits at 4 o'clock with the winding and time-setting crown at 2 o'clock. This format of crowns makes for an excellently sporty look, a great alternative for the collector who has an abundance of chronographs. Some brands will run with a 2 and 3 o'clock format. There also exists a rather smart diver, the IWC Aquatimer, which is equipped with an internal *and* external rotating bezel. The internal chapter ring is operated by turning the external bezel and the two are coupled via a ratchet / clutch.

Option 2 is the locking bezel, immortalised by the OMEGA Ploprof, a monster with an orange anodised release pusher, which holds the bezel locked in place until it is depressed. This is one of the more practical options for a thick-suited and rubber-gloved professional diver.

Above: The Maurice Lacroix Pontos S Diver features an internal bidirectional rotating bezel, which is operated via the screw-down crown at 2 o'clock. The case is also fitted with a discreet helium escape valve at 9 o'clock. © 2016 Maurice Lacroix

Opposite: The Audemars Piguet Royal Oak Offshore Diver has a screw-down crown at 10 o'clock that operates the internal rotating bezel. © 2016 Audemars Piguet, Le Brassus

Right: The unmistakeable OMEGA Ploprof will turn heads at any black tie event.   © 2016 OMEGA SA

Opposite: The IWC Aquatimer Automatic with SafeDive mechanism. The ratchet / clutch system of the SafeDive enables the user to turn the external bezel in any direction but it only engages with the internal register when rotated anticlockwise.
                    © 2016 IWC Schaffhausen

Helium Escape Valve

The diving bezel, although not mechanically part of a watch movement, can still be loosely described as a complication; and aside from the few earliest waterproof wristwatches (such as the Rolex Oyster and the Panerai Radiomir) they are quite frequently featured on any watch that is marketed by boasting the depths that it can reach. The escape valve, developed in the 1960s by Rolex in collaboration with Doxa, is designed to allow helium to release once it has permeated the watch under the changes in pressure / air mix of a saturation dive and subsequent decompression chamber. The watch may have the greatest water resistance, but it will be no match for helium, which possesses the smallest particles of any natural gas. In a deep dive environment like a diving bell (not typical for a recreational diver) the air will be helium-rich and over time will work its way into the watch; return to the surface too fast and the pressure will cause the crystal to launch from the bezel. The escape valve resolves this issue and can be *manual* by way of an additional crown at 10 o'clock, or *integrated* using an unassuming circular cut-out on the caseband at 9 o'clock. It's a great solution to a problem faced by less than 1% of dive-watch wearers, and is therefore a great example of a watch complication that has a highly functional façade but has its appeal in its existence rather than its use.

Incidentally, since 2012 the deepest diving watch on the market has been the mighty Rolex Deepsea Challenge, which was strapped to a small vessel manned by James Cameron and reached nearly 11,000 of its 12,000-metre depth limit.

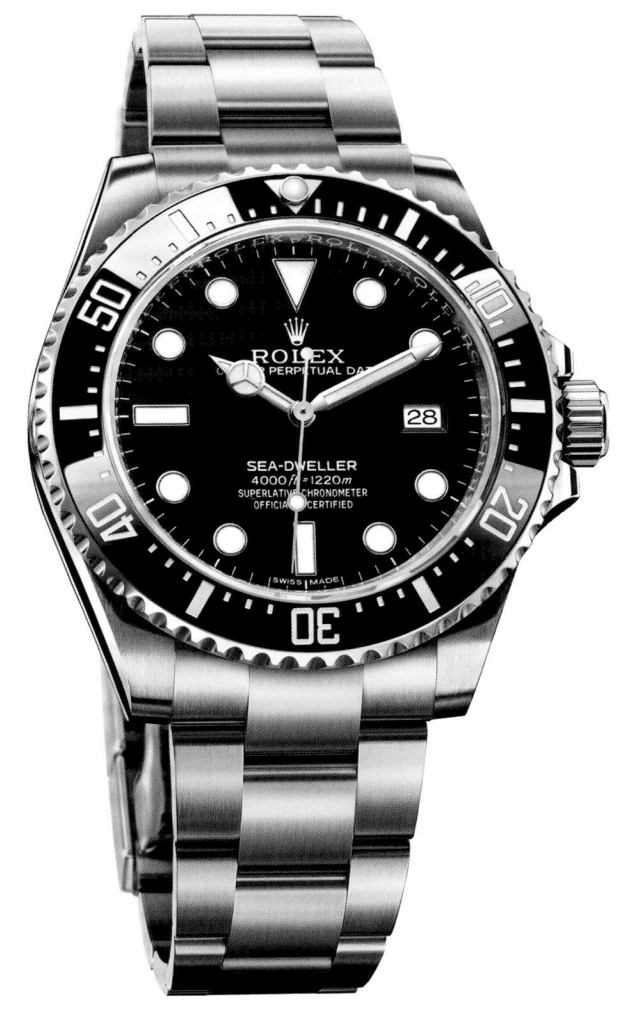

Right, above: The Rolex Sea-Dweller 4000, equipped with a helium escape valve integrated within the caseband. The watch will withstand submersion to a depth of 4,000 feet.   © 2016 Rolex

Right, below: The Rolex Deepsea Challenge is not a regular production model, but a series of three specialist tools designed for the 2012 Mariana Trench dive. There are slightly thinner Deepsea production models available which can achieve 12,800 feet of depth.   © 2016 Rolex

Opposite: The OMEGA Seamaster Planet Ocean features a screw-down crown at 10 o'clock which operates a helium escape valve. The diver must unscrew the crown in order to activate the function. The watch retains its waterproofing, but the valve is now open to release internal pressure.   © 2016 OMEGA SA

Depth Gauge

The depth of one's dive is an important reading to monitor. However, as with most diving complications, today's diver will prefer to rely on his diving computer to track depths, oxygen levels, dive time, etc. Nevertheless, and in the spirit of embracing their obsolescence, a good selection of mechanical depth meters exist that adorn mechanical dive watches.

Some of these gauges have different mechanics and / or different means of display. Take the Jaeger-LeCoultre Master Compressor Diving Pro Geographic, which houses the mechanism in a compartment located outside the core movement, along the caseband at 8 – 10 o'clock. The compartment features an opening covered by a membrane that contracts with pressure and causes the depth indicator hand to progress anticlockwise. The membrane can be pressed with the fingertip to show the gauge in action. Conversely, the Oris Aquis Depth Gauge has built its gauge into the sapphire crystal and allows the water to enter into a channel within the crystal, keeping the complication entirely separate from the movement. The greater the pressure the further into the watch the water will venture, anticlockwise, and the channel in the crystal is frosted making for a visual contrast when it is filled with water – so it is the water itself that marks out the depth on the register. Both the Oris and the Jaeger-LeCoultre are great, but some will take issue with there being an unsealed channel in their

Above: The Jaeger-LeCoultre Master Compressor Diving Pro Geographic. In addition to a mechanical depth gauge, the watch also features a wheel for a second time zone at 9 o'clock, which is selected using a city wheel behind a widened aperture at 6 o'clock. The Compressor range features wing nut 'compressor keys' on the crowns, which allow the fourth gasket to be compressed, to maximise the waterproofing and lock the crown in place. The white arrow indicates that the crown is locked and indicates the direction for the key to be turned to unlock the crown. Turning the key 180° will reveal two black-coloured arrows indicating that the crown is unlocked and ready to be operated.
© 2016 Jaeger-LeCoultre

Right: The Blancpain X Fathoms is where the mechanical watch meets the dive computer. © Image courtesy of Dr. Magnus Bosse, molecular biologist and moderator at the international watch community PuristSPro.com

Opposite: The Oris Aquis Depth Gauge is perhaps the most unassuming watch with a depth meter, opting for a non-mechanical solution within the crystal. © 2016 Oris

watch, and some will struggle with both models' inabilities to retain a reading of the maximum depth.

This is where the IWC Aquatimer Deep Three steps in. It runs a mechanical depth gauge similar to that of the Jaeger-LeCoultre. A notable extra is the maximum depth reading, and also the adjustment crown. The gauge has a red and a blue indicator; when the depth begins to decrease it leaves behind the red indicator, which acts as a record of your greatest depth during the dive. It can be reset by way of the pusher at 2 o'clock. As ambient air pressure can alter the initial reading of the gauge, there is the added bonus of an adjustment crown at 9 o'clock. The crown is used to realign the indicators to mark true zero when at the surface of the dive location. While the additional SafeDive internal / external rotating bezel further contributes to making this a truly

awesome mechanical dive watch, there is perhaps one notable competitor.

The Blancpain X Fathoms, which at an epic 24mm thick, is as close to a mechanical dive computer for the wrist as one can get. The mechanical depth gauge of the X Fathoms has three depth indicators. The blue indicator has a sensitive 0 – 15m depth scale, whereas the yellow indicator runs with fewer graduation markings from 0 to 90m across the same 270° arc. The third, red, indicator is the maximum depth memory. All three indicators work very well together and contribute to an astonishing six centrally mounted hands; but it is perhaps the 5-minute retrograde countdown timer at 10 – 11 o'clock (activated by the pusher at 10), used for timing decompression, that ices the ultimate-wrist-bound-mechanical-diving-tool cake.

Tidal Range / Tide Indicator

One could argue that a tidal range or tide indicator function on a watch is actually an astronomical complication because it indicates the fluctuating gravitational forces of the Moon and Sun and the Earth's rotation. But the tides are a terrestrial manifestation of these celestial phenomena and tend to serve the interests of fishermen and surfers more so than astronomers.

The tidal range is quite simply the tide level at any given location, which will fluctuate from high to low. To best understand a tide complication, it is useful to have an appreciation of the tides themselves. The Moon appears to orbit the Earth once every 24 hours and 50 minutes (its actual orbit is explained in Chapter 2.7). The Moon exerts a gravitational pull on the Earth, a weak one; but when it is combined with the even smaller gravitational pull of the Sun, and the spin of the Earth on its axis, the force has its greatest potential to distort the way that water sits on the surface of the Earth.

Because of this force, the tide is 'high' when the moon is either directly overhead or on the far side of the Earth — in other words it occurs twice in every Moon orbit, so every 12 hours and 25 minutes. The simplest of tide indicators will be a chapter ring with 'High' at 12 and 'Low' at 6, geared to the centre wheel at a ratio that enables a full rotation every 12 hours and 25 minutes. The user simply synchronises the indicator to local high tide.

However, there exist fluctuations in the regular High – Low tide range that can be registered in a tide complication. Take for example 'neap' tides and 'spring' tides. These are high tides that are subject to the *phase* of the moon — which actually means that they are subject to the Sun, as it is the position of the Sun that determines the amount of the Moon's surface that is illuminated. In short, when the Sun is aligned to the Moon (New and Full Moon) the power of the gravitational pull is at its highest and this causes the highest tides, known as a spring tide. Conversely, when the Sun is perpendicular to the Moon and Earth (the Moon is waxing or waning) the forces work against each other and consequently the high tide, a neap tide, is less impressive.

Therefore one can plot a tide register that works in conjunction with the cycle of the Moon, and this is well demonstrated in the Oris ProDiver Pointer Moon which maps out the full tidal range. However, this complication will tell you the *days* when one can expect neap or spring tides, not the exact times of the high or low tides. This additional information can be gleaned from a watch that has a tide indicator *and* a moon phase – a beautiful example of the latter being the Christiaan

Above: The Oris ProDiver Pointer Moon. The orange, arrow hand at the centre of the dial indicates the phase of the moon and when read against the orange marked scale one can determine the strength of the high tides each day, from minimum (neap), to average, to maximum (spring).   © 2016 Oris

Opposite: The IWC Aquatimer Deep Three has a mechanical depth meter with memory.   © 2016 IWC Schaffhausen

van der Klaauw Real Moon Tides, which possesses an extremely accurate moon phase via a large rotating globe and a high / low tide indicator that 'floods' the aperture. The user combines the two readings to determine the strength of the high tide.

There is a watch that is perhaps unrivalled in its ability to perpetually display all relevant tide information via a mechanical movement. The Corum Admiral's Cup AC-One 45 Tides has three tide-related sub-dials: one (at 6 o'clock) indicates the time of the next two high tides via a concentric disc that rotates by the requisite 50 minutes each day and has a hand to indicate the current 24-hour time; a second sub-dial (at 9 o'clock) indicates the ebb – flood flow status (ebb is outgoing high tide, flood is incoming high tide) of a given tide cycle as well as the exact moments of high and low tides; and a third sub-dial (at 12 o'clock) indicates the phase of the Moon and the resulting 'coefficient' of the tide. The coefficient is essentially a measure of the magnitude of the high tide and runs from 20 (very low neap tide) to 120 (very high spring tide).

One final alternative complication is the tide bezel. This can operate with a regular hour hand and an internal or external rotating bezel. The bezel has a High Water marker, which is aligned to the time of the last known high tide at the desired location. These complications are designed to project only one 12 hour and 25 minute tide cycle, unless they are combined with an internal bezel to mark out the corresponding high tides of each day, in which case they can be used to track the tides for up to two weeks. There are also models with rotating bezels that have their own tide hand that complete a full rotation of the dial every 12 hours and 25 minutes (and therefore run perpetually); however these are extremely rare in mechanical watches.

Left: The Christiaan van der Klaauw Real Moon Tides. A wonderfully artistic display of both the moon and tide phases. But do not assume that the accuracy of this complication has any artistic licence. Beneath the dial sits an astonishingly accurate moon phase complication. Whereas a standard moon phase mechanism will lose a day every 2.5 years, this model will remain accurate for 11,000 years!
© 2015 Christiaan van der Klaauw Astronomical Watches

Opposite: The Corum Admiral's Cup AC-One 45 Tides ia a wrist-bound nautical machine. The three central hands could be removed and its usefulness would be undiminished thanks to the 24-hour hand. On this watch it is currently 10:08am. It is a flood tide at present and when the high tide comes at around 14:30 it will be of low / neap strength.
© 2016 Corum. La Chaux-de-Fonds - Suisse

Left: The Sinn 142 St II GZ. The HW1 triangle is aligned with the time of the most recent high tide. A little over halfway along the circumference (to represent the 6 hours and 12.5 minutes of a high-to-low tide cycle) is the Low Water marker (NW), and back past the original marker is a number 2 High Water marker (to represent the 12 hour and 25 minute full cycle).   © 2016 Sinn Spezialuhren GmbH

Opposite: The Heuer Solunar. Align current day and time of high tide to the internal bezel. By aligning the High Tide marker on the outer bezel to the corresponding point of the inner bezel the flow status of that tide cycle can be read. The second high tide of that day can be read against the intermediary dash on the internal bezel, then the first high tide of the following day and so on for up to two weeks so long as the sequence starts on the white Monday.

© 2016 TAG Heuer

2.3 Power and Performance Indicators

Power Reserve Indicator

The hours or days that a watch can run from fully wound is known as the power reserve. The power reserve indicator is the display of the movement's state of winding and can give a reading as binary as a high / low scale or as specific as the exact number of hours or days left in the tank. The indication is traditionally displayed on a fan-form register, often at 10 or 11 o'clock, but there are more exotic indicators that operate as linear scales, apertures that pass from one colour to another, even three-dimensional registers.

Whereas the reserve of a quartz movement is measured in years rather than hours, the reserve of a mechanical movement is measured in hours or days. The indicator is a function not just favoured in, but born of, the mechanical movement. There are purists who believe that the function is only truly necessary on manually wound mechanical watches, as automatics were developed to be a solution to the same problem that the reserve indicator serves to manage – the stopped watch. Many people choose a manually wound movement specifically because they want to feel a close connection to the running of the movement, the need to maintain its power, the idea that the movement is not actually powered by the mainspring but by the twist of your index finger and thumb. Nevertheless the indicator can still be found in certain automatics, perhaps rightly so, as the more sedentary wearer is still at risk of the watch stopping.

Above: The Breguet Classique 3137 has an engine turned fan-form power reserve indicator at 10:30, informing the wearer of the state of wind within its 45-hour reserve.
© 2015 Christie's Images Limited

Left: The F.P. Journe Tourbillon Souverain has opted for a symmetrical fan-form reserve indicator at 12 o'clock. Whereas the more common display indicates the number of hours remaining in the reserve, this displays the elapsed hours since the watch was fully wound. This was the format of choice for 19th century marine chronometers. © 2015 Montres Journe SA

Opposite The linear reserve indicator such as the one seen on the Panerai Luminor 1950 10 Days GMT Automatic Acciaio. The p.2002 movement achieves this by using a rack instead of a wheel to drive the needle. © 2016 Officine Panerai

Right: The Jaeger-LeCoultre Master Compressor Extreme Lab 2 displays the 60-hour reserve on a 180° arc across the top of the dial. It is achieved by way of six apertures and a two-tone disc with internal teeth driven by the reserve gears.   © 2016 Jaeger-LeCoultre

Opposite: The reserve indicator of the Carl F. Bucherer Patravi EvoTec Power Reserve carves a subtle arc and combines a High / Charge / Low scale with a white-to-red aperture.

© 2015 Carl F. Bucherer

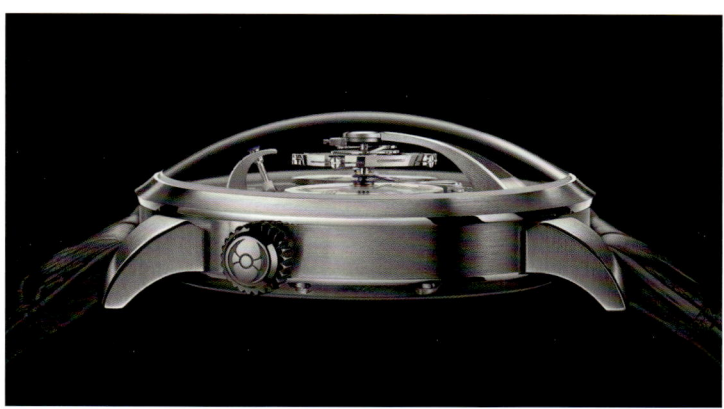

Above and right: The MB&F Legacy Machine No.1 takes further advantage of the domed crystal by using a three-dimensional reserve indicator. © 2016 MB&F

Opposite: The reserve indicator on the caseback of the Ulysse Nardin Freak Blue Phantom shows the approximate state of wind. A large aperture allows the wearer to peer directly into the skeletonised barrel that occupies the entire diameter of the caseback. It is particularly useful given that the mainspring is wound by twisting the bezel of the caseback itself. In this picture the spring is bunched at the outer wall of the barrel and is therefore unwound. © 2016 Ulysse Nardin SA

The indicator mechanism is surprisingly complicated and thoroughly deserves its status as a complication. It is reasonable to assume that all that is required is a reduction gear train attached to the barrel, however the complication arises due to the fact that the barrel drum remains static while the ratchet wheel winds the mainspring, and the ratchet wheel is static while the barrel drum releases its energy to the gear train. In order to convert these two inputs into a single indication, it is necessary to deploy a differential gear that moves the indicator 'up' when the ratchet wheel turns and 'down' when the barrel turns.

As can be seen, there is a lot of variety in terms of the amount of dial 'real-estate' that the power reserve indicator is granted. Some plus / minus displays are very small, nestled into the dial to allow the more important registers their full span. With these watches the accuracy of the register is often foregone in favour of simply notifying the wearer that it's time for a wind. Others make a grand statement of the function enabling the wearer to identify exactly how many hours of power they have left, or just making it clear that knowing the state of winding is of great importance, secondary only to time itself.

Left: The Moser & Cie Endeavour Centre Seconds indicates its seven-day power reserve via the caseback.
© 2016 Moser Schaffhausen AG

Above: The Patek Philippe 5146 enables the wearer to take a simple power reading at 12 o'clock without distracting from the annual calendar and moon phase indications. It's an automatic so why does it need the reserve indicator? With four separate pushers discreetly integrated within the caseband at 2, 4, 8 and 10 o'clock to adjust the month, date, moon phase and weekday respectively the wearer might not want to run out of power too often.
© 2015 Christie's Images Limited

Opposite: The Panerai Calibre P.2002 / E, as featured in the Luminor 1950 Equation of Time 8 Days Acciaio, indicates its impressive eight-day power reserve via the caseback.
© 2016 Officine Panerai

Above, left: The Czapek & Cie Quai Des Bergues No.29 uses a double-ended power reserve indicator to express the state of wind in terms of days and the respective day of the week. The watch is therefore designed to be wound once a week, on a Sunday.   © 2016 Czapek & Cie SA

Above, right: The Roger Smith Series 2 is an entirely handmade timepiece and features a fan-form up-down reserve indicator.
                    © 2016 Roger W Smith Ltd

Opposite: The A. Lange & Söhne 1815 Up Down is a classic example of a traditional alternative to the fan-form register. This style harkens to marine chronometers and is particularly popular with the Saxon and Northern-Swiss manufacturers. The indicator sweeps a large arc of more than 300° to track its state of wind across the 72-hour power reserve.   © 2015 A. Lange & Söhne

Torque Indicator / Dynamograph / Trust Index

The power of a mechanical watch comes from a mainspring that is wound in its barrel by hand or by an automatic rotor. This is the power that drives the wheels and pinions all the way to the escape wheel at which point it is distributed to the balance axis and lever pallet. The escapement is designed to regulate the release of power, otherwise the watch would run as fast as the spring was capable of unwinding. But this regulation is not perfect. Even the most accurate mechanical watches will run at a daily error rate of a second or two. Temperature, friction and gravity will impact the performance on any given day, as will the torque that is being delivered by the mainspring.

Whereas the power-reserve indicator gives a reading of the state of wind, the torque indicator gives a reading of the quality of that power. In recent years different brands have used different names, such as 'dynamograph' and 'trust index', to describe this function. In essence, the torque indicator provides a reading of the current level of torque coming from the mainspring. Whereas the power reserve has a linear path from high to low, the torque curve is smoothest between approximately 90% and 30% wound, it drops off dramatically when the reserve dips below 10% and hits the roof when it is in the top 10%. As discussed in Chapter 1.3, the ideal level of torque is the mid-to-high range and as horizontal (constant) a line as possible. It is possible to mechanically limit the mainspring to operate within this sweet spot, or something more complex (like a fusée & chain or a remontoire) can be used. The torque indicator is an interactive indicator, inviting the wearer to manage their state of wind so that the torque levels are kept constant. For example, one might have a 45-hour reserve indicator but decide to stop winding at 40 hours because the needle of the torque indicator is edging towards the red.

This is not a common complication, not least because it is even more complicated than a power reserve indicator. Unless one is going to make a song and dance of the torque indicator it is easier to stick with a reserve indicator and a slipping spring. But for those that dare, the torque indicator is driven by the recoil of the ratchet wheel on the mainspring barrel. The ratchet wheel is attached to the mainspring barrel arbor; as it rotates the mainspring is tightened around the arbor. The click is used to prevent recoil and so in a movement with a torque indicator it is replaced with a mechanism that performs the same basic function of the click, but does more. Instead of simply wedging its beak in

Above: The Bell & Ross BR01 Tourbillon calls its torque indicator a 'trust index' and positions it across the dial from the reserve indicator so the two can be seen interacting with one another.
© 2016 Bell & Ross

Opposite: The Audemars Piguet Jules Audemars Grande Sonnerie Carillon Dynamographe. This is a sonnerie watch; it chimes the time in passing. The 'couple' indicator is actually a dynamograph, which is actually a torque indicator.   © 2014 Christie's Images Limited

between the ratchet wheel tooth and its arm, the click has several teeth and a blade 'reference spring' to which it transfers the mainspring barrel torque. Instead of stopping the recoil, it acts as a gear and the reference spring stops the recoil. The spring is calibrated to move a lever in response to the varying distance that the spring is bent. As the mainspring unwinds, the reference spring will receive less and less torque until the click is no longer under any pressure and the needle on the torque indicator drops to zero.

One addional complication worth noting is the winding-efficiency indicator. Neither a power reserve indicator nor a torque indicator, this gives a reading of the efficiency with which the mainspring barrel has been wound. The complication exists in the URWERK UR-210, which gives a reading for the efficiency within the past two hours. It's a highly useful tool when you consider that the watch also features an activity-level rotor damping system. For more on the watch see Chapter 2.9.

G-Sensor / Accelerometer

When a watch is being regulated by a rapidly oscillating wheel and spring one might imagine that sudden shocks can have a detrimental effect on the performance of the watch. While this is true, shock and G-force resistance are featured in many modern watches; certainly those watches with a sporty or 'tool' design. For example, an OMEGA Seamaster

or a Rolex Datejust is designed to withstand the momentary G-force of up to 20G in a strong golf drive. OMEGA test their assembled watches to endure up to 100G during an accelerated simulation of 10 years, as well as more focussed tests of resistance to big shocks of 500 – 5,000G (it sounds huge, but it is in fact a drop from waist height onto a hard floor). Shocks are absorbed by a variety of means and in a variety of places, but perhaps the most important area is the balance pivot. Breguet invented the pare-chute system in 1790, which involved holding the cone-shaped arbor pins in place by cone-shaped, spring-mounted cups. The Incabloc was introduced in 1934 and is today the most common system, its lyre-shaped spring seen visibly on the jewels of most balance pivots. Like the pare-chute, the pivot and its jewel are allowed to fall out of place momentarily before being guided back into position by the spring.

When it comes to mechanically resisting, embracing and displaying G-force, Richard Mille is arguably the first name

Right: The Richard Mille RM56-02. The irony can't be ignored when talking about the G-force and shock resistant properties of a sapphire crystal case and a movement with sapphire crystal bridges. Although the RM56-02 could be cleaned with sandpaper and it would cause no harm, it would not be a pretty sight to drop it on marble flooring. In truth this watch is designed with transparency and visual weightlessness in mind, rather than rugged shock-resistance. Nevertheless, the movement has a fascinating shock-absorbent property; the baseplate has been suspended within the case by a single piece of braided steel cable and a series of tensioners and pulleys. A small arrow at 12:30 indicates the amount of give in the cable. © 2016 Richard Mille, Horometrie S.A

Opposite: The Richard Mille RM38-01 is known as the Tourbillon G-Sensor Bubba Watson. You swing, take note of which bush the ball went into, and refer to the G-Sensor at 12 o'clock which will be reading the peak acceleration that the watch experienced during the swing. A press of the pusher at 9 o'clock and the needle of the G-Sensor will snap back to zero.

© 2016 Richard Mille, Horometrie S.A

that comes to mind. With many of their movements literally suspended by bridges or cables, there are particular models dedicated to sports personalities that feature G-force indicator complications. These accelerometers comprise 50 parts, measure less than 20mm wide, and are designed to mechanically record the G-force acceleration that the watch (and attached human) experiences while cornering, braking and swinging a club. Other sensors are designed to indicate when the architecture of the movement is being rendered unstable by excessive Gs.

Thermal Indicator

Generally speaking modern day movement materials, such as Nivarox and silicon can eliminate the performance-hampering effect that temperature fluctuations have on the watch. Today the human body is likely to be far more sensitive to environmental temperature than any timepiece; that is, of course, unless the watch indicates the hours by way of the meniscus between two fluids in a linear capillary. If that is the case, then the watch has been made by the leaders in hydro-mechanical horology, HYT. Although the liquid has been treated so that its ordinary movement through the capillary is not affected by cold temperatures, the elevated pace of hand-setting can put the mechanical bellows into stress as they cope with a colder and denser liquid. Therefore the H2 watch is equipped with a thermal indicator, designed to notify the wearer when the temperature is sub-optimal for hand-setting. Moving from white to blue when the temperature drops below 15°C (59°F), the function doubles as a too-cold-to-get-out-of-bed indicator.

Crown Position / Function Indicator

Aside from the escapement, the most complicated and damage-prone elements of a simple watch are probably the crown, the keyless work and the thin winding stem that connects the two. The keyless work facilitates the winding of the mainspring, the changing of the time and the date. It is one of the few mechanisms of the watch movement that is exposed to the brute force of the human touch. The crown might need to be unscrewed, pulled once, twice, three times, and twisted clockwise and anticlockwise while switching between and operating the mechanisms. Not surprisingly some manufacturers have made a feature of this multi-purpose mechanism by placing a crown position indicator on the dial. The most common setup involves a three-mode indicator and a pull-out crown, although there

Above: The HYT H2. The thermal indicator is located at 9:30 on the dial. If the movement temperature exceeds 15°C the indicator points to the white sector; if the temperature drops below the optimal 15°C the indicator points to the blue sector and the user should avoid any manipulation of the watch; instead they should put it on and let their body raise the temperature of the movement before resetting it once the indicator has moved back to white. There is also a crown position indicator located at 3 o'clock.
© 2016 HYT S.A

Opposite: The Richard Mille RM36-01 literally puts G-force front and centre. The accelerometer is placed right in the middle of the dial and the hour and minute hands have to perform acrobatics to stay out of the way. A white arrow under the complication indicates the direction that the device is 'facing'. By rotating the bezel the entire apparatus also rotates, allowing the wearer to position it exactly as needed. The reset button for the accelerometer protrudes from the crystal. The power reserve indicator can be seen at 1:30, with the function indicator at 3:30 and its associated pusher at 4.
© 2016 Richard Mille, Horometrie S.A

are certain movements that leave the crown in the same position and alternate the mode by depressing a pusher. It is usual to see the three modes identified as H, N and R; these stand for Heure (or hand setting), Neutral (the crown is disengaged) and Remontage (winding the mainspring).

Electronic Rate Meter and Hairspring Adjustment

In 2014 the team at URWERK created a watch with an integrated 'Electro Mechanical Control' unit, named the EMC. The unit is powered by a hand-wound generator that enables a tiny optical sensor to read and display the exact oscillating rate of the balance wheel.

In regulating a watch, which is among the final steps in the manufacturing process of a mechanical watch, the rate is tested and adjusted, usually in five positions. The goal here is to achieve isochronism, a consistent rate independent of changes in amplitude. The watch is rotated and tested to ensure that it is regulated to average out the effect of being upside-down, flat on its face, etc. When an adjustment is necessary it will take place via the regulating micro-screws that are located on the circumference of the balance wheel (with a free-sprung balance) or via a regulator index on the balance cock that extends or shortens the length of the hairspring (with a regulated balance). There also exist balances with both systems. So if the watch is running fast and the rate needs to be slowed, either the micro-screws are unscrewed in order to increase the inertia of each oscillation, or the set screw is turned, moving the two holding pins so that the effective length of the hairspring is increased. These adjustments are designed to find the movement's 'sweet spot', to minimise the accumulated impact that gravity has on the rate.

The EMC enables its wearer to conduct rate tests as and when they please. When the function is activated, a transmitter and receiver that sit on either side of the balance wheel perform an assessment of the 12 oscillations that should occur during a three-second period in order to determine the rate variance. The user untucks the crank from the right side of the case, gives it approximately 20 rotations, presses the button at 8 o'clock and the dial at 11 o'clock provides the precision reading (in + / - seconds per day). Should the rate be unacceptably fast or slow, the user can flip the watch over and turn a screw on the case which connects to the regulator, meaning the user can adjust the hairspring length without even having to take the caseback off.

Above: The Audemars Piguet Royal Oak Concept GMT Tourbillon, with H / N / R crown position indicator.
© 2015 Audemars Piguet, Le Brassus

Opposite: The URWERK EMC. At 51mm long it may seem huge, but considering it functions as a watch, timing diagnostic system, and watch repairman, it is actually incredibly small. Want something like this but with no electronics? The UR-105M has no rate meter, but retains the fine adjustment screw on the caseback.
© 2016 URWERK

Oil Change / Running Indicator

There are several similarities between a mechanical movement and a combustion engine. Take for example the exhaust, which allows the engine to expel excess energy generated as a consequence of its primary goal: propulsion. The French word for escapement, *échappement*, is also the word for the exhaust of a car engine. And one can see the similarity when one considers that the impulse delivered by the escape wheel tooth to the pallet in the escapement is the final step in a release of energy from a coiled mainspring. Everything over and above the actual moment of contact is essentially wasted energy – exhaust.

An additional similarity is that both mechanical movements and engines comprise many moving parts that are made less efficient by the force of friction and the wear of component parts. There are ways that both engines and movements have evolved to lessen the impact of friction: making components out of exotic materials that generate less friction, improving the compatibility of wheel teeth and pinion leaves to microscopic levels, using pivot stones on workhorse arbors, and then there is oil. A movement, just like an engine, requires that certain components, in certain places, are lubricated to avoid excessive contact and abrasion. In time the lubricant will dry or become clogged, and this is one of the more significant reasons why a mechanical watch will need regular servicing (which involves the total dismantling of the movement, cleaning and replacement of lubricants). Some owners, as with their cars, will tend to push the envelope with regard to these scheduled services, but URWERK have developed the mechanical-watch equivalent of the warning light on the dashboard. The 'oil change' function is somewhat exclusive to the avant-garde designs of URWERK (it's also seen on the Harry Winston Opus 5 but this also was designed by URWERK's Felix Baumgartner and Martin Frei). In reality it is little more than a calendar complication, calibrated to a five year service interval. The more cynical enthusiast might suspect that it is more of a post-sale marketing tool to push the wearer back in for a costly service. But they would be ignoring the reality of lubrication deterioration and would be downplaying their responsibility for the long term care of their timepiece. It is also arguably more conservative to set the date at 'running years' as opposed to 'years since purchased'. After all, the manufacturer's recommended service intervals will be based on solid use.

It is worth mentioning that URWERK's pocket watch (the UR-1001) takes tracking the running life to the extreme, with two registers to measure the passing of the centuries of use up to its first millennium – at which point it will be due the mother of all services, presumably by a robot watchmaker.

Above: The URWERK UR-110. The 5-year oil change meter is a disc located at 6 o'clock on the dial (well, 6 o'clock were it a normal watch). © 2016 URWERK

Opposite: The caseback of the URWERK UR-1001 is a running-life dashboard for the timepiece. It features a 5-year oil change dial, a 100-year running indicator with 5-year increments, and a large, linear 1,000-year running indicator with numerals for each century and markers at 50-year increments. If ever there was a watch that demonstrated the relativity of time and the ability of man-made objects to far outlast the man that made them, this is it.

© 2016 URWERK

2.4 Complications for the Explorer

Navigational Complications

In the days before GPS technology an accurate chronometer was a vital navigational aid. Marine chronometers were fairly large clocks, often mounted within a wooden box by gimbals that absorbed some of the gravitational effects of being at sea. The invention and successful development of the marine chronometer has been attributed to John Harrison, an 18th century English carpenter. It took Harrison, and many others, many years to create clocks that were capable of maintaining acceptable accuracy because of the limitations of clock-making at the time, and the constant threat to stability that being at sea caused to a movement. Chronometers were revolutionary things, demonstrating staggering accuracy despite the elements. Today's (COSC) chronometer certifications are an echo of the noise caused by man's development of the chronometer and the navigational problem that it sought to solve. So what *was* the problem?

To identify one's location without GPS one needs to know: latitude, longitude and altitude. Altitude at sea was always an obvious 'sea level', and latitude could be determined by matching the position of the sun at noon, or stars at night, to a chart. With this information it was possible to determine where one was within 90° north or south of the equator. But obtaining an accurate reading of longitude remained an issue for many years and at the cost of countless lives and ships. It was agreed that the key to unlocking longitude was time. As the Earth rotates 360° of longitude in 24 hours, or 15° per hour, with the right supplementary information one can use time to calculate a position within 180° east or west of the meridian. A quick note, both longitude and latitude are measured in degrees, minutes and seconds. Each degree has 60 minutes, each minute has 60 seconds. The longitude of New York city, for example, is 74° 0 minutes 59 seconds west of the Prime Meridian.

If, for example, the solar time at one's present location is known (derived from the Sun) and it is possible to determine the time at a point of reference (Greenwich Mean Time - GMT) then one's longitude can be calculated by comparing an event in the present location, such as the position of the Sun, to how that event would occur at the fixed location (GMT). Although there were exceptionally complex methods by which GMT could be calculated using the lunar distance, and although these were made easier by the introduction of almanacs with pre-populated tables, using a reliable chronometer to track GMT and calculate longitude became the preferred method by the late 19th century.

Although the actual navigational methods are fairly complex, the role that the chronometer played in the process was simple — it needed to tell the time accurately and consistently. This period of time in horology was the height of the race for accuracy in mechanical movements. Today's chronometers are exceptionally accurate (for mechanical watches — they don't stand up to quartz, and pale in comparison to an atomic clock), but despite this there are no widely followed standards higher than those imposed by the prestigious observatories of the 19th and 20th centuries. The Marine Chronometer and Observatory Chronometer paved the way for time-driven navigational complications, introducing technologies that still exist in the mechanical wristwatch of today.

- **Hour Angle** — Developed in the 1920s in a collaboration between Charles Lindbergh, Naval Navigator P.V.H. Weems, and Longines, the Hour Angle watch became the first wrist-bound instrument designed to calculate exact longitude. The watch required a time signal to confirm that the watch was running at exact GMT time, and an ability to calculate the solar time of one's exact position, as well as the 'equation of time' for that day (for a full explanation of the equation see Chapter 2.7).

  There is an internal rotating chapter ring at the centre, which contains two registers — one is the traditional 60-second register and the watch is equipped with a 'Weems second-setting complication' which enables synchronisation of seconds on the move. The exact Greenwich Mean Time would be transmitted to the pilot by radio signal, and in order to adjust the watch quickly with minimal crown-fiddling (imagine wearing large

gloves, flying a plane, and possibly mixing a Gin & Tonic) the user could pull the crown and rotate the internal chapter ring to align with the seconds hand. This meant that any seconds of accuracy lost during the flight could be rapidly clawed back without having to alter the running minutes or hours. The other scale on the central dial runs from 1 to 15. As it takes 24 hours for the Sun to circumnavigate the 360° 'celestial sphere', each hour that passes will represent 15° of this journey. The register represents the 15° of 'arc' that the Sun completes every hour and is therefore read against the minute hand.

The 180° scale follows the same concept but in terms of the 12-hour cycle of the hour hand. Each time the hour hand passes an hour numeral the respective degrees of arc have increased by 15°. Therefore, when the hand completes a 12-hour cycle, the arc will have covered 180°. Then there is the Roman numeral indication for the running hours and finally, the rotating bezel, which looks intimidating but is actually just another adjustment module for the equation of time. This last adjustment makes sense given that the entire concept of the hour angle is one's true relative position to the Sun compared to the true relative position at Greenwich. The exact time at Greenwich needs to be adjusted to the local true solar time at Greenwich.

Let's run a simple example. You are flying eastward along the equator (0° latitude). The time on your watch is set to GMT and reads 10:08 and 42 seconds AM (as pictured). The Sun has reached its highest point in the sky so you are aware that it is local apparent noon and a great opportunity to make a simple longitude calculation. The time signal comes through and you are already synchronised to the second (so no need to use the Weems second-setting). So you know the local true solar time is 12:00 and the GMT *mean* solar time is 10:08. To adjust this to reflect true solar GMT you refer to an almanac which provides the equation of time for GMT that day. Each minute + / - in the equation would equate to one bezel click anticlockwise or clockwise respectively. If the equation included seconds these would be

translated into minutes of arc using the seconds and 1–15 register at the centre. To keep it simple let's say the equation for the day is zero. You can now compare the information. First, you can see that the hour hand has reached 10, which is 150°, then you read the minute hand against the outer bezel, providing another 2° and zero minutes of rotation. Finally, read the seconds hand against the internal 1-15° register, which gives you 10.5 minutes of rotation. Therefore you are at a longitude of 152°10'30", which places you over the Pacific Ocean, about 500 miles off the north-east coast of mainland Papua New Guinea.

- **Slide Rule** — Owners of a Breitling Navitimer or a similar pilot's tool watch, will have one of the most visibly noisy watches around when it comes to registers. Not only do they have the usual chronograph and tachymeter of most sports watches, but there are two further registers adorning the outer chapter ring and the rotating bezel. Alternatively there is the Sinn 903 ST, which is neither coincidentally nor illegally identical to the Navitimer on account of an intellectual property fire-sale that occurred when Breitling temporarily buckled under the pressure of the quartz crisis in 1979.

So how do we make sense out of the noise? If all of the chronograph registers and the tachymeter are removed, what's left is a slide rule. Anyone who studied mathematics before calculators will be able to use these with relative ease. For others it will require getting the manual out (the Breitling manual does a decent job of explaining it). The slide rule can be used to calculate ground speed, fuel consumption, rate and distance of altitude change (climb / descent), as well as kilometres-to-metres conversion. For example, if distance and time are known then ground

speed can be calculated. Align the distance (bezel) with the time in minutes (inner dial) and the 'mph' marker at 12 o'clock will indicate the ground speed on the bezel (as the slide rule is not particularly concerned with decimal places, common sense will need to be applied to the reading).

- **Compass** — There is a simple way in which *any* watch can be used as a compass. The approach differs depending on your hemisphere.

    For the northern hemisphere remove the watch and point the hour hand in the direction of the sun. If it is PM then determine south by plotting the point anticlockwise between the hour hand and 12 o'clock. If it is AM then determine south by plotting the point clockwise between the hour hand and 12 o'clock. If running Daylight Saving Time then use the 1 o'clock position for the above calculations instead of 12.

    For the southern hemisphere point the *12 o'clock* register in the direction of the Sun. The midpoint between the hour hand and 12 o'clock is *north*.

    Some watches take this concept and push it a step further, into a simple complication, incorporating it into their dial / bezel. Take the Richard Mille RM 60-01, which has a UTC (or GMT) hand on a 24-hour register and a bezel that has the four cardinal points (N, S, E and W) and two sets of 24-hour registers for the northern and southern hemispheres. The user aligns the UTC hand to the sun, and adjusts the bezel so that the UTC hand is displaying local time for the applicable hemisphere on the bezel. The user then has their bearings.

Above and below: The Terra Cielo Mare Orienteering BP. The user points the hour hand to the sun. The crown at 2 o'clock is used to rotate the inner bezel and the hour hand is aligned to the respective time on the bezel for the northern hemisphere (blue numerals) or the southern hemisphere (yellow). The bezel now indicates your four cardinal points.   © 2016 TCM Srl

Opposite: The Sinn 903 ST.   © 2016 Sinn Spezialuhren GmbH

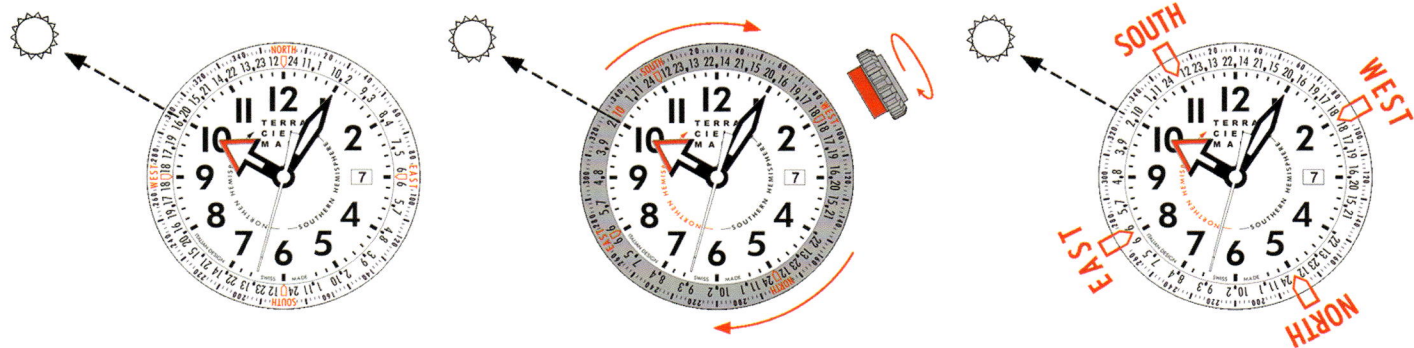

The major benefit of these complications is that they can be sensitive to hemisphere, but they have one fundamental inaccuracy; they do not account for the difference between mean solar time and true solar time. In other words, you might have your clock set to GMT, but if you are on the far eastern or the far western point of the GMT time zone, you will have significantly different experiences of the apparent motion of the sun and the northerly direction in relation to it. Remember, the hour angle principle, whereby the sun moves at 15° of arc every hour, therefore any location separated by exactly 15° of longitude will be exactly 1 hour of true solar time apart. For example, let's assume that it is 12:00 in Greenwich, England. Although they share the same GMT mean solar time zone, at the far eastern point (say Inékar, Mali) and far western point (say Reykjavík, Iceland) the local true solar time will be 12:12 and 10:36 respectively. It is understandable therefore how, despite both being in the northern hemisphere and sharing a time zone, the position of the sun and the respective true north will be a little off from either location. One special watch was designed to handle this issue.

The Arnold & Son True North Perpetual allows the user to adjust for local longitude, as well as the equation of time, in order to identify the true north using the watch. It is calibrated to the northern hemisphere. First, the crown at 8 o'clock is used to adjust to exact local longitude. This causes the internal rotating bezel to rotate and is read by tracking the small arrow at 6 o'clock against the degrees indicated in the black section of the ring. If you are located 5° east of the formal longitude of the time zone (GMT=0°, GMT+1=15°, etc.), you rotate the bezel so that is moved to 5° from True North in the easterly direction of the bezel. Then it is as simple as pointing the 24-hour sun hand to the direction of the Sun and you have yourself a True North bearing. The watch is even capable of adjusting the difference between the mean solar time and the true solar time. This is important because, depending on the time of the year, the apparent sun will cut a faster or a slower path across the sky versus the mean solar time. The watch has an equation of time register at 7 o'clock, which indicates

how many minutes deviation there is at any given day. What is particularly special about this watch is the way this equation adjusts the reading of the sun hand. The thin disc marked 'Sun Slow / Sun Fast' at 12 o'clock is connected to the outer disc, and will move the respective true solar time according to the equation. So a +10 minute equation will mean that the true solar time is running ten minutes faster than mean solar time, and this will be translated to a two-notch clockwise adjustment of the chapter ring.

Above: The Arnold & Son True North Perpetual.
© 2014 LuxWatch.com, LLC

Opposite: The Richard Mille RM 60-01. A very useful compass complication, able to be used in both hemispheres. The central red UTC hand is adjusted by the pusher at 8 o'clock. In addition to the orienteering functions the watch has subsidiary seconds at 3 o'clock, a big date at 12 o'clock, month indicator at 4 o'clock, central flyback chronograph seconds, with a sub-dial at 9 o'clock that can be read as a 60 minute countdown register (reading the yellow dial against the yellow arrow) or regular 60-minute chronograph register (reading the yellow 60 marker against the green register). © 2016 Richard Mille, Horometrie S.A

and altitude have a relationship. Gravity affects air in the same way that it does other matter, like seawater for example. The air that we experience at ground level is under pressure from the vast quantities that are piled up on top of it. Similarly, at the top of our atmosphere the pressure is at its lowest, with very little else but infinite weightlessness above. It is this reduction in pressure that causes hot air to cool down, and is why you need a thick sweater on if you are going to climb Everest.

- **Altimeter** — We have already touched upon the mechanical depth gauge, and the altimeter is very similar in functionality and display. Surprisingly this complication was only introduced to a mechanical watch in 2014, less surprisingly the innovation was pioneered by a brand with respectable pilot-watch heritage and with an existing depth-gauge model in their inventory (although it employs different technology). The Oris Big Crown ProPilot Altimeter watch is a 47mm, unapologetically pilot-centric, watch with readings for both the air pressure and the altitude. As is the process with aneroid barometers, the altitude is manually 'set' based on the known altitude or air pressure (the altitudes are easy, and if you are in communication with a radio tower they will read you the official local pressure). Before setting, a large crown is unscrewed to allow air to enter the case via a membrane, and a red indicator along the base of the crown communicates to the user that the 100m waterproofing has been temporarily suspended. From this point the cells are capable of tracking the changes in air pressure, and the corresponding altitude reading, on an accurate scale.

- **Barometer** — As mentioned above, the air pressure reading is the primary reading of an aneroid barometer; yet it is often referred to as an altimeter, and this may simply be a consequence of our preference for altitude over pressure readings. If the barometer were to have feelings one would expect it to be somewhat begrudging of the limelight that the altimeter borrows and flaunts. Who really cares about air pressure? Meteorologists do. Air pressure is one of the core determining factors of the weather. Therefore, if altitude can be ruled out, then any

Altitude and Pressure Complications

Whether flying a light aircraft, jumping out of one, or skiing down a mountain, it may (or may not) be important to be able to read the altitude or air pressure via a watch. As with many other complex functions, todays electronic watches offer an abundance of relatively inexpensive options. But when it comes to mechanical ones, the playing field is sparse. The notable mechanical models employ barometric aneroid cells — these are constructed out of a particular alloy that enables the cell (with the aid of a spring) to contract and expand when the air pressure increases or decreases respectively. The altitude reading of a barometer is implied by the change in air pressure. Why? This is because air pressure

Above: The Oris Big Crown ProPilot Altimeter.　　　© 2016 Oris

Opposite: The Breva Génie 01.　　© 2015 Breva Geneve SA

changes in air pressure will be the cause of, and result in, changes in weather. You can trust a company like Breva to have come up with the weather-predicting barometer complication in their first model, the Génie 01 uses aneroid cells to an effect that is similar to the Oris ProPilot. However, instead of using air-pressure as a base-setter or inferior reading, the Génie inverts this and it is the altimeter that plays second fiddle. The user adjusts the altimeter, by pressing the pusher at 2

o'clock, to align to the correct local altitude. Then, by unscrewing and depressing the pusher at 4 o'clock, the external air pressure floods the watch movement, and affects the aneroid capsules. The subsequent reading is made on a dial with weather markings associated with their equivalent pressure levels (H = Sun, L = Rain / Storm). This process is not going to make smartphones or TV Weathermen redundant, but it's a fun approximation.

2.5 Additional Time Zone Complications

When the wristwatch was conceived there was not a great deal of global travel, nor was the world strung together by cables, satellites and cell towers. Even if one *could* deduce that it was 9pm back at home while out hunting white rhino in Namibia, there wasn't much one could do with that knowledge. Today, many more people are separated from their line managers or family members by oceans, not postal codes; travel is for business, for pleasure, to expatriate. It is clear to see why time zone complications are so much more important today than they were in the past.

However the journey does in fact start at the dawn of the portable clock and pocket watch. It was specifically *because* of the lack of connectedness in the past that until the late 19th century there were literally hundreds of *local* time zones based on true solar time (see Chapter 2.7). Venturing into the next Swiss Canton meant entering a different time zone. Not a simple 60-minute adjustment, but an entirely independent time zone based on the local sunrise and sunset and whatever inaccuracies the local clock tower added in between. Some of the earliest pocket watches with time zone complications managed these difficulties by using time zone wheels with a vast array of locations at 30-minute intervals, or by providing the movement with multiple independent gear trains allowing for independent timekeeping on multiple dials. This helped the owner keep track of the fact that it was 12:17 in Geneva and 12:32 in Zug.

Standard Time and Civil Time

With the advent of passenger train travel in the mid-19th century, more and more people were able to cover greater ground faster, and the confusion regarding what time it was grew exponentially. Imagine putting together a train schedule for a 3-hour journey that stopped in seven different time zones. In 1883, after 50 years of excessively complicated timetables, the US railroad system decided to divide the country into four time zones (where previously there had been hundreds). With train crews relying on their timepieces

to get a train to its station on time it is no wonder the railroad watch became the forefront of accuracy and reliability; Webb C. Ball, and his subsequent 1891 Ball Watch Company, eventually became synonymous with those qualities.

In 1884, the International Meridian Convention took place in Washington, DC and a 24-hour global time zone concept was proposed, with Greenwich as the Prime Meridian (Greenwich Mean Time, GMT). Today, we refer to this civilised grouping of time zones as 'civil time'; not only does it make life easier, but it makes the time zone complication more useful and legible on a watch.

Dual Time

The simplest way for a traveller to manage time zones is to simultaneously track the relationship between local time and home time (or home time and an additional reference time when they are not travelling); this is known as the dual time complication.

The dual time complication often gives rise to an additional supplementary complication, the day / night (6pm to 6am) or AM / PM (12am to 12pm) indicator, because the wearer will need to know if it is day or night at the location they are not presently in. The indicator is not exclusive to dual time watches, as it can still be a useful addition to a single time zone watch –

if a watch with a date function needs resetting, the wearer will want to make sure that it is set to the correct half of the day otherwise the date will switch in the middle of the day.

At first glance the Maîtres du Temps Chapter Three looks like a fairly simple but elegant date and moon phase complication. But when the integrated crown pusher is depressed, apertures on numerals 12 and 6 open to reveal day / night and dual time roller indicators. The Chapter Three is the result of a collaboration between Kari Voutilainen and Andreas Strehler.

© 2016 Maîtres du Temps

The Jaeger-LeCoultre Master Hometime features a centrally mounted dual-time hour hand, subsidiary seconds, date and a double-ended day / night indicator at 10 o'clock.   © 2016 Jaeger-LeCoultre

The Patek Philippe ref.5524 displays home time via an
additional (skeletonised) tapered baton hour hand.
Two apertures display the day and night for each
location. The local time hour hand is adjusted by the
two pushers at 8 and 10 o'clock.

The day / night or AM / PM function can be indicated by way of a sub-dial and a hand that completes a rotation every 24 hours. Alternatively it can run on a disc with pictorial representations of day and night, made visible through a semicircular aperture that looks like a moon phase indicator. There are also models that use a roller through an aperture, a simple dark / light aperture, or a double-ended hand with a sun and a moon at either end.

Back to the dual time complication and its variety of forms:

• **Additional Central Hour Hand** – One of the most common dual time formats uses a second central hour hand, coloured or skeletonised in such a way as to distinguish it from the running hour hand. With this layout the additional hour hand can be neatly hidden behind the running hour hand when the traveller is home. When they find themselves entering a new time zone, the traveller advances / retracts the local time hour indicator by the requisite hours. This is made possible either by a pusher (usually at 10 or 2 o'clock, with occasional models featuring additional anticlockwise pushers at 8 or 5 o'clock), which moves the hand by an hour on each depression, or by the crown. Some variations run an additional central hour hand that takes 24 hours to complete a rotation and has a 24-hour concentric chapter ring within the main dial or engraved onto a fixed bezel. A benefit of this format is that you do not need an additional day / night indicator, but the compromise comes with an inability to hide the hand when not needed.

Right: The A. Lange & Söhne Saxonia Dual Time features an additional alpha-shape hand in blued steel to represent home time. A 24-hour day / night indicator is located at 12 o'clock. The pushers at 10 and 8 o'clock advance and retract the gold hour hand of local time. © 2015 A. Lange & Söhne

Opposite: The Zenith Elite Dual Time has an elongated blue 24-hour hand with skeletonised arrow-tip for the second time zone and a pusher at 10 o'clock to advance the time. © 2016 Zenith

The IWC Portofino Midsize Automatic Day & Night
has an inner concentric chapter ring for the 24-hour
home time hand. The local time and home time are
adjusted via the crown.   © 2016 IWC Schaffhausen

The Rolex Oyster Explorer II, with iconic 24-hour orange hand for the reference time. While this is a fine example of a dual time complication, it is equally a watch for the explorer. The watch is designed to be used as a highly legible am / pm indicator for the local time of an explorer in a place of such extremes that one could not visibly discern the difference. The 12-hour hand can be set independently of the 24-hour hand should the wearer wish to use it as a dual time indicator. © 2016 Rolex

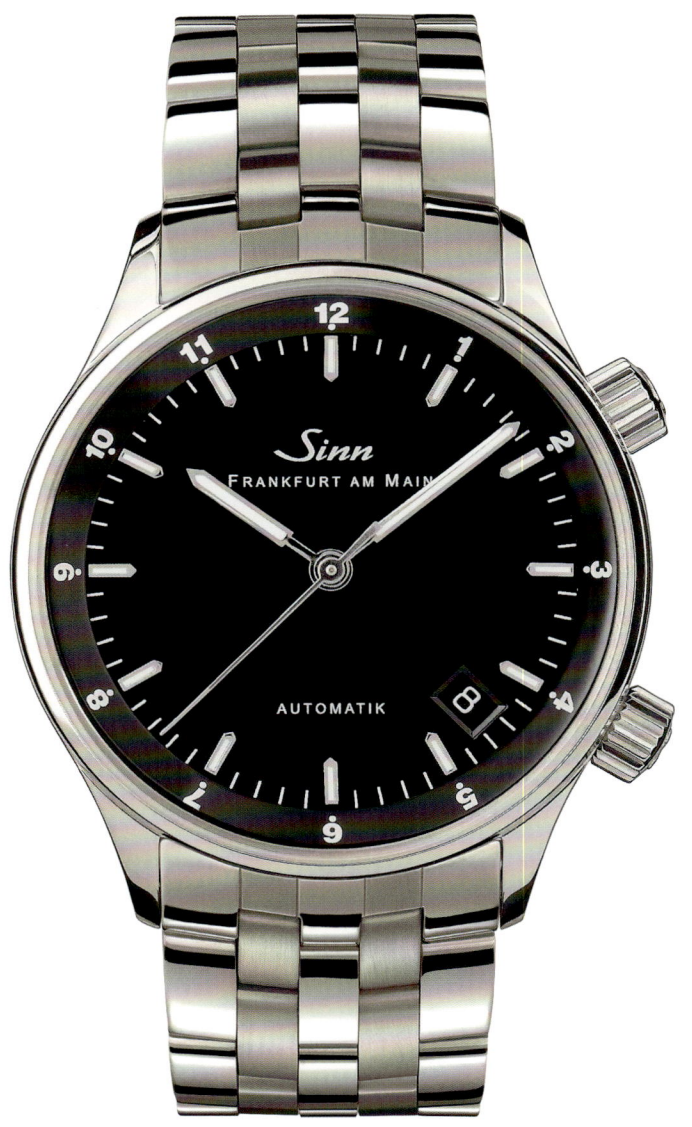

Above, left: The Sinn Frankfurt Financial District Watch has an internal rotating 12-hour bezel, operated by the crown at 2 o'clock.
© 2016 Sinn Spezialuhren GmbH

Above, right: The OMEGA Seamaster 300 'SPECTRE' Limited Edition. We appreciate that he is a naval officer, but bearing in mind Bond spends more time travelling than he does underwater, it makes perfect sense that he would wear a 12-hour rotating bezel rather than a diving bezel.
© 2016 OMEGA SA

- **12-Hour Rotating Bezel** — Other dual timers might rely on a rotating bezel to derive a second reading from the regular hour hand. It's a simple solution: take a regular two- or three-hander, add a rotating bezel with 12 hour markers, and the reference time can be adjusted with a simple click of the bezel. As with a diving bezel, the register can be placed on an internal or external rotating bezel.

- **Dual Time Sub-Dial** — The dual time function is also made possible by way of a subsidiary dial. The dial can employ a 12- or 24-hour register; the former is often supported by a day / night indicator. In many cases the second time zone is adjusted by way of one or two pushers, which can be located anywhere on the caseband.

Left: The Vacheron Constantin Overseas Dual Time is a sporty example of a 12-hour dual time sub-dial with additional day / night indicator. The crown adjusts the two time zones, and the pusher at 2 o'clock adjusts the date.   © 2015 Vacheron Constantin

Below: The Girard-Perregaux Traveller Large Date, Moon Phases & GMT does exactly what it says. The 24-hour dual time sub-dial is adjusted by the pusher at 4 o'clock.   © 2015 Girard-Perregaux

Dual Time with City Aperture — Another dual time complication uses a city wheel behind an aperture calibrated to the second time zone indication. This is a highly useful format in that it has a 'memory' of the time zones, so all the traveller needs to know is their city. It is close to what we call a world time watch, but the aperture and sub-dial (or additional hand) give the user a one-at-a-time view of the zones. The city wheel is progressed via a button, the crown or an additional crown. As each new city appears in the aperture the reference time will advance to the next time zone. Most models will add Daylight Saving Time adjustments so that the city does not inadvertently show the wrong time. The city wheel itself will have 24 cities as representatives of the 24 time zones, however, there do exist one or two watches that add more cities, allowing for the 10 zones (such as India) that are offset by half-hour increments. Very few are sensitive to the three zones (such as Nepal) that are offset by 15-minute increments.

The Glashütte Original Senator Cosmopolite is possibly the ultimate dual time watch. The destination / reference time zone sits front and centre on the main dial, with a day / night indicator at 9 o'clock. There are two apertures at 8 o'clock that enable the user to set the time to either STD (standard) or DST (Daylight Saving Time). The 37 locations on the city wheel include the usual 24-hour zones, the 10 half-hour zones, and the 3 quarter / three-quarter zones. The home time dial is at 12 o'clock and features a curved power reserve aperture and a pinhole day / night aperture. The crowns at 8 and 4 o'clock change the time zone and set the reference time, with the crown at 2 o'clock for home time setting and mainspring winding.

Above: The Jaeger-LeCoultre Master Geographic displays the city through a widened aperture at 6 o'clock. The widened aperture, and the two alternating rows of cities, allows the user to alternate between standard and Daylight Saving Time. When a city is observing DST, align the arrow at 6 o'clock to the black extension on the left of the city name. The city reference time is indicated on the 12-hour sub-dial at 6 o'clock, with a small day / night indicator at 9 o'clock on the sub-dial. The city wheel rotates anticlockwise with a turn of the crown at 10 o'clock while the hour hand on the sub-dial advances.   © 2016 Jaeger-LeCoultre

Opposite: The Glashütte Original Senator Cosmopolite.
          © 2016 Glashütter Uhrenbetrieb GmbH

- **Multiple and / or Independent Dials** — Sometimes a watch is simply equipped with more than one dial — neither is primary, neither is central, giving the user free reign to assign whatever time zone to them that they wish. Typically they will be managed by two separate crowns, and they may have two entirely (or partially) independent movements. The benefit of these dials is that they can be set independently, which allows the user to track countries that operate outside of the 24 hourly zones, like Venezuela (GMT-4h30') and Nepal (GMT+5h45').

Some people, especially those without the eyesight of a hawk, prefer larger dials. How can two full-sized dials be placed in a watch without making the case unacceptably large? Put one on the other side of the case, as with the Jaeger-LeCoultre Reverso Duo. The Reverso is a marvellous invention, created in the 1930s to cope with the violence suffered by watches on the polo field. The case could be flipped so that the steel caseback faced outward and the glass was protected. What was initially developed to be a solution to a problem soon became a novelty. With the development of sapphire crystal it was unimportant for the average, non-polo-playing

Above: The Jaeger-LeCoultre Reverso Duo. On one side of the case you have an elegant art deco dial with hours, minutes, and subsidiary seconds, which would be set for local time. On the reverse is a new dial, with a 24-hour reference sub-dial; it is adjusted easily by way of the pusher on the caseband. The Duo offers the wearer a discreet home time or reference time that can be totally concealed when desired.   © 2016 Jaeger-LeCoultre

Opposite: A particularly fine example of a two-zone watch with independent dials is the Arnold & Son Double Tourbillon Escapement Dual Time which has two dials, one with Roman and the other with Arabic numerals. The dials are powered by the same double-barrelled mainspring, but regulated by their own tourbillon, which sit on the front of the dial. © 2015 Arnold & Son

wearer, to be overly protective of the glass. This provided Jaeger-LeCoultre with untapped real estate on the reverse of the dial to make functional. There are many iterations of the Reverso today, but as a dual timer the Reverso is extremely useful.

Finally, for something a little different, Jacob & Co have invested much of their identity into dual / multiple time zone models and perhaps one of their more considerable complications is found in the Jacob & Co. Epic SF24. The watch presents the dual time display not via an additional hand, dial or rotating bezel, but by way of a large 'split-flap' display in a module that sits above 12 o'clock. The styling plays on the kinds of split-flap displays that you might find in train stations and airports and offers a rotation of 24 cities with a jumping numeral for the hour.

World Time / Universal Hour

The world time, or universal hour, complication doesn't require that the user selects a destination. There are no adjusters necessary (though often they are provided) and no sub-dials. Instead the main dial has a 24-hour chapter ring, with two colours to represent day / night and world cities aligned to a numeral. As the hour hand on the dial progresses, the 24-hour ring rotates anticlockwise. With this layout, the user can read all 24 time zones at a glance without having to push or twist anything. On most models, the user first adjusts the city wheel so that the local time zone is aligned with the marker on the wheel (usually a small red arrow at 12 or 6 o'clock). Then the regular timekeeping hands are adjusted to tell the correct local time. When the user travels to a new time zone, the city wheel is adjusted so that the new city (or respective time zone) is aligned to the marker.

The world time watch is easy to spot. In addition to the city wheel, the centre of the dial is often adorned with a world map as viewed from the northern axis, with lines of longitude running through it to align with the 24-hour markers. The map is sometimes made partially transparent and enhanced with a day / night disc, which rotates beneath it. The dial may feature a more abstract design or enamel painting, and they are occasionally given some degree of customisation here or there. At the request of a collector, or for a limited boutique edition, some models might replace the standard representative city with an alternative city. Other models rename the cities to correspond with racecourse or racetrack names.

Above: The Vacheron Constantin Traditionnelle World Time features a colourless 24-hour wheel, thanks to the day / night indication projected beneath the sapphire crystal map. The city wheel accommodates the regular 24 time zones, and the 13 'special cases' in blue. The red Istanbul is a good example of a customised dial. The time setting and adjustment of the city wheel are controlled via the crown.   © 2016 Vacheron Constantin

Opposite: The Jacob & Co. Epic SF24, a departure board for the wrist.   © 2016 Jacob&Co.

The Patek Philippe ref.5131. As it is not used to align to the time zones, this model offers a number of variations on the orientation of the map. There are even editions that feature paintings of scenery; all are executed with great skill in cloisonné enamel. The reference zone is indicated at 12 o'clock. The button at 10 o'clock advances the city wheel and 24-hour wheel anticlockwise, while the hour hand advances clockwise. This allows the wearer to adjust reference zones at the click of a button.

The Montblanc Heritage Spirit Orbis Terrarum World
Time combines a day / night map with a day / night
24-hour wheel and opts for a cleaner 24-city
designation. The pusher at 8 o'clock advances the city,
the 24-hour register, the map, and the hour hand
clockwise so that a new reference city can be aligned
to the marker at 6 o'clock.   © 2016 Montblanc

The Globe

While the 24-hour wheel and rotating map at the centre of some world timers give the user a good sense of the global passage of time, nothing beats the actual rotation of a globe. A watch that employs this to magnificent three-dimensional effect is the Greubel Forsey GMT. Those familiar with the brand will notice that, in addition to the usual black-polished bridges, asymmetric case and the 25° inclined 24-second tourbillon, is a rather large and magnificently anodised titanium globe. It is mounted with the northern axis perpendicular to the dial. Around the equator is a 24-hour register, and in line with the daylight portion of the register is a crystal window in the caseband, which bathes the globe in 'daylight'. The globe works in conjunction with a more traditional 24-hour city wheel on the caseback as well as a subsidiary GMT dial at 10 o'clock. What makes this watch stand out from (the very few) other globe world-timers is the amount of the globe that is visible to the naked eye, thanks to the very deep, partially skeletonised movement and caseband window.

Left: As the Reverso did for the dual time dial, the Jaeger-LeCoultre Reverso Squadra World Chronograph gives the city wheel a dial of its own so that the cities can be labelled radially like longitudinal wheel spokes. This again makes for a discreet and highly legible world timer. © 2016 Jaeger-LeCoultre

Opposite: The Montblanc Collection Villeret Tourbillon Cylindrique Geosphères Vasco da Gama has centrally mounted local time, a 'home time' dial at 6 o'clock, and two partial spheres, cut at the line of each Tropic, showing the northern and southern hemispheres with synchronised two-tone 24-hour registers. The pusher at 8 o'clock adjusts the local time without disturbing the other indicators. © 2016 Montblanc

Above and opposite: The Greubel Forsey GMT. The world time disc on the caseback has an inner ring for summer time, which can be applied to those lighter-toned cities that operate Daylight Saving Time.   © 2016 Greubel Forsey, Art of Invention

Above: The Jaeger-LeCoultre Duomètre Unique Travel Time uses the dual-wing movement (separate mainsprings and gear trains joined by one regulator) to display two independent dials. In addition, at 6 o'clock sits the tip of a northern hemispheric globe, functioning as a guide for the setting of the reference time. Each depression of the time adjustment pushers at 8 and 10 o'clock will rotate the globe accordingly and the marker at 6 o'clock will let the user know that they have selected the correct time zone. A list of cities and the r respective time zones is engraved along the rim of the caseback. © 2016 Jaeger-LeCoultre

Opposite: The Cecil Purnell World Time Bi-Axial Tourbillon. It is equipped with a bi-axial tourbillon and a rotating northern hemispheric globe with 24-hour time zone register. There is no dual time register or city wheel, so the user will need to use the globe as the sole indicator of additional time zones. © 2016 Cecil Purnell

GMT / UTC

Greenwich Mean Time (GMT) or Coordinated Universal Time (UTC) is a common label although many are better described as dual-timers. A GMT features a second centrally-mounted hour hand, which rotates once every 24 hours and is designed to be set to GMT. It is used in conjunction with a 24-hour bezel. The complication was developed by Rolex, in co-operation with Pan Am in the 1950s, so their pilots could track their progression through multiple time zones, using Greenwich Mean Time (GMT) as a base.

To use the GMT like a true 1950s pilot, the running hours / minutes hand is set to local time, and the GMT hand (the long arrow-tipped hand) is set to GMT by aligning it with the 24-hour markers on the bezel. As the flight enters a new time zone the bezel is twisted by as many increments as the time zone relates to GMT (clockwise for -GMT, anticlockwise for +GMT). Thus, to establish what time it is in New York, simply rotate the bezel clockwise by 5 hours.

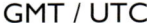

Above, left: The OMEGA Seamaster Planet Ocean 600 M GMT with its central 24-hour hand and rotating bezel.   © 2016 OMEGA SA

Above, right: The Bell & Ross BR 01-93 GMT 24 H has a large orange 24-hour hand and internal fixed bezel. © 2016 Bell & Ross

Opposite: The Rolex GMT Master II 'Pepsi' in white gold.
© 2016 Rolex

The Jaeger-LeCoultre Master Calendar demonstrates a handsome triple calendar and a good example of a moon hand and concentric date ring. The dial is meteorite.

2.6 Calendar Complications

It is commonplace for a modern mechanical movement to have a 31-day date wheel, usually displaying the function at 3 o'clock or between 4 and 5; occasionally at 6. This is known as the simple calendar. Some of the most popular mass-produced movements include date wheels as standard and as such this familiar dial template can be seen on a very large number of diverse timepieces. Even with brands that manufacture their own movements the date function is often the very first complication added to the hours / minutes / seconds and is a typical feature on the entry-level range of models. These are simple complications, with a reduction gear running from the motion work of the movement, usually the hour wheel. The 31-day date wheel is a disc with 31 internal teeth, held in place by a jumper, and driven by a finger on a wheel that rotates once every 24 hours. The teeth of the 24-hour wheel and the driving wheel are meshed under tension by midnight and usually by 1:30am the jumper will have snapped the wheel into position. Other forms have no jumper and instead they directly drive a date wheel with 62 teeth by way of a Maltese cross and pinion. This is less desirable because there is a lengthy transition period.

The date wheel of a simple calendar turns every day ad infinitum, indicating a new date each day, therefore the wearer will be required to adjust the wheel five times per year.

Displaying the Date

There are more complicated calendar mechanisms that can accommodate these irregularities. However, whether a movement features the simple or more complex calendar complications the day of the month can be displayed in a variety of forms over and above the simple date wheel / aperture. Here are some of the most common:

- **Chapter Ring** — Using a circular scale from 1 to 31 the watchmaker can display the date alongside the minute track of the main dial. The date is indicated by an additional hand, mounted concentrically with the hours and minutes of the timekeeping function. The hand is often differentiated from the minute hand, the shank might be notably thinner and instead of a natural taper or an arrow head, the hand might be adorned with a crescent (moon hand) or a perpendicular line (hammer hand). An

Left: The Cartier Rotonde de Cartier Annual Calendar is a fine and concealed application of the hammer hand, albeit for the day of the week rather than the date. The date is displayed in two large apertures at 12 o'clock, and the month is displayed through a widened aperture. Vincent Wulveryck © 2016 Cartier

Right: The Eterna Super Kontiki Chronograph features two subtle enhancements to the simple calendar date window. First, the date disc is colour-matched to the dial, and second, the numerals are set out on the disc in such a way that they are perpendicular when at 6 o'clock. The end result is aesthetically pleasing both in terms of symmetry and overall design consistency.
© 2016 Eterna SA

alternative option is to isolate the date ring to a sub-dial. This format is favoured with particularly complicated watches as the space within the sub-dial can be granted to an additional date-related function like the phase of the moon or leap year indicator. The gearing on such a concentric or eccentric display is very similar to the wheel / aperture option, with the exception of the teeth. The wheel of a date hand has outward-facing teeth, and the date wheel has inward-facing teeth.

- **Retrograde Date** — Not exclusive to displaying the date, a retrograde indicator of any function is appreciated by many enthusiasts as being particularly visually pleasing. Instead of the scale being placed along the circumference of a dial, it can be flattened completely or set out along a bow shape. The hand will track its course from start to finish before it sweeps back to the start in a flash. On occasion a watch might have a date wheel displayed through a widened aperture, providing a view of several dates at once. This may have the look of a retrograde display but it is not, because the key action of a retrograde display is the returning of the hand to the start position when it reaches the end of its scale.

- **Big Date** — Popularly applied and perfected by Saxon watchmakers, the big date display allows the use of big bold numerals and is made possible by two overlapping or closely positioned date wheels, one for the single units and one for the tens. The latter is sometimes a square or a cross, rather than a circular disc, because it is only displaying 0, 1, 2 and 3. The date is displayed through two closely positioned regular-sized date apertures or one large panoramic aperture. The mechanism is more complicated because it must choreograph the two discs' different rates of rotation.

The Vacheron Constantin Patrimony Contemporaine Retrograde Day Date with retrograde displays for both the day and the date on one dial (a platinum dial in this instance).
© 2015 Vacheron Constantin

Above, left: The A. Lange & Söhne Grand Lange 1 Lumen is a good example of the big date using a divided aperture. It also gives a small insight into the workings of the two discs beneath the smoked sapphire dial. The tens are rotated on a small 'cross' disc that sits within the circumference of the larger disc for the units.

© 2015 A. Lange & Söhne

Above, right: The Glashütte Original Panomatic Lunar. This is a slightly different execution of the big date. It is a single aperture, and the two discs can be seen running side-by-side.

© 2016 Glashütter Uhrenbetrieb GmbH

The dial-side of the Zeitwinkel 275° Saphir, and its movement, the ZW0103, shows two overlapping date discs. Running beneath each disc, and fastened by three screws, is a jumper spring, which allows the wheels to snap into place, rather than roll.

© 2016 Zeitwinkel Montres SA

Types of Calendar Mechanism

Having established how the day of the month can be displayed, it is important to understand quite how complicated it can be to deliver a calendar indication that does not need to be manually adjusted at the end of certain months, especially February. If our calendar was based on a consistent number of days in each month, and no leap years, it would be fairly simple to build a movement with a perpetually accurate calendar function. But even with the best efforts of Pope Gregory XIII in 1528, today's framework still requires that four of our 12 months have only 30 days. And then there is February, which has 28 days for three years and 29 on the fourth. The calendar is a good calendar, and was a small tweak to the Julian calendar, which was put in place by Julius Caesar in 46 BC but was 11 days out of synch by the late 16th century.

Nevertheless, the difference between a watch movement with a simple calendar function and a perpetual calendar is considerable both in terms of the additional parts required and the ultimate price tag. Each can be differentiated by how frequently they rely on the user to manually adjust them:

- A **simple calendar**, as noted above, will only display the day of the month, therefore it will require that the user adjust it five times a year, for each of the 30-day months (April, June, September and November) and February. There are very many examples of a simple calendar, with displays ranging from chapter ring, to big date, to retrograde.

- A **triple / complete / full calendar** watch has a more sophisticated display than the simple calendar, but still requires the same frequency of manual adjustments. In addition to the day of the month, a triple calendar will display the month, and the day of the week. When the watch includes a phase of the moon display, it might also be referred to as complete or full.

The Rolex 8171 Triple Calendar Moonphase 'Padellone'. It's a gorgeous and highly sought after vintage triple calendar, especially in steel.   © 2015 Christie's Images Limited

Above: The OMEGA de Ville Hour Vision Annual Calendar does without the day of the week but is still an annual calendar. The caseband of the Hour Vision is made from sapphire crystal, allowing for an unusual view of the side of the movement.   © 2016 OMEGA SA

Opposite: The Parmigiani Fleurier Tonda Quator is an annual calendar with retrograde date, day of the week sub-dial, and a northern and southern hemisphere moon phase.
© 2016 Parmigiani Fleurier SA

- An **annual calendar** will account for the four 30-day months but will need a manual adjustment at the end of every February (hence being 'annual'). An annual calendar can be displayed by apertures, chapter rings or retrograde displays for the month or the day of the month. There are a small number of watches (such as the Breitling Navitimer 1461) that allocate 28 days to February and therefore only need to be adjusted on the leap year. These are not annual calendars, but quadrennial calendars.

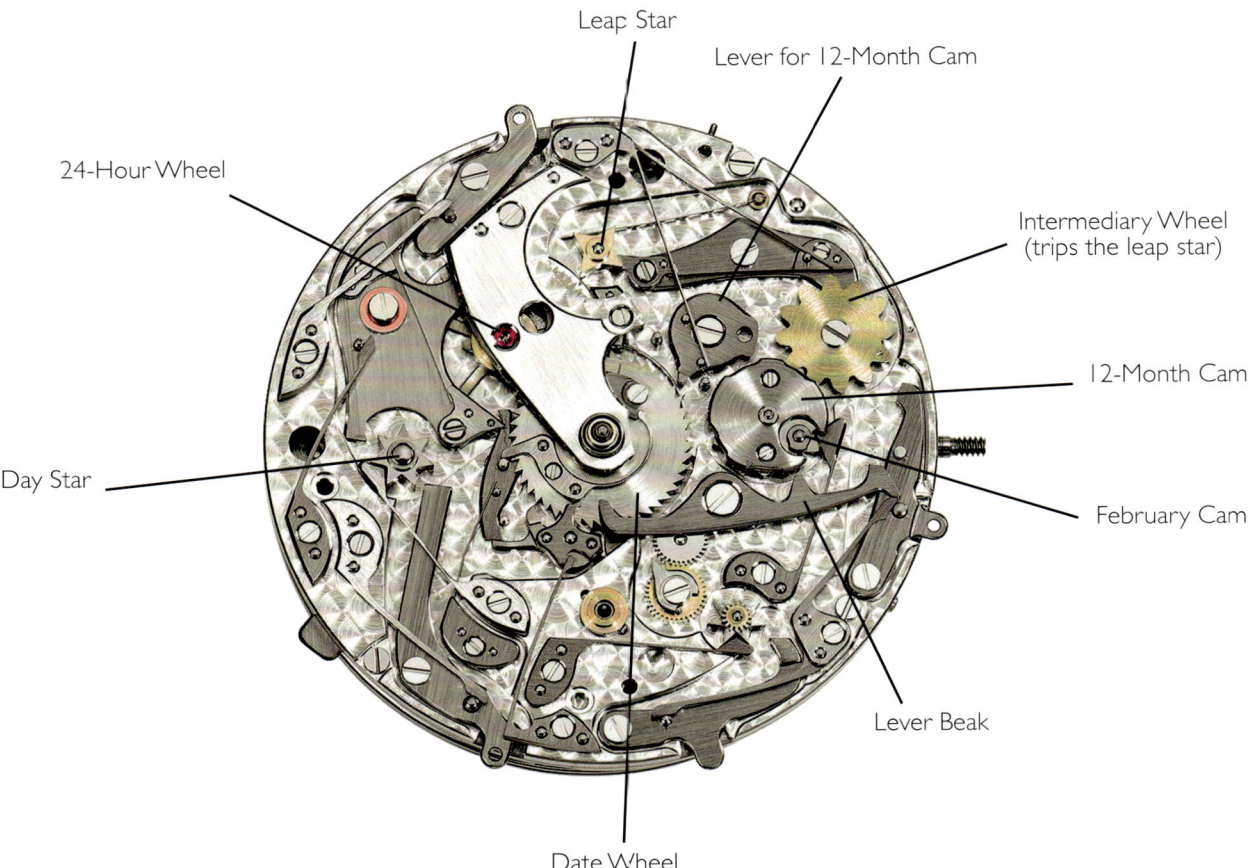

24-Hour Wheel

Leap Star

Lever for 12-Month Cam

Intermediary Wheel
(trips the leap star)

12-Month Cam

Day Star

February Cam

Lever Beak

Date Wheel

- Saving the best for last, the **perpetual calendar** is something of an unattainable complication for many, with very few available for less than $15k, even in the pre-owned market. The perpetual calendar is designed to run according to the Gregorian calendar with *almost* no requirement for manual adjustment. The only time that this is necessary is on the few occasions when the fourth year is *not* a leap year.

  The astronomical year (think of the Earth circling the Sun rather than a printed calendar) is 365.2422 days long. The Julian calendar was introduced to get as close to this figure as possible, by introducing the leap year principle, which gives the average year

under the Julian calendar a value of 365.25. But this meant that the Julian calendar was still running ever so slightly faster than the astronomical calendar – about 0.75 days per century, or 11 minutes per year. The Gregorian calendar brought the average days per year down to 365.2425, and this was achieved by ignoring the leap year rule when: a) it was the start of a new century, *and* b) the date could not be divided by 400. It's still not perfect but now it overruns the solar calendar by only 1 day in every 3,322 years!

Back to watches. A perpetual calendar is smart enough to know when a month is just 30 days long, and when it is a regular leap year, but it needs a nudge on the first year of three out of every four centuries. Therefore on the morning after 28 February 2100 the date will skip to 1 March, and so on until 2400 when there is a well-deserved century off.

Often displayed in a similar fashion to the full calendar, the perpetual is usually differentiated from the more basic calendar mechanism by the presence of a leap year indicator. This will sometimes take the

The Patek Philippe Calibre R 27 PS QR is a minute-repeating perpetual calendar and is similar to the "LU" version found in the ref. 5104p. Note that both this movement and the Vacheron Constantin 2253 have integrated the February/leap cam with the 12-month cam. © 2016 Patek Philippe SA

form of a small aperture that turns blue or red on the leap year, or a small sub-dial split into four sectors (1,2,3,L or, with a red, 4). Alternatively, but less common, the months are placed into 48 chapters, again with four overarching sectors. Some leap year indicators are hidden on the back of the movement, some are implied by virtue of a digital year indicator, and others are excluded altogether requiring some dexterity from the user when setting for the first time.

How does it work? The mechanism is governed by either a 12-month or 48-month cam and the chosen cam is often identifiable by the way the month is displayed on the dial. If it has a 48-month indicator it is a 48-month cam, if it has a leap year indicator it is a 12-month cam. The mechanism relies on a reduction gear train to drive a 24-hour wheel. The 24-hour wheel has a finger that actuates a lever with several beaks; the beaks drive star wheels for the day and the date. The month wheel (and cam) is driven by a finger on the date wheel that engages it once a month. If it is a 48-month system it will have further reduction gearing. A 48-month cam has four levels of depth profile, for 28, 29, 30 and 31-day months. Each slot in the cam increases or decreases the effective length of the beak that drives the date wheel. This causes the beak to accelerate the date wheel, when necessary, by several days at once so that it can jump from 30 to 1 at the end of June, for example. The deeper the slot in the cam, the more of a jump the date wheel will make at the end of the month. The 12-month cam works on a similar, but simpler, basis. The leap adjustment is made possible by a cam on a leap year wheel, which is driven by the month wheel at a ratio of 4:1. The leap cam limits the beak once every four years so that it cannot drop to the very base of the slot on the month cam.

Right, above: The Patek Philippe Calibre 240 Q is a perpetual calendar movement with a 48-month cam mechanism.
© 2016 Patek Philippe SA

Right, below: The Vacheron Constantin Calibre 2253 features a more traditional perpetual calendar mechanism with a 12-month cam that is usually hidden beneath the equation of time and sunrise cams (but is exposed in this particular image).
© 2015 Vacheron Constantin

Above, left: The IWC Portugieser (previously named Portuguese) Perpetual Calendar. As well as 7-day power reserve indicator and moon phase, the watch has a perpetual calendar and keeps the leap adjustment in cycle thanks to a digital year indicator.

© 2016 IWC Schaffhausen

Above, right: Introduced in 1941, the Patek Philippe ref. 1526 was the brand's first serial production perpetual calendar. The 1526 and its successors for the next 40 years would display the complication without leap or year indication. Although today the 1526 is more likely to be found in a vault than on the wrist, it was designed for frequent use; as such it would be highly unlikely for the owner to lose track of the year it was last running to. © 2014 Christie's Images Limited

Opposite: The H. Moser & Cie Endeavour Perpetual Calendar places the leap year indicator on the movement side to retain the use of the function, but leave the dial uncluttered. © 2016 Moser Schaffhausen AG

Above: The Jaeger-LeCoultre Gyrotourbillon 1 features a leap year indicator on the bridge side of the movement and adds a month indicator so that the year can be set without having to refer to the dial side. © 2016 Jaeger-LeCoultre

Opposite: The MB&F Legacy Machine Perpetual is perhaps one of the most unusual displays of a perpetual calendar, featuring an exposed mechanism, enamel dials, and the trademark suspended balance wheel of the Legacy Machine range. The novelty of this watch is not limited to its aesthetic. The movement employs a 12-month cam, which can be seen behind the month dial. Whereas a typical 12-month mechanism uses the depth of the cam to reduce the days from a 31-day month, this cam is inverted, increasing the days from a 28-day month. © 2016 MB&F

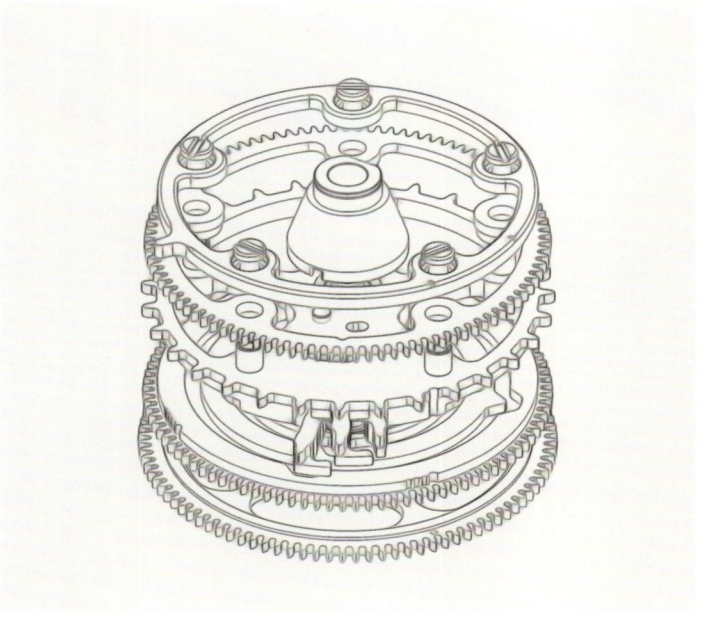

Above: The Greubel Forsey Quantième Perpétuel à Équation. For those more familiar with the hugely impressive trademarks of the brand, you might take for granted the power reserve indicator, the 24-hour widened aperture at 7:30, even the tourbillon positioned at a 25° tilt. You will certainly notice that this appears to be an interesting aperture display of the perpetual calendar; one that can be adjusted with exceptional ease by selecting the QP setting on the crown pusher and adjusting accordingly.

© 2016 Greubel Forsey, Art of Invention

Right and opposite: What will particularly impress will be the way in which the solstice, equinox, season and equation of time are displayed via a single rotating disc and scale on the caseback alongside the digital year indicator. The truly impressive thing about this mechanism lies beneath. The full set of calendar cams, including the equation, are layered co-axially into what Greubel Forsey refer to as a "computeur mécanique". Not only does this preserve space, but it makes the function particularly easy to set without causing undue trauma to the mechanism.

© 2016 Greubel Forsey, Art of Invention

Quick Date Setting

Some watches with a date display have a 'quick date' setting function, which allows the user to directly set the date via the crown without having to rotate the minute and hour hand many, many times. Other watches will allow quick date correction via a pusher in the caseband. Although it is vital for a calendar complication, the quick date mechanism can cause havoc with the regular date mechanism when it is in the period of transition. During this time the date gears mesh with the motion work and cannot move freely or be decoupled when the crown is pulled. Although the date might not change until 1 or 2am the transition can start as early as 9pm. If the quick date setting takes place during this time the movement will likely be damaged. Easy to remember not to change the date between those hours of the day, but less so when the watch stops at 1am and needs to be reset three days later.

There are watches that elaborate the driving finger of the date wheel, so that it can buckle to a date setting without jamming the gears. If it is not known whether a watch has this function, it is best to avoid setting the date between 9pm and 2am. When picking up a stopped watch, step one is to manually progress the minute and hour hands so that they pass 12; if the date does not click forward then the hands have just passed 12 o'clock noon and it is safe to set the date.

Jumping Mechanism / Flash Calendar

The jumping mechanism gets more attention when it is used for the hours register, yet it is far more common as an enhancement to the date function. Arguably it is overlooked because the jump of the date happens overnight, whereas the jumping hour (or minute) can be observed throughout the day.

Watches with jumping mechanisms (also known as flash calendars) reduce the period of transition to a very brief period within which the date snaps into place. The mechanism features a cam (on the 24-hour wheel), lever and spring. The spring is progressively loaded so as not to disrupt torque, and eventually there is so much power built up in the spring that a well-timed unlocking causes the date wheel to rocket forward before locking once more.

Above: The A. Lange & Söhne Lange 1 Tourbillon Perpetual Calendar applies the jumping mechanism to its big date windows, the retrograde day display *and* the rotating month ring on the circumference of the dial. It's a wonderful dance that will have the wearer regularly staying up until midnight at the end of the month to see it in action.   © 2015 A. Lange & Söhne

Opposite: The H. Moser & Cie Endeavour Perpetual Calendar is an extremely understated perpetual calendar. The month is indicated by the small central hand, with each hour marker representing a month. The leap year, as we have just seen, is displayed on the caseback. The power reserve indicator continues the theme of subtlety, at 9 o'clock. The watch features a fairly complex flash calendar that uses a series of cams, levers and springs to progressively build up the energy required to simultaneously switch the date (and month if necessary) at exactly midnight.   © 2016 Moser Schaffhausen AG

Above, left: The Vulcain Cricket. Press the pusher at 2 o'clock, the crown pops out for alarm setting (indicated by the arrow-tip hand). Press the crown back in when set, wind the crown anticlockwise to power the alarm mainspring, and go about your business. © 2016 Vulcain S.A

Above, right: Both the rather rare 1967 Jaeger-LeCoultre Memovox Polaris and the modern 'Tribute to Polaris' (as pictured) are highly attractive alarm watches with internal rotating bezel (adjusted by the crown at 3 o'clock). © 2016 Jaeger-LeCoultre

Opposite: The Ulysse Nardin Sonata Streamline features an alarm countdown sub-dial at 11 o'clock, alarm setting sub-dial at 1 o'clock, home time sub-dial at 6 o'clock, big date at 4 o'clock and alarm function indicator at 9 o'clock (adjusted by the integrated crown pusher). The two pushers at 4 and 8 o'clock set the travel time, indicated on the main dial, backward or forward. The crown at 3 o'clock alternately winds both mainsprings bi-directionally. Unlike many other alarm functions, the Sonata uses a hammer and cathedral gong to make the wearer feel particularly special. The centrifugal governor, which is explained in Chapter 2.8, is visible through the dial at 8 o'clock. © 2016 Ulysse Nardin SA

Alarms and Diary Alarms

In the age of smartphones and tablets there is little need for another device to compete with the beeps and buzzes of daily life. However there is something personal and immediate about a wrist-bound device to remind one of particularly important events, and although this is perhaps mastered by the smartwatch, there is something pleasingly tactile about the setting, and the setting off, of a mechanical alarm. The alarm complication is not particularly common, with manufacturers preferring to attain the complex heights of sonneries and minute repeaters. Patented in 1908 and put into production in 1910 by Eterna, the alarm was not a new concept for horology but it had a slow introduction to the wrist. By the early 1950s, with some small improvements to the complication (such as a shriller ring and an automatic variant), there were two brands leading the charge for alarm watches. First was Vulcain, with its Cricket, and then Jaeger-LeCoultre with its equally iconic Memovox.

Anyone familiar with an alarm clock will be comfortable with the basic operation of these watches, but there are differences. With the Eterna, the alarm and timekeeping functions were powered by the same mainspring, whereas the Vulcain and

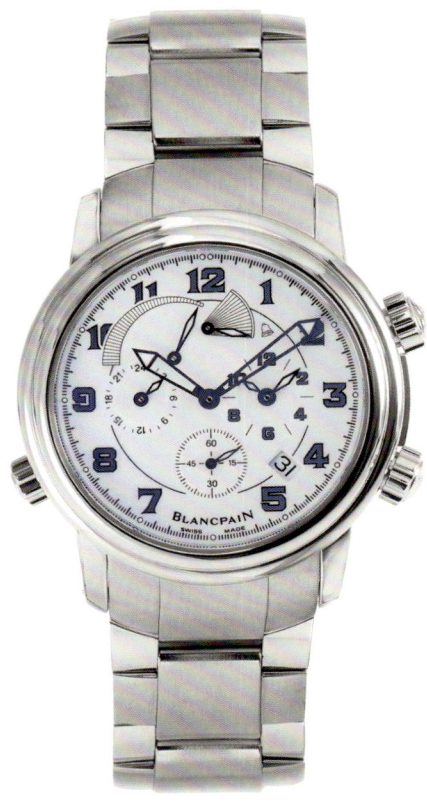

Above, left: The Blancpain Léman Réveil GMT features a 24-hour second time zone indicator at 9 o'clock, hours and minutes alarm setting sub-dial at 3 o'clock, as well as an alarm reserve indicator and function indicator at 11 and 1 o'clock. The crown at 4 o'clock sets the alarm, the crown at 2 o'clock sets the running time, and the screw-down pusher at 8 o'clock turns the alarm on and off.
© 2014 Christie's Images Limited

Above, right: The Glashütte Original Senator Diary combines a widened 24-hour aperture, divided into 15-minute increments, and a date sub-dial at 9 o'clock, enabling the wearer to set their alarm to a specific time and *date*. The pusher at 8 o'clock selects the function, which is displayed by the small aperture within the date ring. The crown at 10 o'clock winds the alarm and rotates the functions through alarm date setting (d), alarm hour setting (h) and alarm on (bell symbol). The pusher at 8 o'clock turns the alarm off (bell with a strikethrough). © 2016 Glashütter Uhrenbetrieb GmbH

Opposite: The Jaeger-LeCoultre Master Compressor Extreme with Alarm has a widened double-digit aperture for the alarm setting (at 9 o'clock), which is set and wound via the crown at 2 o'clock. The crown at 10 o'clock adjusts the 24-hour city wheel and its guard doubles as an alarm on / off switch. An added benefit of the Master Compressor Extreme range is the quick strap change mechanism which saves time and tools if you are the type of enthusiast who likes to switch straps on a whim. © 2016 Jaeger-LeCoultre

Jaeger-LeCoultre had (and still have) two independent mainsprings. The Cricket uses one crown, which can be twisted in both directions to wind either mainspring; the Memovox has two separate crowns for winding at 2 and 4 o'clock. The alarm indicator of the Eterna was a hammer hand, which was operated by rotating the bezel; the Cricket has a dark tipped arrow hand and is operated by the crown when a button at 2 o'clock is depressed; the Memovox features a large concentric disc with a printed arrow that is set by the crown at 2 o'clock. There also exist alarm watches that display the alarm setting on an independent sub-dial or through widened apertures. Some enable the function to be turned off, indicating the alarm status through an aperture or on a fan-form dial, while others are silenced by simply not winding the mainspring of the alarm.

What if the wearer wants their alarm to go off on a specific day, for a specific event? This is where the diary alarm comes into play and the Glashütte Original Senator Diary is one of the few watches with such a function. Using a 1-31 subsidiary chapter ring and a widened aperture to set the alarm time in 15 minute increments, the Senator Diary boasts the ability to set a single event reminder up to 30 days in advance. Its 80-second chime will ensure that no matter what they are up to, so long as they are wearing the watch, it will get the owner's attention.

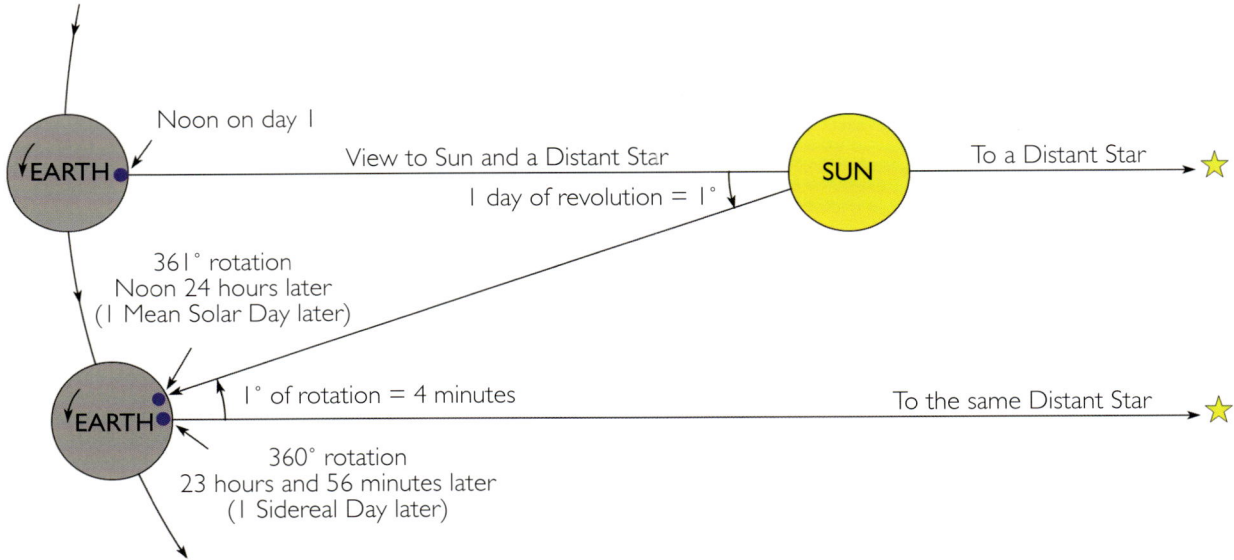

2.7 Astronomical Complications

The relationship between timepieces and astronomy is as old as horology itself. Even before clocks gained the necessary accuracy to be taken seriously as timekeepers, the mechanical principles were being employed by astronomers to bring to life their vision of the pre-Copernican solar system. The position of the planets, their relation to one another and to the stars, was a fundamental fascination of pre-Enlightenment man. This was a time when mankind struggled to come to terms with the growing understanding that they, and the Earth they inhabited, were not the centre of a celestial dance, but flotsam in a storm of unimaginable scale and origin. Despite coming to terms with this concept there is still something awe-inspiring, romantic, and even mystical about a watch that can translate some of this celestial dance onto the dial.

In order to explain astronomical complications, there are some basic principles that need to be covered.

Above: The sidereal and mean solar day

Right: The reverse dial of the Patek Philippe Sky Moon Tourbillon 5002 is a classically executed 24-hour sidereal time and sky chart pairing. (For a view of the front dial, see Chapter 2.11.)

The Solar and Sidereal Day

Imagine time before there was timekeeping. No concept of seconds, minutes or hours. How is it possible to create order out of that? An initial observation might be that the Sun rises, sweeps across the sky, and then sets, plunging everything into darkness. This phenomenon happens at a fairly uniform frequency and is known as a solar day.

When the Sun is down, the stars light up, and, like the Sun, they also trace a path across the night sky, although not the same path. Over successive nights it can be observed that any given star in the sky will pass back over (or very close to) its originally observed position at roughly the same time. This is known as a sidereal day.

Although at first a sidereal day and a solar day appear to be the same length, over time it becomes clear that this is not the case — stars that appear on the eastern horizon at dusk are significantly farther into their westward course just a few weeks later. This is because a sidereal day is around 4 minutes less than a 24-hour mean solar day. Imagine a child on a merry-go-round and at each 360° rotation they touch their mother's hand. What if the mother moves? The child is no longer rotating exactly 360° before they touch their mother; they rotate a little more or a little less depending on her direction. This is similar with the Sun. The Earth is not only spinning on its axis anticlockwise (northern hemisphere) like a merry-go-round, but it is also orbiting the Sun anticlockwise. Therefore each day, in order for the sun to cross the same reference line as yesterday, it will take more than 360° of spin. Whereas if we were also viewing a star that was in a similar position to the Sun, due to the vast distance between us, and the fact that we are not orbiting it, the star would reappear at its originally observed position 4 minutes before the Sun.

Sidereal Time

Certain watches with astronomical complications will display sidereal time. While this is of some use to the modern star-gazer in tracking their favourite constellation; it was particularly important for navigation in the pre-GPS days. The

most useful way to display sidereal time is via a 24-hour chapter ring — not 12-hour because there is no day or night in sidereal time. Sidereal time is based on an astronomical event observed from Greenwich, UK, and is expressed in 24 hours in terms of one's relationship to Greenwich. Local sidereal time can be set based on one's longitude in relation to Greenwich, or alternatively it can be set to correspond to one's own observation of a star using 00:00 as a time marker.

The sidereal chapter ring may be concentric with the running time, or on a sub-dial. There are even watches that display sidereal time via an orbital escapement, which rotates around the dial once every sidereal day — the escapement itself representing

The Arnold & Son DBS Equation Sidereal uses two entirely independent movements. The left side of the dial is calibrated to sidereal time, and the right to mean solar time. The sub-dial at 12 o'clock gives a 24-hour reference to both 12-hour time indications, which is particularly important for the sidereal time being that there is no day or night in space. © 2015 Arnold & Son

The front of the IWC Sidérale Scafusia does a very clean job of displaying sidereal time on a sub-dial. The sidereal and solar gear trains share the same 100-part constant force tourbillon escapement. Note what appear to be two sets of escape wheels and levers. In fact there is just one 15-toothed escape wheel, which has a spiral spring remontoire (providing the constant force to the balance wheel via the lever). The six-toothed wheel on the other side of the balance axis is actually responsible for driving the carriage and recharging remontoire every second. This gives the tourbillon an unusual dead second mechanism. The six-toothed wheel is unlocked and locked by way of a lever that connects with a triangular cam on the escape wheel.

© 2016 IWC Schaffhausen

a star's apparent motion. The Jaeger-LeCoultre Master Grande Tradition Grande Complication, covered in Chapter 1.4, is one such watch that beautifully executes an orbital flying tourbillon on a concentric 24-hour sidereal chapter ring.

On occasion the sidereal and solar displays are regulated by two independent escapements, on others they use two separate gear trains with different tooth ratios and a unified regulator.

Solar Time and the Equation of Time

The sundial is the purest representation of solar time. Unlike sidereal time, solar time is the foundation of the time that is tracked on a wristwatch. Using the sun to determine the time of day is as old as human history. The apparent motion of the sun across a celestial sphere didn't just confirm man's mistaken belief that the Earth was the centre of all things but provided anyone with a pole or an obelisk with the ability to mark out and observe the relative uniformity with which each day passed.

The time between each solar 'noon' – the moment at which the sun is at its highest point – is referred to as a solar day. But the true solar day is not precisely 24 hours long, it fluctuates. This is the result of two phenomena. First is the distance / speed of the Earth's orbit around the Sun at any given time of year. The Earth does not orbit the Sun in a perfect circle. Rather, the orbit is an ellipse and the speed of the orbit increases the closer the Earth is to the Sun (early January being the peak). When this speed and direction of orbit are combined with the Earth's consistent speed of axial rotation, the apparent motion of the Sun will be faster or slower. Because the Earth both rotates and orbits the Sun in an anticlockwise direction, the faster the orbit the slower the Sun will appear to be moving.

The second phenomenon occurs due to the Earth's 23° 'axial tilt' as compared with the axis of its orbit around the Sun. Depending on where the Earth is during its orbit, its tilt will be positioned differently relative to the Sun, and will cause the Sun to reach its highest point in the sky at a different place in the sky (plotting these differences throughout the year would result in a figure of eight, known as an analemma). It is not as simple as the Sun reaching a higher or lower point (the Sun's declination), it also peaks to the east or west of the meridian, and it is this lateral phenomenon that has an effect on the equation of time. If the Sun needs to peak further in the west than the day before it will take longer to get there and will therefore lengthen the solar day.

Because of the accumulated effect of these two phenomena, at any given day the true solar time will be running a little faster or slower than the day before.

The Breguet Perpetual Calendar Equation of Time uses a traditional fan-form sub-dial at 1 o'clock for the equation.

A regular watch does not mimic the apparent motion of the Sun (true solar time) but instead runs to a uniform mean solar day lasting 24 hours. As discussed in Chapter 2.5, this averaging out of the true solar time is further extended to what is called civil time, whereby large areas of individual local mean times are grouped into 24 shared time zones of 15° longitudinal increments. Without civil time a country like France would have two borders separated by 13 minutes of mean solar time and as many time zones in between as there were minutes, seconds, and even fractions-of-a-second! It is therefore worth noting that, when talking about the difference between true solar time and mean solar time, there will be a third dynamic at play: the difference between the mean solar time of the exact longitude and the civil time of the time zone.

The difference between mean solar time and true solar time is represented by the equation of time. The equation was particularly useful as the world transitioned from the sundial to the clock and those concerned about the reliability of the latter kept an eye on it with the former. The equation follows the same fluctuating pattern each year, with very small deviations. At its most extreme, true solar time is around 16 minutes and 30 seconds faster (in early November) or 14 minutes and 5 seconds slower (in mid-February) than mean solar time. A watch with an equation of time complication will provide a day-by-day reading of this difference. Its needle is connected to a lever and a special kidney-shaped cam that rotates once per year. It is usually presented on a fan-form dial with a -15 to +15 scale to represent the minutes that true solar time will be running in comparison with mean solar time.

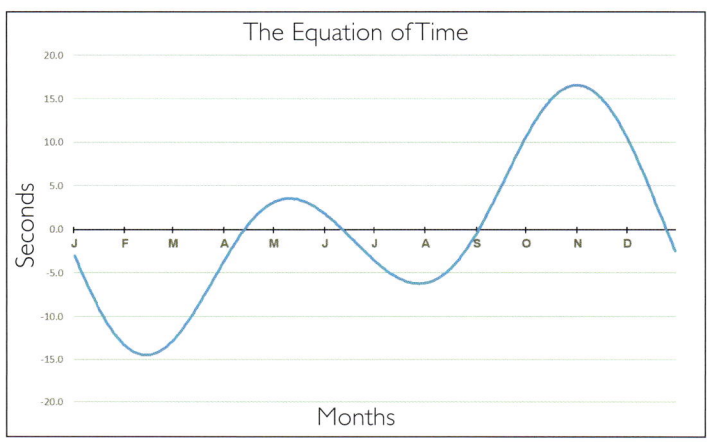

Above: The Blancpain Equation du Temps Marchante presents the equation both via the fan-form register at 1 o'clock and via the solar minute hand that visually displays the difference as compared with the regular minute hand.   © 2015 Christie's Images Limited

Left: The equation of time.   © 2016 Ryan Schmidt

Opposite: The Panerai Radiomir 1940 Equation of Time 8 Days Acciaio displays the equation of time subtly along a linear register.
© 2016 Officine Panerai

Opposite: The Audemars Piguet Royal Oak Equation of Time features a perpetual calendar (sub-dials at 12, 1 and 6 o'clock) and moon phase. The central blue hand and the sub-dials at 3 and 9 o'clock indicate the equation of time, and sunset and sunrise times, respectively. The cams are tailored to the wearer's intended longitude, with the location and hour angle printed on the rehaut at 1 o'clock.   © 2015 Audemars Piguet, Le Brassus

Above and left: Although it is not a wristwatch one cannot ignore the beautiful symmetry of the George Daniels Space Travellers' Pocket Watch. The watch is a staggeringly impressive play on the relationships between sidereal, true solar and mean solar time. Two mainsprings power independent gear trains with escape wheels regulated by the same balance wheel. Daniels needed the assistance of a mathematics professor in order to calculate the ratio for both sidereal and mean solar trains to share the same escapement. The right dial displays mean solar time, with a subsidiary seconds dial and annual calendar in the aperture at their intersection. The left dial displays 24-hour sidereal time, with large moon phase aperture, a subsidiary seconds dial and age of the Moon in the aperture at their intersection. At 12 o'clock sits the equation of time. Daniels recreates an old-world process that involved setting a precision clock by conversion from sidereal time. The central 60-second chronograph can be calibrated to record a mean solar or sidereal minute.   Image Credit: Sotheby's

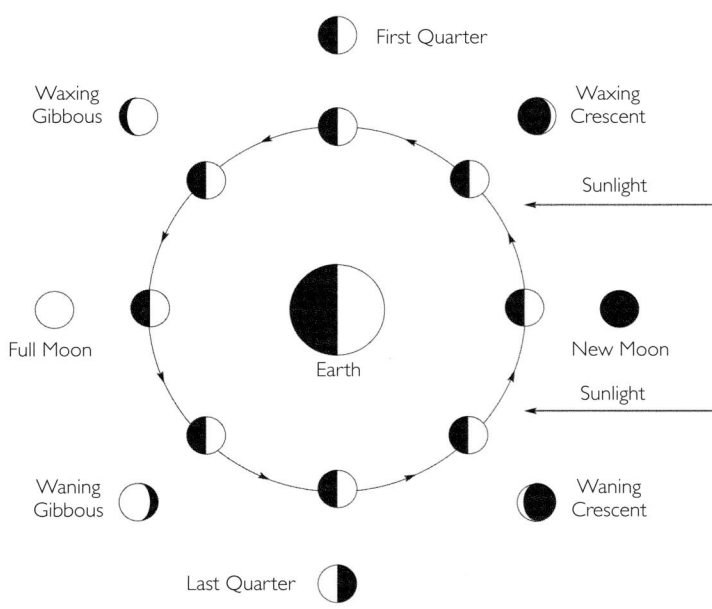

First Quarter

Waxing Gibbous

Waxing Crescent

Sunlight

Full Moon

Earth

New Moon

Sunlight

Waning Gibbous

Waning Crescent

Last Quarter

The inner circle shows how the Moon is illuminated by the Sun.
The outer circle shows how the Moon appears in the sky.

The Moon Phase Indicator

The moon phase is the most common astronomical complication. This is likely due to its simplicity of execution (at least relative to its other astronomical siblings), its visual impact, and the sheer romance and mystery that the Moon evokes.

The Moon orbits the Earth every 27 days. Depending on the position of the Sun, Moon and Earth, the surface of the Moon that faces the Earth will reflect some, all or none of the Sun's light onto the Earth. This lunar cycle has four phases: new (no illumination), first quarter (half of the facing surface is reflected), full (all of the facing surface is illuminated), and third quarter (the other half). It 'waxes' in the first two quarters, and 'wanes' in the second. The cycle takes place over 29.53 days. Why not 27? Because in the 27 days that the Moon has orbited the Earth, the Earth has also been orbiting the Sun in the same anticlockwise direction. Therefore the lunar cycle that creates the phases is not simply its orbit, but the time it takes to align with the Earth and the Sun.

On a wristwatch the phase of the moon is most commonly presented through an aperture. The full Moon is placed on a disc and the aperture is curved at the entry and exit so that the Moon appears to wax and wane as it comes into view. On occasion the phase will be indicated by a hand, which points to a depiction of the phase on a sub-dial, by a disc on a lever that moves past a circular aperture of the same size, or by a rotating sphere coloured dark and light on each half.

As the exact lunar cycle lasts 29.530588853 days the simplest way to deliver this mechanically is to use two images of the Moon on a 59-toothed wheel with teeth that are driven by a single finger attached to the hour wheel. This means that each moon on the disc will pass through the aperture every 29.5 days. Because of the 0.03-day difference the indicator will have lost a day of accuracy if it ran solidly for 3 years.

Driven by the desire to obtain perfection, watchmakers have created more accurate moon phase indicators. These are achieved by geared transmission, the simplest of which can improve accuracy so that the mechanism runs fast by only 57.2 seconds each cycle. Around 122 years would pass before the mechanism had lost a full day of accuracy. Bearing in mind that there will be several services during this period, this is a perfect moon phase. Regardless, a number of manufacturers have breached the 1,000-year accuracy mark with others venturing past 3,000, 14,000 and even 2.045 million years; an absolutely staggering feat. Amidst all of the celebration and fanfare being showered upon these watches, spare a thought for the poor moon phase corrector button as it will be one of the most redundant mechanisms on a modern watch.

Above: The phases of the moon as experienced by the view from Earth. The diagram demonstrates why a new moon is not visible to us at night, however it also suggests, incorrectly, that the waxing and waning crescents will be a daytime-only phenomenon. This is not entirely true; because of the sheer distance between the Sun, Earth and Moon, there is a delay in the rising and setting of the Moon and the Sun. This allows us to briefly observe the waxing and waning crescents shortly after dusk and before dawn, respectively.   © 2016 ACC Art Books

Opposite: Andreas Strehler Sauterelle à Lune Perpétuelle is a titan in terms of moon phase accuracy. Its mechanism is capable of delivering an accurate moon phase to the nearest day for 2.045 million years. The watch also features an eccentric dial and a one-second spiral spring remontoir d'égalité on the fourth wheel at 10 o'clock which doubles as a dead second.   © 2015 Andreas Strehler

Left and below: The De Bethune DB28 Digitale embodies a host of features worth mentioning. The moon phase is indicated by a rotating sphere made of palladium and blued steel at the centre of the dial. Aside from being visually beautiful the moon phase mechanism is accurate to 1,112 years. Moving on to the rest of the watch, the crown at 12 o'clock, the jumping hours, the rotating minute disc, and the blued titanium with white gold stars are all notable. The skeletonised lugs are articulated at 3 and 9 o'clock so that the watch sits snug on the wrist. The view of the movement reveals a very unusual silicon and white gold balance wheel (disc).

© 2016 De Bethune SA

Opposite: The Piaget Emperador Coussin XL Large Moon Enamel is a fine piece of champlevé enamel art illustrating a map of the silk route. It is also a great example of a large moon phase indicator by way of a rotating paddle. The movement features two dark paddles which rotate around the central axis of the dial and pass beneath the 12mm aperture. The mechanism is a basic gear transmission, meaning 122 years of accuracy. You and your watchmaker could keep this running all your life and it would still be your grandchildren who would need to adjust the mechanism by one day.

© 2016 Piaget

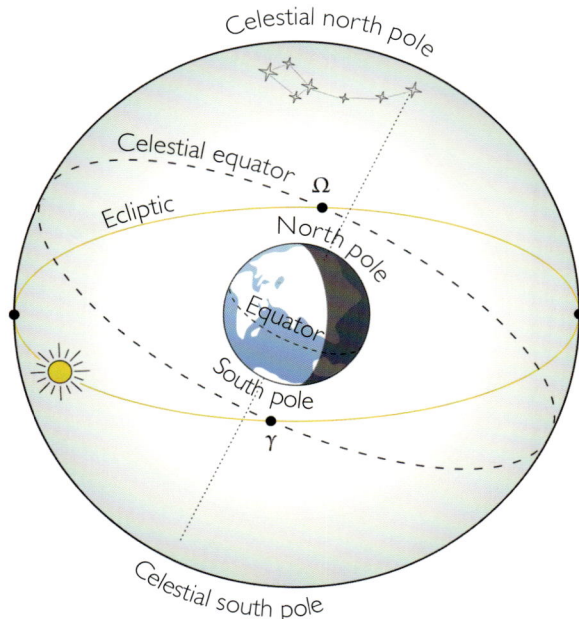

Celestial north pole

Celestial equator

Ecliptic

Ω

North pole

Equator

South pole

γ

Celestial south pole

The Celestial Chart / Sky Chart / Astrolabe

There is perhaps no greater natural wonder than experiencing the Earth's movement through the dance of the stars, and so a complication designed to replicate this movement will need to be very special. The watch is such a small space in which to allow creativity to breathe, yet somehow the celestial chart and astrolabe defy this, and instead give the wearer a sense that the dial is merely a porthole through which the wearer can glimpse the universe.

- **Celestial Chart / Sky Chart** – Simply put, the chart gives its wearer a reading of the constellations that will appear in the night sky at a particular time and latitude. They are calibrated to one of the two hemispheres (northern and southern) as both will have opposing celestial poles (rotational axes) from their respective positions. As the sky chart is highly location-specific, they require tailoring to the location of the wearer, or alternatively might provide the chart of a particularly important location. The sky chart is presented through a 'planisphere', which is a large elliptical aperture, under which a larger rotating disc features key constellations of the night sky. The aperture is eccentric too, but overlaps with the axis of the disc beneath. To the observer, the night sky pivots on an invisible axis known as the celestial pole (the rotational axis of the Earth). The axis of the disc beneath represents the celestial pole and as such the degree of

eccentricity that the aperture has in relation to it will be a reflection of the latitude that the chart is designed for. The chart might be labelled with the four cardinal points, with north and south inverted. This allows the wearer to face north, hold the chart above their head and have the correct bearings from this inverted view. Alternatively east and west might be inverted, requiring the wearer to face south for their star-gazing.

Although they look the same, there are two types of sky chart complication. One will perform a single rotation every year and provide a depiction of the night sky at a fixed daily time. The other will perform a rotation once every sidereal day and therefore represents a real-time depiction of the sky. The former is an easier task, requiring the same reduction gearing as a month wheel. The latter is a more significant undertaking in that the disc will require far more complex gearing ratios to translate the regular train into a sidereal one. Both lock stunning. One of the best examples of the latter is the Patek Philippe ref. 6102P Sky Moon. It features a blue sapphire crystal background with moon aperture, a moon disc beneath it, and a sapphire crystal disc with the constellations on one side and the Milky Way on the other. The elliptical is printed on the underside of the main crystal. These layers combine to provide depth and mystery to the complication. Aside from being stunning, it is also impressively accurate. The sky chart rotates once per sidereal day, the moon phase is accurate to one day in over 1,000 years, and the passage of the Moon across the sky runs a 24-hour and 50-minute cycle. The result is a real-time depiction of the night sky (from Geneva's longitude) including the location and phase of the Moon. The crown at 2 o'clock manages the timekeeping and the winding, the crown at 4 o'clock manages the Moon and sky, and a pusher at 9 o'clock changes the date (as told by the centrally mounted moon-tipped hand).

Above: The Celestial Sphere, featuring an equator, ecliptic and celestial North Pole.

Image: Equatorial coordinate system (celestial)
© 2016 Joshua Cesa, www.joshuacesa.org

Opposite: The Patek Philippe ref. 6102P Sky Moon.
© 2016 Patek Philippe SA

The Van Cleef & Arpels Midnight in Paris depicts the night sky as
viewed from Paris at night. It therefore rotates once a year rather
than once every sidereal day. The elliptical is illustrated by a large
clear aperture surrounded by opaque sapphire crystal. The hinged
'officer' caseback conceals a date wheel, a meteorite plate and a
winding mechanism for setting the date. © 2016 Van Cleef & Arpels

The caseback of the IWC Sidérale Scafusia reveals an exceptional sky chart. The tailored co-ordinates are printed in yellow at 12 o'clock and represented within the yellow ellipse (the red circle is the apparent orbit of the sun). A thin disc indicates the day of the year at 12 o'clock in hundreds, tens and single days at 1 o'clock. The leap year is indicated at 11 o'clock. Within the chart, the red arrow indicates the current mean solar time and the yellow arrow indicates sidereal time. On the periphery the sunrise and sunset times are indicated by red arrows. Incredibly the crystal on the chart darkens during nocturnal hours. © 2016 IWC Schaffhausen

• **Astrolabe** – The astrolabe dates as far back as 150 BC, was widely popularised in early 15th century France, and during the 16th century settled into the form in which it is found (albeit rarely) in today's wristwatch. It is a hugely impressive device considering the relative simplicity of its component parts. The astrolabe is a large disc-shaped planisphere; it features a base plate, an additional cut-out rotating plate, a hand, and a rotating device on the back. The base plate is mapped out with a series of celestial co-ordinates that are specific to the latitude of the owner and features a zenith (the point in the sky aligned to the rotational axis of the Earth), the azimuths (degrees of longitude) and altitude (degrees of latitude) in the celestial sphere. The top plate enables the user to differentiate between the seen and unseen portions of the sky at a given time and also identifies key constellations. Knowing the date and using the hand one could determine certain celestial events, such as sunrise

and sunset times, or the times that certain stars would be visible. Using the rotating device on the back, a star could be sighted in the sky and its respective altitude and azimuth calculated. Knowing the date, and sighting a star, one could determine the exact solar time.

How does the astrolabe operate as a mechanical watch complication? It features the same set of co-ordinates, the rotating plate, and the hand; but with

The Vacheron Constantin Maître Cabinotier Astronomica is an extremely complicated watch with strong astronomical tones. The dial side is crammed with a perpetual calendar (three sub-dials and aperture at 1 o'clock), an equation of time (10:30), a power reserve indicator (9 o'clock), a sunrise and sunset (8 and 4 o'clock), and a tourbillon (6 o'clock). The caseback shows a detailed sidereal sky chart calibrated to Geneva latitude, the large central hand indicates the date and zodiac sign, the smaller hand indicates the moon phase. There is also a minute repeater, as hinted at by the slide.   © 2014 Vacheron Constantin

the latter in constant synchrony with the passage of time it serves to provide the wearer with the exact co-ordinates of stars at a given moment, sunset and sunrise times, the respective season and zodiac sign. When additional hands are mounted to the astrolabe dial, the watch is capable of even more.

Few watches have even come close to exploring the depths of the astrolabe as the Ulysse Nardin Astrolabium Galileo Galilei (pictured). The mean solar time is read from the baton hour and minute hands against the 12-hour Roman numeral bezel. The hand with the counterweight sun indicates the month on the outer chapter ring and the zodiac sign on the ecliptic. It provides an approximate date, but it is precisely calibrated against the sun hand so that it never needs adjusting and is therefore a truly perpetual calendar. The weekday is in the aperture at 6 o'clock. The sun hand can also be read against the 24-hour bezel to indicate the true solar time. Wondering why the difference between that time and the mean solar time of the regular hands is so significant? It is not just the equation of time, but also the difference between the current time zone and the true solar time of that exact longitude. When the sun hand, the ecliptic, *and* the horizon line on the left or right side of the dial intersect, it will be the exact time of sunrise and sunset, respectively. As the intersection of the sun hand and the ecliptic move along the grey area between the horizon line and the edge of the darkest portion of the dial, this is the period of astronomical dawn and dusk. The equivalent lunar indications are given by the hand with the counterweight moon. The axis of the dial represents the earth, and the tips of the sun and moon hands indicate whether the Sun and Moon will be visible at the same time. Whether the sun hand is behind or ahead of the moon hand will determine if the Moon is waning or waxing, respectively. When the two hands align it is a new moon, when they directly oppose each other it is a full moon. When the dragon hand converges on the new moon or full moon you have yourself a solar or lunar eclipse, respectively. Using the azimuth and altitude grid on the dial it is possible to determine the exact location of a given star as identified on the grid, or of the Sun and Moon by the position of

their respective hands intersecting with the ecliptic on the grid. If one considered 12, 3, 6 and 9 o'clock, to be South, West, North and East, respectively, then compass direction can be determined by pointing the sun hand at the Sun or the moon hand at the Moon. The concentric circles of Cancer, the Equator, and Capricorn and their intersection with the ecliptic and the sun hand will indicate the summer solstice, equinox and winter solstice.

The intimidatingly complex dial of the Ulysse Nardin Astrolabium Galileo Galilei.   © 2016 Ulysse Nardin SA

Sunrise and Sunset

Understanding the apparent motion of the Sun from a given latitude, and with the use of a tool such as an astrolabe (or its electronic equivalent) one can calculate the varying times of sunrise and sunset at any given time of year. Not least because it relies on their complex calculations, the sunrise and sunset indicator complication is usually provided as part of a wider set of astronomical complications. The sunrise scale will usually range from 4 to 9, and the sunset scale from 16 to 21. The sunrise and sunset times are each managed via a location-specific cam.

Orrery / Planetarium

In 1704 two great watchmakers, George Graham and Thomas Tompion, made a mechanical model of the solar system. The model was developed by instrument maker John Rowley and presented to the Earl of Orrery, after whom the device was named.

The modern orrery mechanically depicts the tilt of the Earth, the Moon's orbit of the Earth, and the planets' orbits of the Sun. In watchmaking terms a planetarium is used interchangeably with orrery. The complication typically places representative planets on discs which move concentrically around a representation of the Sun. It is the most literal use of planetary wheels that one is likely to find.

Above: The sunrise (left) and sunset (right) mechanism for the Audemars Piguet Calibre 2120 / 2808, as featured in the Royal Oak Equation of Time. Each dial has its own cam, tailored to the location of the wearer. The cam for the equation of time can be seen on the front of the sunset wheel. The two indicators shift each day and are driven by the date wheel at 6 o'clock.
© 2015 Audemars Piguet, Le Brassus

Opposite: The Jacob & Co. Astronomia Tourbillon features a double-axis tourbillon, a third axis if you include the central one around which the majority of the movement rotates every 20 minutes. The Earth does spin on its axis, but rather than being orbited by the Moon (a 280-facet diamond) it dances with it around the central axis. It is not scientifically accurate, but it is certainly captivating. It is set and wound via two crowns concealed within the caseback.
© 2016 Jacob&Co.

Above and opposite: The Graham Tourbillon Orrery. The Sun is represented by the diamond stud at the centre of the tourbillon bridge and the Earth orbits the Sun every 365 days in between the zodiac and Gregorian calendar rings. Mars is also featured, with its 687-day orbit. Perhaps the most impressive element is the tiny Moon that orbits the Earth on its 27-day cycle. The phase of the Moon can therefore also be read — when it is between the Earth and the Sun it is new, when behind the Earth it is full. The back of the watch features 100 years etched on the circumference of the crystal. There is a marker on every 7th and 25th year so that the wearer can make an adjustment to the Moon and Mars at 4 and 10 o'clock, respectively, to retain accuracy. The crown at 2 o'clock adjusts the planets along the date wheel.   © 2016 Graham 1695

Left: The Christiaan Van der Klaauw CVDK Planetarium is the smallest mechanical planetarium in the world. The watch places six planets on a sub-dial at 6 o'clock, which is marked with the signs of the zodiac and equivalent degrees of the circumference. You might expect such a complication from Van der Klaauw, the brains behind a number of other in-house astronomical complications as well as the Van Cleef & Arpels Midnight Planétarium.
© 2015 Christiaan van der Klaauw Astronomical Watches

Opposite: The Van Cleef & Arpels Midnight Planétarium places six precious stone planets on rotating discs topped with solid aventurine. The shooting star on the dial rotates every 24 hours and can be used to indicate the time. The bezel moves the red arrow around the date ring and is used to set a 'lucky day' upon which the Earth will be sitting beneath the star etched into the crystal. The back of the watch features a month / date indicator at 6 o'clock and year indicator at 3 o'clock.
© 2016 Van Cleef & Arpels

2.8 Chiming Complications

The earliest clocks were built from materials that were heavily affected by temperature fluctuations, they employed technology that was somewhat basic and the deviation in terms of exact measurements was a matter of the nearest millimetre as opposed to micron. As a result, the earliest clocks were developed with only a single hand for the hours, or no hands at all. Their purpose was not so much to enable a person to understand the exact time at any given point, but to sound out the call to prayer or other important communal events. These clocks provide something of a historical context for the chiming / striking pocket watches and wristwatches of today, but the complication was actually developed to solve an environmental problem; it was developed for darkness.

In the late 18th century, houses and streets were dimly lit by gas lamps and candles. Should one wake in the middle of the night, or find oneself away from the immediate illumination of a street lamp, a watch would be useless. Houses in England did not light up until the mid-to-late 19th century, and luminescent paint for hands and markers followed shortly thereafter, so it was with more than novelty and historic homage in mind that the chiming mechanism was born in the wrist / pocket watch. The user would activate the mechanism and the chimes would be orchestrated in such a way that the hours, quarter hours (or tens), and even minutes of the current time could be sounded out in the darkness.

The chiming complication falls into two distinct functional categories: the repeater and the sonnerie. The repeater chimes the time on demand, the sonnerie does so in passing at predetermined intervals. The earliest configurations used hammers and bells, but in today's chiming complications they use hammers and gongs. The gongs are thin, elongated and hardened rods that occupy a portion of the circumference of the movement (usually at the base, sometimes under the dial, sometimes above) and are only attached to the movement at one end. The hammers are simply hammers held in place by two counter-springs. Typically there are two hammers and two gongs, one that creates a treble note and the other a deeper, bass note. Using a two-note format you can create three indications: the single bass (usually hours), the single treble (usually minutes), and the combined (quarter hours or tens of minutes).

How does a chiming mechanism work? Answering this comes in two parts: how the mechanism tracks the time and how it is translated into strikes. To track the time the chiming

Above and opposite: The F.P. Journe Répétition Souveraine has a subtle repeater slide at 10 o'clock and displays the two hammers through the aperture at 9:30. The dial side of the movement boasts the key workings of the repeater, except for the governor, which spins wildly on the bridge side.   © 2015 Montres Journe SA

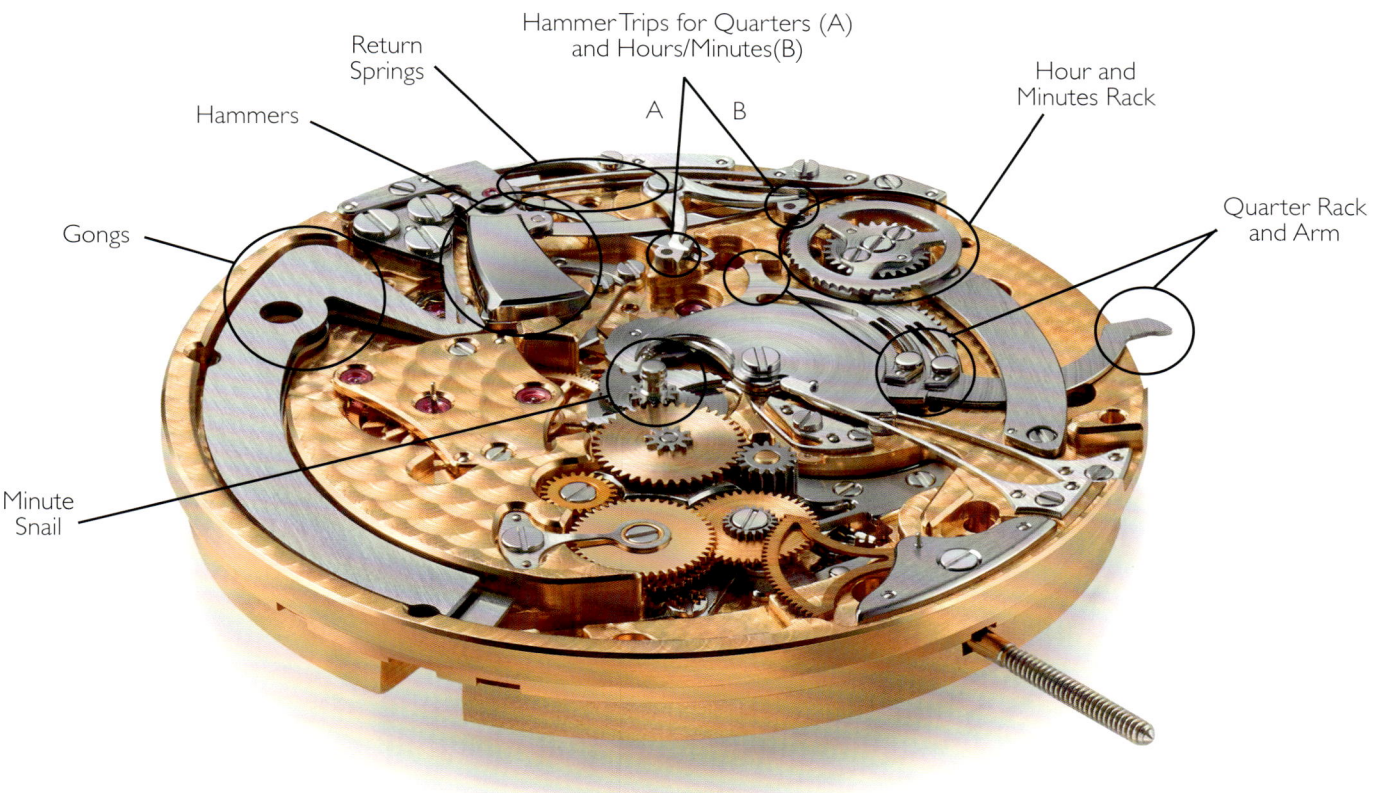

Gongs

Hammers

Return Springs

Hammer Trips for Quarters (A) and Hours/Minutes(B)

A   B

Hour and Minutes Rack

Quarter Rack and Arm

Minute Snail

mechanism uses a series of snail cams that sit on the wheels of, or are driven by, the regular timekeeping mechanism. First there is a 4-step 'quarter snail' cam, and a four-blade wheel with 14 teeth on each blade which looks like a ninja throwing star, called the 'minute snail'. These rotate with the centre wheel and therefore perform one full rotation per hour. Then there is a 12-point star wheel, and a 12-step 'hour snail' mounted nearby. The cannon pinion has a single tooth that engages the star wheel each hour, causing it to rotate and snap into place thanks to a blade spring 'jumper'. The mechanism is driven by the second wheel of the gear train which can keep stock of the exact time in hours, quarter-hours and minutes.

How does this tracking translate to strikes? When the repeater slide is pulled back its mainspring is charged and the rack for the hours / minutes / quarters is cocked into starting position. The exact starting position will determine the number of hammer actions that will be tripped when the repeater mainspring is released and the rack is driven back to its resting position. Each rack has a beak and it is this beak that connects with its respective snail cam, which determines the starting position of the rack. So if it is the third quarter of the hour, the beak of the quarter rack will travel back to the third-

of-four starting positions and because it will connect with the third 'deepest' step of the quarter snail it will pass through positions 3, 2 and 1 as it is released. Conversely, if the time is less than 15 minutes past the hour, the starting position of the rack will be at its shallowest and it will not pass any of the other positions. Why is this important? The racks are equipped with teeth, each one corresponding to an hour, quarter and minute, respectively. When the repeater slide is released the mainspring drives the repeater gear train; the racks return to their resting positions and while doing so their teeth pass a hammer trip. The trip is held in place by a blade spring and is somewhat similar to the click on a mainspring barrel; when the teeth pass in one direction (cocking the racks) the trip lets the teeth pass with a click; when the teeth pass in the other direction, the trip engages with the tooth and transfers an impulse to one of the hammer's two counter-springs. This causes the hammer to pull back, snap forward, and hit the gong, before resting away from the gong thanks to the other counter-spring. Modern repeater sliders also possess an 'all-or-nothing' safety mechanism which means that the repeater will not function unless the slider has been pulled all the way, appropriately positioning the racks.

Repeaters

A repeater enables the wearer to activate the chiming mechanism on demand, usually by way of a slide lever on the caseband. These slide levers are prominent and enable the watch enthusiast to quickly pick one out from the crowd, however there are also one or two models with more concealed levers or push buttons. The slide lever is important because the action of the slide will *wind* a separate mainspring. The mainspring is immediately released by way of a 'centrifugal governor' that spins at a high rate until the mainspring is spent. The governor acts as a constant flow escapement relying on the centrifugal force and / or air resistence to dampen its release. The governor is a toothless wheel with two spring-mounted weights that separate as the wheel spins, altering its moment of inertia and effectively smoothing out the release of mainspring power across the torque curve. It is a perfectly effective escapement for the short burst of a repeater, but would be far less accurate for timekeeping than existing escapements. The only criticism of the centrifugal governor is that it generates an audible whirring, which competes very slightly with the sound of the chimes.

Repeaters are categorised by the level of detail that their mechanisms indicate. A common minute repeater will have two gongs and two hammers to chime the hours, the quarter hours and the minutes. There also exist decimal minute repeaters, which are the same with the exception of a 10-minute indication instead of a quarter hour. This would be achieved quite simply by adding two additional steps to the cam and teeth to the rack. There also exist, particularly in vintage pocket watches, 5-minute repeaters, half quarter repeaters and quarter repeaters, which will chime to indicate the time down to the nearest 5 minutes, 7.5 minutes and 15 minutes, respectively. Until a second-repeater is invented, the quarter or decimal minute repeater is the most accurate, and preferable, format.

Right: The exquisitely handmade Voutilainen Decimal Repeater with 24-hour time for the running time or an additional zone. The repeater mechanism is operated by a traditional slider at 9 o'clock. Note the fine mix of guilloché engine-turning on the dial.
© 2013 Christie's Images Limited

Opposite: The caseback of the Ulysse Nardin Hannibal Minute Repeater reveals a beautiful and traditional minute repeater mechanism. The racks can be seen at 9 o'clock and the four blades of the minute snail can be made out at the centre.
© 2016 Ulysse Nardin SA

Sonnerie

While a repeater will chime to indicate the time on demand, a sonnerie will chime 'in passing'. On a sonnerie there is no slide lever, which typically means that the regular mainspring is *shared* with that of the timekeeping function or is independent. In either case the mainspring needs to be hand-wound to ensure that it will continue to function, and if it is shared with the timekeeping function a low reserve could cause the whole watch to stop. It is therefore common for a sonnerie to take power from an independent mainspring, and extremely common for any sonnerie to have a power reserve indicator as well as a 'silence' mode in order to allow the wearer to manage power.

Right: The Audemars Piguet Jules Audemars Grande Sonnerie Carillon Dynamographe has three hammers and gongs. The sonnerie has its own mainspring with reserve indicator at 1 o'clock, and can be alternated from silent to petite sonnerie to grand sonnerie using the switch at 2 o'clock. The regular timekeeping function has a second mainspring and a dynamograph to keep track of the torque. The pushbutton at 10 o'clock prompts a repeater function; note that it is a button rather than a slider and therefore does not charge the mainspring. Instead, the mainspring of the sonnerie is charged by turning the crown clockwise, and the mainspring of the timekeeping function is charged by turning anticlockwise.   © 2015 Audemars Piguet, Le Brassus

Opposite: Patek Philippe 5104p. With a simple, three-hand watch the dial side of the movement is more or less featureless. But when a minute repeater, perpetual calendar and moon phase are added to the movement it explodes with levers, racks, and cams. With so much complication in action, concealing it behind an opaque dial is an injustice to the watchmaker. The 5104p sports many of its perpetual calendar components on the dial and uses translucent registers (with blue indicators passing beneath them) to draw as much attention to the components as to the readings they deliver. Patek Philippe has the reputation of producing some of the finest repeaters. The CEO, like his father / grandfather / great-grandfather before him, personally quality-checks the tone of the repeater before the watch leaves the manufacturer.

© 2016 Patek Philippe SA

Right: The exquisite dial-side movement of the Audemars Piguet Millenary Minute Repeater (the watch is shown in Chapter 1.2). It features a repeater mechanism with two hammers and two blued gongs, and a direct impulse double-hairspring 'AP' escapement.

© 2015 Audemars Piguet, Le Brassus

Below: The Girard-Perregaux Opera 2 sports a tourbillon, perpetual calendar, minute repeater and skeletonised dial to show off the mechanism beneath. The Opera 2 has four hammers and four gongs and can therefore be referred to as a Westminster chime repeater. It is seen here resting on its repeater slider.

© 2015 Girard-Perregaux

There do also exist some repeaters that operate in this fashion, as opposed to a slide-activated additional mainspring. Take for example the A. Lange & Söhne Zeitwerk Minute Repeater. It has a pusher at 10 o'clock instead of a slider. Although this is a repeater and not a sonnerie, the Zeitwerk repeater is powered by the regular mainspring. This requires diligent power management but is made easy for the wearer due to the safety mechanism that disables the repeater when the reserve drops below the red dot on the indicator.

There are two kinds of sonnerie, the petite sonnerie, and the grande sonnerie, although in most modern manifestations a sonnerie will come with both functions and the user may alternate between the two. The petite sonnerie will chime the hour on the hour and (in most cases) the quarter hour every 15-minute period in-between. The grande sonnerie will chime the full time every 15 minutes, but unlike the repeater it will chime the quarter first and then the hour. A grande sonnerie might also include a minute or quarter repeater, which is activated by a button (as opposed to the slide lever). As the sonnerie and repeater chime in a different order this is more complicated to execute than it may seem. There are other, more basic, variations of sonnerie that chime the hours on the hour only, or a single chime every hour.

The dial of the A. Lange & Söhne Zeitwerk Minute Repeater gives clean views of the extremely polished hour hammer (left) and minute hammer (right). This is a decimal repeater so the two hammers also combine to ring out increments of 10 minutes. The gongs can be seen too as they coil around the edge of the dial. Many images of the Zeitwerk will read 7:52; this is a nod to the clock towers of a bygone era that would chime 8 minutes before the start of the opera.   © 2015 A. Lange & Söhne

Carillon, Westminster and Cathedral

You might notice some additional words creeping into the names of certain chiming watches. Aside from whatever fancy superlatives the manufacturer chooses to add (some watch names need two breaths to read aloud), the extra words may be indicating another level of technical complexity based on the quality or quantity of gongs and hammers. A carillon, for example, is a chiming watch that features more than the traditional two hammers and gongs. When a watch crams in a fourth pair it is often referred to as a Westminster chime watch, named after the great Big Ben clock tower of the Palace of Westminster, which plays an iconic four-note tune. When the repeater function is activated in a carillon or Westminster sonnerie, the chime structure will usually use the bass note for the hours, a cascading three or four-note tune for the quarter, and the treble note for the minutes. When a chiming watch boasts a sound that particularly reverberates and amplifies, it might be referred to as a cathedral repeater. Cathedral repeaters feature gongs that are longer than the circumference of the movement itself, requiring an impressive doubling back or overlapping, not unlike the game 'snake' that was featured on the cell phones of a particularly common pre-smartphone brand – cause the gongs to touch and the game is over.

Above and opposite: The Christophe Claret Allegro Minute Repeater. Each of the two cathedral gongs makes two laps of the circumference, giving the repeater its rich tones. The pusher at 2 o'clock adjusts the big date, and the pusher at 4 o'clock adjusts the dual time hour hand and corresponding day / night aperture (in the sub-dial at 3 o'clock). The large opening in the dial at 6 o'clock gives a clear view of the racks and the hammer trips.

© 2016 Christophe Claret

The Bvlgari L'Ammiraglio del Tempo Minute Repeater. The movement boasts a cylindrical balance spring and detent escapement as well as a remontoire on the fourth wheel (seen at 4 o'clock close to the centre of the dial) which charges itself twice every second. The repeater is a four-gong / hammer Westminster mechanism. The lug at 7 o'clock is actually not a lug but a concealed slider; it is a great design element that preserves the iconic Daniel Roth case shape (the eponymous brand was bought by Bvlgari in 2000).   © 2016 Bulgari S.P.A

Innovations in Repeater Technology

The few manufacturers who are capable of producing great repeaters have a hard enough time retaining the technology and expertise, let alone improving upon it. Brands must look after their specialist watchmakers capable of building and repairing these treasures; there aren't many of them. Despite this being an archaic complication for an antiquated device, there have still been some notable innovations in the chiming complication.

Chiming hammers are fairly consistent in their design. They are top-heavy with a little beak for the impact. They are held in place by two springs, one of which is triggered by the trip mechanism when the rack tooth passes it. Although they are already designed to provide the gong with a strong, concise tap before resting away from the surface, the traditional hammer burns a lot of kinetic energy. The trebuchet hammer, introduced by Jaeger-LeCoultre, does a fine job of mitigating this waste. The principle follows that of the trebuchet catapult, whereby the arm of the catapult uses a rope extension to create a sling-shot effect, dramatically increasing the velocity of the projectile. In the same way the trebuchet hammer is articulated so that it 'whips' the tip of the hammer into the gong. The result is the sort of clarity and strength of tone that one would hope to hear from a particularly fine chiming mechanism.

Other notable innovations have taken place in the realm of sound amplification and resonance, the acoustic goal of the chiming watch being to create an auditorium within the case. This is achieved by using the right material and by giving the movement room to cultivate strong sound waves.

The Jaeger-LeCoultre Hybris Mechanica à Grande Sonnerie is an exquisite perpetual calendar with flying tourbillon and sonnerie. Although this alone is highly impressive, what makes the Hybris Mechanica one of the most complicated watches in the world is the combination of its functions and the way in which they are displayed and operated. This watch is further explored in Chapter 2.11.

© 2016 Jaeger-LeCoultre

Although high-density materials are better at directly conducting sound waves, the case of the watch must prioritise amplification over conduction in order to deliver the best acoustics; after all, the audience is only able to enjoy this show from outside of the auditorium and therefore the auditorium must operate as a speaker, a tool designed to project and amplify sound waves. If the sound is immediately channelled out of the watch, it may be loud, but it will sound dull. The ideal material is hard, but not dense. Consequently, it is not unusual for the cases of minute repeaters to be steel and there are even some cases made from carbon fibre or titanium.

To further boost acoustics the gongs might be set on the dial side of the movement so that the sound waves can be directed to the space in-between the dial and the crystal, avoiding the various levers, cams and wheels that either dampen the sound or produce their own in competition. In fact, there exist repeaters with the gong 'heel' fixed to the surface of the sapphire crystal itself. This allows the crystal to resonate with the gongs and amplify the sound; a huge benefit of this approach is that the case can be waterproofed (a waterproof case dampens the tone of the traditional repeater) because the sound is exiting through the crystal rather than a series of small side doors in the auditorium.

Right, above: The Hublot Classic Fusion Tourbillon Cathedral Minute Repeater Carbon embraces the light-but-hard qualities of carbon in order to allow the vibrant sound of the cathedral gongs to emanate from the case to the ear. The slider is aesthetically integrated with the bezel lug at 9 o'clock. © 2016 Hublot

Right, below: The Jaeger-LeCoultre Master Grande Tradition Minute Repeater. The 'crystal gong' system of Jaeger-LeCoultre involves fixing the gong 'heel' directly to the sapphire crystal, which is coated in a metallic foil. The entire crystal resonates with the strike of the gong. © 2016 Jaeger-LeCoultre

Opposite: The four trebuchet hammers of the Hybris Mechanica à Grande Sonnerie can be seen via the caseback. They strike their four gongs to sound out the full Westminster chimes; in full sonnerie mode (indicated at 5 o'clock) the independent power reserve (indicator at 6 o'clock) will last 12 hours.
© 2016 Jaeger-LeCoultre

Right The dial-side calibre 182 of the Hybris Mechanica à Grande Sonnerie reveals the 'infernal tower', a vertical stack of the various snail cams that deliver the time to the repeater mechanism. The tower sits towards the centre of the movement and can be identified by its top layer, the large minute snail (it has 15 steps because the quarter snail handles the rest).

© 2016 Jaeger-LeCoultre

Below: The Breguet Tradition Répétition Minutes Tourbillon 7087 affixes the gong heels to the rehaut (the internal bezel) and domes the crystal to maximise the resonant effect of the chimes. The hammers are positioned beneath the gongs and strike vertically, sending the sound waves to the firmament. Turning over the watch reveals some familiar racks and cams, as well as a chain transmission that links the chiming mainspring to the rack. The escapement of the repeater mechanism, which is not visible, features a 'magnetic governor' whereby the wheel is slowed down by magnetic fields instead of centrifugal energy. The peripheral winding rotor is barely noticeable.

© 2015 Ian Skellern

Finally, the escapement of the chiming mechanism, the governor, has experienced some exotic iterations in recent years. Ordinarily, the mechanism uses sprung weights and their centrifugal force to slow down and regulate the rotations. However, for some the noise created by the spinning is unacceptable. Instead, silent governors have been developed that work on air viscosity or by magnetic friction. A repeater with a silent governor will have minimal audible overture and intermission to the performance.

The Credor Minute Repeater. The spring drive movement, with its glide wheel, makes for a silent canvas upon which to paint a fine decimal minute repeater. The silence remains even after the repeater slide is released thanks to the silent governor, an extremely thin constant flow escape wheel that relies on air resistance to brake its speed of rotation. The result is one of the clearest chimes one can experience.

Common Hour / Minute Hands
1. Baton / Pencil
2. Lozenge
3. Lance / Alpha
4. Sword
5. Dauphine
6. Spade / Pear / Poire
7. Skeleton / Squelette
8. Leaf / Feuille
9. Arrow
10. Stick / Post
11. Blunt
12. Tapered Baton

Signature Hour / Minute Hands
1. Mercedes (Rolex)
2. Plongeur / Ploprof (OMEGA)
3. Breguet / Moon (Breguet)
4. El Toro (Ulysse Nardin)
5. Voutilainen (Kari Voutilainen)
6. Broad Arrow (OMEGA)
7. Broad Arrow (Greubel Forsey)
8. Smith (Roger Smith)
9. Snowflake (Tudor)
10. Rounded Baton (Patek Philippe and Audemars Piguet)
11. Teardrop (F.P. Journe)
12. Luminous Pencil (Panerai)

Signature Seconds Hands
1. Diamond (A. Lange & Söhne)
2. Milgauss (Rolex)
3. Plongeur / Ploprof (OMEGA)
10. Lollipop (OMEGA, Tudor and Rolex)
11. Star (Zenith)
12. Breguet (Breguet)

2.9 Novelty Indication

A watch without complications is a watch that just tells the time; no bells or whistles. The term 'complication' refers to any additional function that a watch may possess. However, this term was born of a very simple generic watch design, one comprised of concentric hands and markers on a circular dial. What if a watch does not add any additional functions, but instead presents the time in an entirely new format? This is what would be described as a novelty indication, arguably a complication in its own right, not by virtue of its additional functionality but instead as a consequence of its unique manifestation of the passage of time. Although there is something of a boom in novelty indication of ate, these complications are not exclusive to modern watches, in fact some of the earlier pocket watches and clocks provided some quite exceptional alternatives to the 'three-hander' format. As for modern watches, there are a number of small independent brands making waves with their radical designs, but special mention should be granted to the Harry Winston Opus series. Each unusual watch in the series is the result of a collaboration between Harry Winston (the timepiece division was once run by Maximilian Büsser of MB&F) and an independent guest watchmaker (or pair). The result is always unusual and usually extremely unusual. These watches are at the very frontier, a place where technology and the imagination fleetingly overlap, sometimes just long enough for a single prototype to fall into the material realm.

The Hand

Before we consider the ways in which time indication can deviate from the norm, it might be useful to look at what the norm is. Hands are a key design feature of a watch and the greater your appreciation of the variety of options the more likely you will be to identify a watch that hits or misses. There are many ways in which a hand can be shaped, but unless the watchmaker is particularly adventurous they will likely employ iterations of the core hand shapes. The core hand shapes are like different fonts, and the hour and minute hands of each font are like the difference between a capital and a lowercase letter. Some are stark and utilitarian, others are far from that. Of course, in addition to the shape, the material, the colour and the applied luminescent paint can transform the look of the hand; as can skeletonising the hand or extending its counterweight. However nothing defines its character like the shape.

The Single Hand

The single-handed watch is not so much a complication as a *simplification*. The design is a nod to old clock towers of the past; a time when movements were so adversely impacted by friction, thermal expansion and contraction, even the wind, that to add a minute hand would only serve to draw unwelcome attention to its consequent unreliability. Today, with the wide availability of accurate movements, and in a society geared around punctuality, one would think that there would be no need for a single-handed watch. However there is something to be said for a watch that allows the wearer to track the time to the nearest 5-minute increment. It promotes a more relaxed attitude to timekeeping and displays the passage of time with an unrivalled level of calm and simplicity – this is the sundial of wristwatches.

Above: The MeisterSinger No.2 possesses a single hand for the hours and a chapter ring in 5-minute increments.
© 2015 MeisterSinger GmbH & Co. KG

Opposite, left: The common hand types. Almost any type of hand will have its roots in the common types. A watchmaker can broaden an arrow, move the wide-point of a lozenge, skeletonise or embellish with luminescent paint, use counter-balances and extensions in order to create a hand set that best suits the overall aesthetic of the watch. © 2016 Ryan Schmidt / ACC Art Books

Opposite, middle and right: Signature hand types. Although they are essentially a sword and pencil hand, by suspending them from a thin shank the 'plongeur' style is born. Other types, such as 'Breguet' and 'Snowflake', feature simple hands and apply moons or squares to accentuate them. Certain styles have been coined by innovative watchmakers, others by iconic watches; and while they might exist elsewhere, they have become the signature of that brand or model. © 2016 Ryan Schmidt / ACC Art Books

The Regulator

If you like the look of an isolated hour hand, but you prefer it not to be at the expense of accurate readings, the regulator format is an excellent one. Like the single-handed watch, the regulator dial pre-dates the wristwatch and positions the hour, minute, and seconds hands independently of each other. The term 'regulator' comes from precision clocks of the past that were used to monitor and set other timekeeping devices, although many of these clocks used concentric hands. The most common wristwatch regulator layout mounts the minute hand centrally, and the hour and seconds hands on sub-dials at 12 and 6 o'clock, respectively. The key principle of the regulator is to avoid any superfluous displays or functions in favour of absolute legibility. There is an irony in the fact that it can often take one or two more seconds to tell the time on a regulator than it can on a simple concentric two-handed timepiece. Nevertheless, it remains a handsome and (literally) eccentric design option.

Left: Glashütte Original Senator Chronometer Regulator is entirely focused on legibility and precision. In addition to sporting a regulator dial, the chronometer-grade movement stops and zero-resets the seconds hand when the crown is pulled. As the time is set the minute hand snaps exactly to each minute marker so that the time can be set with absolute precision.
© 2016 Glashütter Uhrenbetrieb GmbH

Opposite: The Patek Philippe 5235 Regulator adds an annual calendar complication but does so without losing the clarity of the regulator display. © 2016 Patek Philippe SA

Retrograde Indication

Invented at the end of the 18th century by Abraham-Louis Breguet, the godfather of watchmaking, the retrograde display provided an ingenious alternative to the overcrowded face of a complicated pocket watch. Where previously a calendar or timekeeping complication would occupy the central dial, or a sub-dial of its own, the retrograde display allows additional functions to be laid out across a linear or fan-form register. This takes up less space and makes for an aesthetic counterpoint to the all-too-familiar circular theme of a watch. The name 'retrograde' does not refer to the linear layout, instead it refers to the way in which the indicator will move back from the end of its scale to the beginning. It is an instantaneous snap that is not unlike the reset of a chronograph seconds hand. Therefore the retrograde display can come in any form, so long as it is not a complete circle, but the most common is the fan.

The Louis Moinet 20-Second Tempograph is a useful demonstration of the retrograde mechanism. The Tempograph has a central seconds hand that continuously runs a retrograde 20-second path on the scale between 12:30 and 2 o'clock. The dial and movement are partially skeletonised to provide a view of the mechanism. The fourth wheel at 8 o'clock rotates once every 60 seconds. It has three sectors that can be used to track which 20-second sector the seconds hand is running. The fourth wheel drives another wheel below it (7 o'clock) at a 1:1 ratio. This wheel is fitted with a three-step cam (so a step every 20 seconds). The cam actuates a pallet and lever to the right, which drive a small intermediary wheel via a rack (between the fourth wheel and the centre of the dial). As the pallet runs along the cam the seconds hand moves across its scale; then the pallet drops off the step and thanks to the spiral spring (centre of the dial) the seconds hand snaps to the start of the scale and immediately continues.

Left, above: The Bvlgari Octo Retrogradi combines a retrograde minute indication with jumping hours.   © 2016 Bulgari S.P.A

Left, below: The Louis Moinet 20-Second Tempograph.
© 2016 Les Ateliers Louis Moinet S.A

Above: The Van Cleef & Arpels Lady Arpels Butterfly Symphony uses a similar mechanism to the Pont des Amoureux but does so to tell a different story. White gold and lacquer butterflies dance around a tree, indicatiing retrograde hours and minutes on the onyx dial. © 2016 Van Cleef & Arpels

Right: The Van Cleef & Arpels Lady Arpels Pont des Amoureux puts the retrograde display into full theatrical effect. The man makes his way to the centre of the bridge every 60 minutes, marking the passing minutes with the flower behind his back, before snapping back to the start. As each hour passes, the woman makes her way to the meeting point, indicating the passing hours with her umbrella. At midnight they share a momentary kiss before they are forced apart once more. © 2016 Van Cleef & Arpels

Wandering Hour / Orbital / Satellite Display

The wandering hour, which dates back to the 17th century, places the 12 hours onto a series of discs that rotate on their own axis as well as a shared axis. The configuration is usually three discs with four numerals on each. The minutes are tracked in a widened aperture across the dial and time is indicated by the hour numeral as it traverses the minutes track; as soon as it reaches the 60th minute the next hour is already lined up for its turn. Alternatively the hour might be framed within a small aperture, which moves along a minute track but consigns the inner workings of the mechanism to mystery. Towards the end of the 20th century, the modern complication was mostly attributable to Audemars Piguet, whose 'star wheel' with crystal discs was often left uncovered so that the wearer could enjoy the sight of all 12 numerals jostling for position. Today there are a number of traditionally executed wandering hours, and a few that give very modern interpretations of the format. Perhaps the most innovative wandering hour specialists are URWERK, whose original UR101 model was a traditional wandering hour aperture and whose recent models add new levels of complexity to their 'orbiting satellites'. Take the UR-202 for example. The hours are set out on three four-sided arms that rotate on their own axis as well as a unified one. What is particularly impressive about the 202 is the cam-actuated telescopic minute hand that extends from each arm so that it meets the exact contours of the minute track before it retracts like the head of a timid turtle.

Left, above: The UR-202 features URWERK's signature orbiting satellite complication, moon phase, and day/night indication. The automatic rotor is controlled by twin turbines, both of which can be seen and adjusted via the caseback. This novel and interactive damping system is covered in Chapter 1.2.   © 2016 URWERK

Left, below: The URWERK UR-210. In addition to the four-sided rotating arms, the UR-210 includes a retrograde pointer and frame that snaps into place as the new hour reaches the minutes track and follows it on its path, marking out the minutes with satisfying legibility. If one looks closely at the centre of the dial one can see the cylindrical copper-coloured retrograde spring. Setting the time on this watch is so much fun it's a surprise that it is equipped with a power reserve indicator (top right). A perfectly functional addition is a winding efficiency indicator (top left) which indicates the amount of automatic winding that has occurred in the last two hours. When it is red the power has been draining without being replenished, when green the winding is optimal. This can be used in conjunction with the rotor damping on the back.   © 2016 URWERK

Right: The Vacheron Constantin Métiers d'Art Savoirs Enluminés – Vultures conceals its wandering hour mechanism beneath a champlevé enamel plate. The discs are skeletonised so as to isolate the numeral as it traverses its 60-minute passage.

© 2015 Vacheron Constantin

Below: The URWERK UR-110 places its minute track along the right side of the watch, ideal for those wearing a cuffed shirt. But the model is not a simple cosmetic uplift, instead the satellite hub features a more complex planetary gearing so that the markers are always positioned perpendicular to the minute track and parallel to each other. As they rotate, the running seconds, 5-year oil gauge, and day / night indicators are revealed on the plate of the dial.

© 2016 URWERK

Digital / Jumping Displays

The phrase 'digital watch' tends to bring to mind LCD-display quartz-regulated watches; watches that are widely available, cheap, but perhaps lack something of the 'soul' of a mechanical watch. However the digital display actually predates quartz. These early models obscured the majority of the dial, revealing the hours and minutes on discs under apertures. There exist watches today that execute digital displays in similar fashion, as well as some others that 'turn it up a notch'. Whereas the analogue display gives time a circular characteristic, and the retrograde display illustrates its linear nature, the digital display presents time as a single moment, one occasionally punctuated by the sudden jump of a numeral.

The MVT0 / D01, by 4N, is one such example of a modern digital / mechanical display. There are three bridges holding discs for the hours, tens of minutes, and minutes. The hours and minutes bridges hold pivoted carriages and each carriage holds four and five pivoted discs, respectively. They rotate as a result of a planetary gear system. The tens of minutes are on a single bridge and pivoted disc. The planetary gears require a massive amount of power, and this is delivered by two mainspring barrels providing a highly impressive 237 hours of autonomy. In order for the balance wheel to remain isochronous the transmission features two spring-loaded constant force wheels, each one loaded by the rotation of its respective set of planetary gears, their constant force enables the balance wheel to oscillate with no sense of the acrobatics going on further upstream.

Left, above: The de Grisogono Meccanico dG, with its analogue and digital display, which can function as dual time displays. The mechanical movement is comprised of 651 parts. Separated from the rest of the movement by a constant force mechanism, the configuration of each digital column is determined by a stack of cams programmed to a binary code. The pushers on either side can manually adjust the hours and minutes.   © 2016 de Grisogono SA

Left, below: The Harry Winston Opus 11. Places a single digit at the centre of an array of 'shards' to indicate the hour and in a subsidiary section at 2 o'clock on the caseband is a jumping tens-of-minutes disc alongside a running minute unit disc. At the turn of the hour the jumping mechanism explodes, the planetary gears dance in the chaos before coming to a halt and indicating the next hour numeral.   © 2016 François-Xavier Overstake

The MVT01 / D01, by 4N. There is something about a case-full of discs and a lone balance wheel that makes a movement appear to be very simple. But this 514-component movement is not simple.

Image Courtesy of 4N

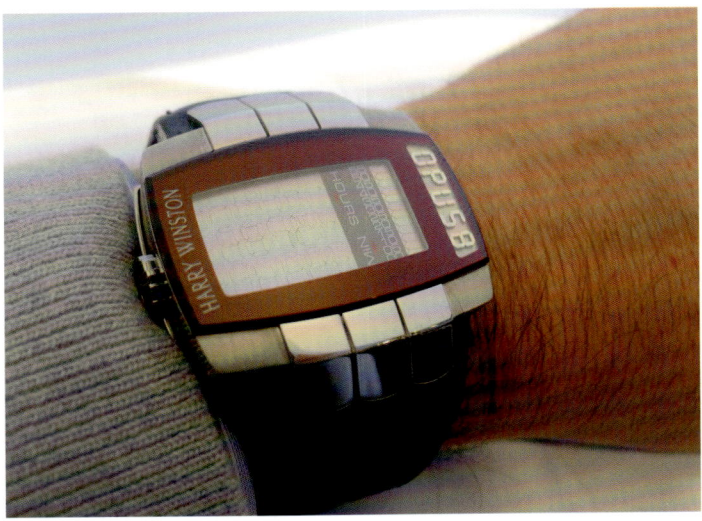

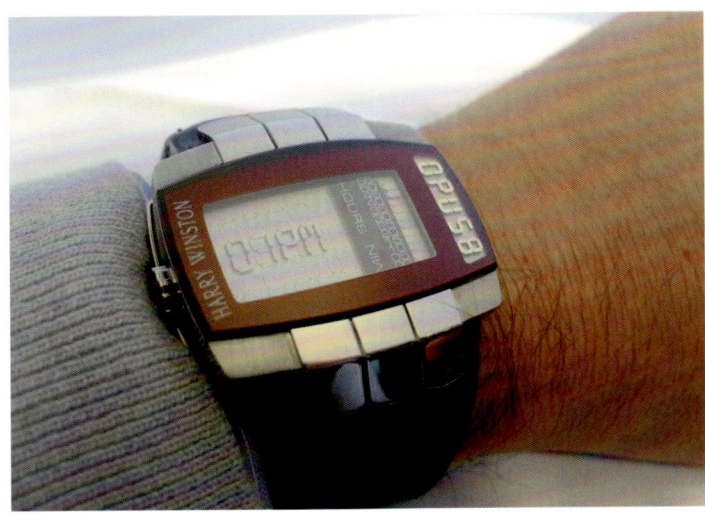

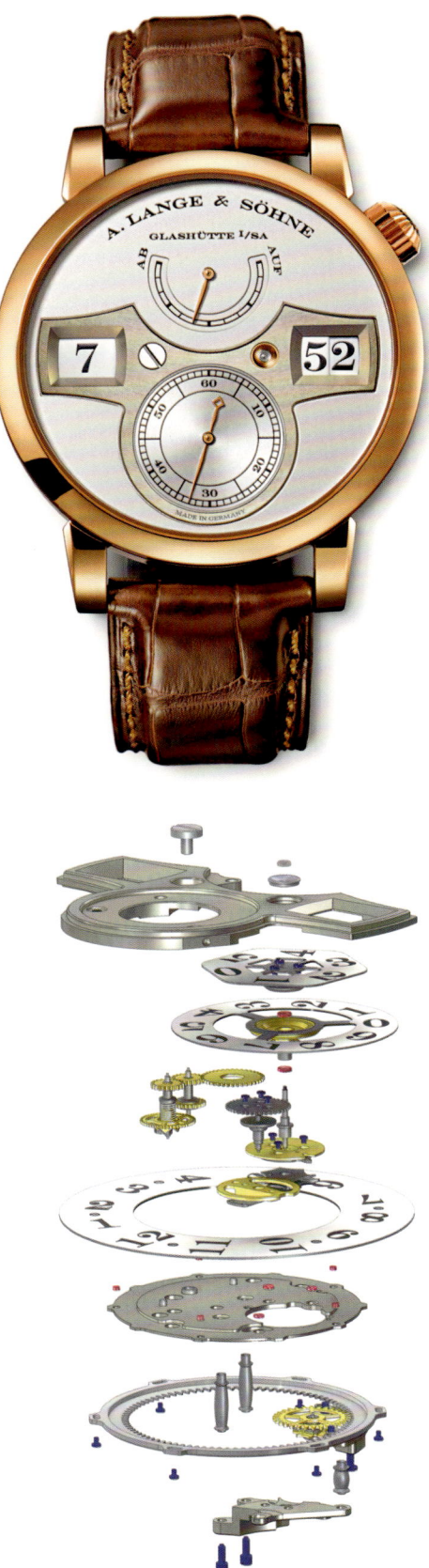

Above: The Harry Winston Opus 8, one of the rarest of the rare Opus models. At first it appears not to be able to tell the time at all; but when the sliding switch at 3 o'clock is activated, the digits of the hour emerge from the digital display module as does an indicator against the linear minutes scale. The time is 1:45 pm. After five seconds the display melts back into the dial. The time is set thanks to a set of additional apertures on the caseback.

© 2016 François-Xavier Overstake

Right: The digital jumping display of the A. Lange & Söhne Zeitwerk is powered by a strengthened mainspring, and the balance wheel is fed constant force thanks to the one minute remontoire. The dial is an elegant and hand-finished mix of digital and analogue. Its wonderful symmetry is kept intact by the mirrored positions of the bridge screw and the pivot stone for the minute discs.

© 2015 A. Lange & Söhne

The Ludovic Ballouard Half Time has a retrograde minute hand at 6 o'clock and a jumping hour indicator at 12. Both mechanisms are beautifully displayed on the caseback. What makes the hour indication particularly unusual is the fact that it features two discs that combine to form the numeral; the outer disc moves anticlockwise, the inner disc moves clockwise. The effect is a chaotic array of illegible figures but for the numeral at 12 o'clock.

© 2016 Montres Ludovic Ballouard

Left: The Harry Winston Opus 3, created in collaboration with Vianney Halter, is the king of jumping digital date, hours, minutes and even seconds. The blue digits indicate 24 hours, the black digits indicate the minutes, and the red digits display the date vertically. The last four seconds of every minute are also displayed through the left hour aperture.   © 2015 Christie's Images Limited

Above: The DeWitt Academia Mathematical displays jumping digital hours and minutes by way of four ornate wheels, one for each numeral. They overlap chaotically behind the smoked sapphire and deliver their choreographed reading of the time through their own aperture.   © 2016 Montres DeWitt SA

Opposite: The MCT Sequential One S100 has a wandering minute display and digital hours. In similar fashion to a revolving billboard, the dial features four slat hour displays. Each display consists of five three-sided slats that rotate to create three numerals. The minutes track runs along a 270° arc; as it passes 30 minutes the hour numeral hidden behind it rotates, and as the hand reaches 60, the *track* snaps 90° anticlockwise. This allows the minutes hand to rotate a seamless 360° (every 80 minutes) while the minutes track is always arranged around the correct hour numeral.   © 2016 Manufacture Contemporaine du Temps

The Tread and Winch

From the fusée and chain mechanism to the belt-driven transmission, there is something fascinating about two wheels being coupled in an alternative fashion to the wheel-tooth-to-pinion-leave approach. They have been seen in power distribution and gearing, but there are watches that draw even greater attention to the technology, by driving the numerals with a winch, or even laying the numerals on the belts themselves.

Above: The Devon Tread 1 may employ a microprocessor, a quartz oscillator, four step motors, and a lithium-polymer rechargeable cell, but the display is undeniably mechanical and impressive. The Tread 1 places the hours, minutes and seconds on four separate fiberglass-reinforced nylon 'time belts' which intersect behind apertures to give a unique time display.
© 2016 Devon Works

Left: The Cabestan Winch Tourbillon Vertical employs the most traditional winch in horology, the fusée and chain (seen along the left side of the watch), which is hand-wound by a crank on the side of the case. What makes the movement and the time display particularly unique is the fact that the mechanism, the entire movement indeed, is flipped onto its side. As a result the indications run along the rim of their driven wheels.

The movement is separated into two halves, the power sits on the left (72 hours of reserve indicated on the fusée cone at the top), and the transmission and escapement sit on the right. The minute and hour wheels are at the top, the motion work sit in the middle, and the second wheel and tourbillon sit at the bottom.
© 2016 Cabestan C.P. Luxe Sàrl

Opposite: The Harry Winston Opus 9 frames two baguette-cut diamond-studded chains, each with a garnet, to act as the indicator for the linear hour and minute tracks. There are two garnets on each chain, as the chain runs a full lap of the movement. This allows the display to run seamlessly without any need for the jump of a retrograde mechanism.
© 2015 Christie's Images Limited

The Hautlence HL2.4 combines a tread display of digital hours with retrograde indication of minutes. The three-dimensional sapphire allows clear views of the tread mechanism, which also serves to rotate the movement (from third wheel to escapement) by 60° on a vertical axis with each jumping (or half-trailing) hour. The 12-link tread mechanism is powered by its own mainspring and the governor, which regulates the speed of the transition, sits at the centre of the dial bearing the Hautlence logo. A large power reserve aperture sits at 6 o'clock.   © 2016 Hautlence

The Hautlence Vortex shares the mechanics of the HL2.4, but the architecture is rotated from portrait to landscape. There are a handful of crystals on the case, pouring light into the movement and offering excellent views. For example the gearing for the tread can be seen through the caseband, and the reverse side of the tread sits alongside an eccentric micro-rotor on the caseback. Every hour the movement is rotated by 60° and the action is managed dampened by 48 rotations of the central governor.

© 2016 Hautlence

Everything Else

There are a handful of watches that offer such unique displays of time that they create their own category. This is where the passage of time is marked by liquid and floating balls, where the display is mechanically interchangeable or where the hands do acrobatics in order to circumnavigate an elliptic dial. These are highly peculiar watches, interconnected only by the uniqueness of their telling of the time.

Left and below: The Christophe Claret X-TREM-1 features a flying tourbillon inclined at 30°, and two black chrome-plated steel spheres that float alongside their respective hour and minute markers. This impressive display is made possible by an enhanced retrograde mechanism. Instead of a traditional hand, the retrograde rack and lever move magnets on a rail along the inside wall of the case. The spheres are held in place within their transparent tubes by magnetic field. The two mainspring barrels power the magnetic slides and the movement independently, linking the two via a pallet lever driven by a star wheel on the main movement to unlock the magnetic mechanism in a regulated fashion.   © 2016 Christophe Claret

Opposite: The Harry Winston Opus 7 was created in collaboration with Andreas Strehler and features an alternating dial complication. With each depression of the integrated crown pusher the disc at 1 o'clock (and the small indicator at 12 o'clock) rotates to provide the wearer with a singular indication of the hours, the minutes, or the 60 hours of power reserve.   © 2015 Christie's Images Limited

Above and opposite: The unmistakeable HYT H2 Tradition. The clear tube capillary is filled with two liquids, one coloured, one translucent, that are pumped by two bellows (seen at 5 and 7 o'clock). The meniscus between the two liquids acts as the indicator for the hours. As the time reaches 6 o'clock the liquid performs a retrograde sweep back to the other side of the 6 o'clock rider so that the meniscus can continue to travel from 6 to 12 o'clock.

© 2016 HYT S.A

Both the Maurice Lacroix Masterpiece Mysterious Seconds (below) and Masterpiece Square Wheel (left) indicate the hours and minutes in a conventional fashion, but they indicate the seconds with great innovation and charm. The Mysterious Seconds uses a double-ended seconds hand that appears to dance across the dial disembodied from any apparent central axis while it traces four linear sets of 15 seconds. The Square Wheel uses an unusually shaped intermediary wheel to drive a square seconds wheel that indicates by way of a window in the wheel.

Above: Harry Winston Opus 13, in partnership with Ludovic Ballouard, tells the time but in a very unusual fashion. The minutes track consists of 60 blades that snap forward with each passing minute while one of 12 arrows hiding behind the large central faceted crystal elongates to mark the hour (the time is 3:16 in this picture). When the 60th minute passes the full dial of blades retract and the dance starts again. © 2013 Ariel Adams, aBlogtoWatch.com

Right: The Harry Winston Opus 14. The home time hours are displayed through the widened aperture on the disc at 9 o'clock. A retrograde red needle indicates the minutes on the large red track. What makes this watch particularly special is not that it also has a date and GMT function, but *how* those functions are displayed. When the display has been selected (on the left caseband), by pressing the pusher at 4 o'clock, an arm retrieves a disc from the stack beneath the main display and deposits it on the dial at 2 o'clock. The user can select between a GMT disc, a date disc and a star disc (which is just for fun). A power reserve indicator at 6 o'clock monitors the power of the disc-change complication.

© 2015 Gary Getz

Above, right: The Ressence Type 3 displays the date, day, hours, minutes, seconds and temperature and does so using a series of planetary gears, concentric and eccentric rotating discs instead of hands. The indications appear to be flush with the crystal. This is made possible by doming the crystal and the discs, and by flooding the upper half of the movement with oil. The submerged components are separated from the movement by magnetic transmission. A system of bellows allows the oil to contract and expand as the ambient temperature changes. Finally, there is no crown, the movement is both wound and set by turning the caseback. © 2016 Ressence

Above left and left: The Ludovic Ballouard Upside Down watch features a regular feuille-shaped central minute hand and a small subsidiary second dial, however the hours do not conform. All but the current hour are upside down. As the minute hand passes 12 the incumbent hour returns to its upside down position and the next one takes office, all in an instant.

© 2016 Montres Ludovic Ballouard

Parmigiani Fleurier Ovale Pantographe places a power reserve indicator at 12 o'clock, a widened date aperture at 6 o'clock and employs two telescopic, titanium, laser cut, hand riveted, cam-driven hour and minute hands that traverse the oval dial without ever failing to reach the markers or lose their respective proportions.   © 2016 Parmigiani Fleurier SA

Above and left: The MB&F HM6 presents an unusual display of the time, using two rotating semi-spherical discs. But this hardly stands out amongst the peculiar case, the central dome with its 'retractable shield' to protect the flying tourbillon within, and the two spherical turbines that rotate in their own respective domes to air-brake the massive swinging rotor that sits behind the caseback.

© 2016 MB&F

Opposite: The MB&F JWLRYMACHINE. With earlier iterations of the HM3 being designed to very subtly resemble a frog, MB&F collaborated with jewellery-house Boucheron to embellish the HM3 with amethyst, diamond, and sapphire in such a way as to transform the watch into a three-dimensional owl. If you stare into its eyes you will be given day / night indication and rotating hours and minutes. From only a certain angle, and from deep beneath the owl's plumage at 6 o'clock, near the crown, is the date indication.

© 2016 MB&F

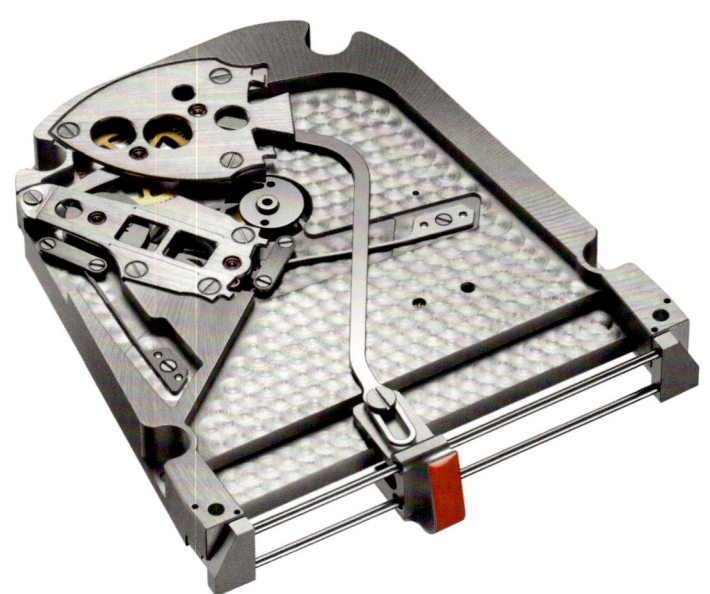

Left and below: The Romain Jerome Spacecraft not only looks like a spacecraft, but it is also quite practical to read the hours while piloting one. The 'dial' is split into two sections, the minutes are displayed by a rotating disc beneath a large aperture on the top of the case. On the caseband at 6 o'clock sits a linear retrograde hour indicator.   © 2016 RJ Watches S.A

Opposite: The URWERK UR-CC1 takes a break from the orbital satellites of its siblings and delivers time in a linear retrograde fashion. The seconds are displayed at the top of the dial both digitally via an aperture and also by linear indication thanks to a spiral indicator on the wheel. The minutes are shown by a continuously moving cylinder behind a linear aperture and the hours are displayed in a similar fashion but with a jumping mechanism. Both have the appearance of a retrograde mechanism when they reach the end of their track, however the cylinders are simply continuing their endless cycle.   © 2016 URWERK

Above and opposite: The MB&F HM5 presents the time in a similar way to the Romain Jerome Spacecraft, but with both the hours and minutes displayed by discs. How is this possible in the format of the case? The discs are actually horizontal and their image is projected and magnified through a prism. The case features louvres, which let in light to increase visibility and are operated by the switch on the right-hand-side of the case. The case also has 'exhaust pipes' that release any water that may enter through the louvres. © 2016 MB&F

2.10 The Whimsical and Playful

Since their inception, the principles of watch and clock mechanics have been used not only to facilitate the telling of time, but also to deliver a visual spectacle; something poetic or whimsical. The power source, transmission and escapement may still be employed, but rather than delivering a wheel-driven reading of time, they are reimagined in order to play music, or to perform a mechanical dance. These creations are not hindered by the high demands that accuracy lays upon timekeeping. This freedom from constraint serves to release the watchmaker from the bindings of isochronism, and in doing so empowers them to create for art rather than objective measurement. From the 18th century automaton to the music box and the watch that suspends time, this chapter sheds light on what takes place in the playground of the watchmaker.

The Automaton

The automaton dates back to early 18th century France, when miniature and life-sized models came to life with the turn of a key. The more impressive ones could be 'programed' to perform unimaginably, seemingly, human tasks. It delighted some and outright frightened others. In some respects the art of the automaton was not unlike horology, and watchmakers such as Pierre Jaquet-Droz put their broader mechanical knowledge to work by building automata outright or incorporating them into their movements. Today, a small number of brands create watches with automata, and despite the rise of the computer, even the robot, there is still something in these small devices that takes the breath from you. Automata and repeaters are a perfect match, and when the former is employed it is often alongside the latter. Not only does the chiming make for an accompaniment to the performance, but both mechanisms can take advantage of the same power and escapement, the automaton can even be directly linked to the racks and hammers so that it dances in time.

Above: The Jaquet Droz Bird Repeater features two hand-engraved 'parent' birds standing over their nest with two chicks and an egg. When the repeater is activated one bird moves its wing, the other offers food to a chick, whose sibling makes a dive to intercept. Just when you think it's over, their youngest is hatched. The fourth wheel is incorporated into the scene, providing the constant flow of a waterfall.   © 2014 Ariel Adams, aBlogtoWatch.com

Opposite: The Ulysse Nardin Hannibal Minute Repeater is a great example of an automaton being integrated with a repeater, in this case a four hammer / gong Westminster repeater. An arm of each of the three figures, as well as the elephant's trunk, are connected to a hammer, animating the chimes in perfect synchrony.
                                        © 2016 Ulysse Nardin SA

Above, left and right: The Andersen Eros plays on what was once a common application of the pocket watch automaton. When viewed from the front the Eros looks like a regular watch, but when the watch is reversed and the button at 8 o'clock is pressed, an additional mainspring brings life to the automata on the back.

© 2015 Christie's Images Limited

Left: The Jaquet Droz Charming Bird features a domed crystal at 6 o'clock, housing a three-dimensional hand-painted bird. When the button at 2 o'clock is pressed it bursts into life, rotating on its axis, flapping its wings, and rapidly opening and closing its beak. The governor of this mechanism orchestrates miniature bellows, making the sound of a whistle as they expel air.

© 2015 Ariel Adams, aBlogtoWatch.com

Opposite: The Richard Mille RM19-02 features a decadent, diamond encrusted case and a lacquered magnolia flower made from 18k gold with a rotating stamen set with precious stones. Every five minutes the five petals open to reveal a flying tourbillon beneath. If the wearer cannot wait that long, the mechanism can be prompted manually via the pusher at 9 o'clock.

© 2016 Richard Mille, Horometrie S.A

Above: The Cecil Purnell Carillon Animated Minute Repeater Tri-Axial Tourbillon delivers all that its name suggests. The animation comes from the three-horse race that takes place on the dial when the repeater is activated. The winning horse will be the result of seven possible outcomes.　　© 2016 Cecil Purnell

Opposite: The Bvlgari Commedia dell'Arte depicts a 16th century Italian theatrical performance. This particular iteration places Arlecchino (Harlequin) at the centre, who indicates retrograde minutes with the flute in his right hand. A jumping hour aperture is placed in front of him. When the repeater is activated Arlecchino moves his left arm whilst his three supporting performers spring to life.　　© 2016 Bvlgari S.P.A

The Music Box

Like the automaton, the music box also has its roots in historical clock and watchmaking, with the earliest iterations dating back to the late 16th century. The principle is similar to the repeater: a power source drives the mechanism and its release of power is made consistent by a governor (the escapement). The mechanism will be familiar to those who have seen music boxes because they are often displayed. It features a rotating barrel (or disc in some cases) laden with small pins. The barrel runs very close to a 'musical comb', a series of elongated teeth that resemble a hair comb; each one is of a different length in order to achieve a different tune. As the barrel rotates, the small pins prick the teeth and they are laid out in such a way that a melody is played.

Left, above: The movement of the Breguet Classique Réveil 'La Musicale' features a large rotating pin disc that doubles as an engine-turned rotating dial when activated (its sequence performs a full rotation so the dial remains aligned). The music box is integrated with an alarm complication and is regulated by a magnetic governor. The alarm hand is centrally mounted and the crown at 4 o'clock both sets the hand and winds the music box mainspring. The mode of the alarm is managed via the pusher at 8 o'clock and displayed through the aperture at 9:30, the power reserve of the music box is displayed in the aperture at 3 o'clock. The pusher at 10 o'clock activates the music box on demand.
© 2013 Ariel Adams, aBlogtoWatch.com

Left, below: The Ulysse Nardin Stranger places the rotating pin disc on the front of the dial and the teeth either side of it. Like the Christophe Claret Orchestra, the Stranger functions as a sonnerie and can be turned on or off by pressing the pusher at 10 o'clock (the mode is displayed in the fan-form dial at 7 o'clock). There is a pusher integrated with the crown that alternates its function from time setting (T), to date setting (D), to winding (W). The pusher at 8 o'clock activates the music box on demand.
© 2016 Ulysse Nardin SA

Opposite: The Christophe Claret Orchestra. The governor sits at 12 o'clock on the dial. There are two melodies that can be played on demand as well as in a sonnerie style with the passing of each hour. The reserve of the mechanism and the selected melody are indicated through the apertures at 11 and 1 o'clock. The mode / melody is selected by the pusher at 10 o'clock and the mainspring of the music box is wound by pressing the pusher at 8 o'clock. The movement also features a detent escapement.
© 2016 Christophe Claret

Games

Although some brands, such as Romain Jerome, have made a name for displaying characters from iconic computer games on their dial, they are simply depictions rather than complex mechanical games. When it comes to complex mechanical games, although there are one or two notable others, there is one brand that has laid all of its cards on the table: Christophe Claret. The brand boasts its own Gaming collection. For the game complication the turn of a card or role of the dice is miniaturised, mechanised, and made magical, but not without a little tongue in cheek.

The Christophe Claret Poker allows three players and a mechanical dealer to enjoy a game of Texas Hold'em. Your cards are revealed through angled slots so that your opponent can't see what you are holding and vice versa. The mechanism is effectively an automaton designed to generate nearly 100,000 combinations for each player. The button at 9 o'clock deals the cards, the button at 10 o'clock is the flop, and at 8 o'clock is the turn and river. With each press of the flop, turn and river, a hammer chimes a gong and the appropriate square disc slides away to reveal the card underneath. The table is 'cleared' by pressing the pushers once more at 10 and 8 o'clock. Although that should be more than enough, the rotor on the back of all three in the Gambling series is designed as a roulette wheel. It has a pointer that rests on one of the numbers and the bezel can be tailored so that any chosen number can be aligned with the 'lucky number' emerald.

The Christophe Claret Blackjack reveals some of its unusual mechanism through a smoked sapphire dial, but employs darkened 'cards' to anonymise the discs. The apertures represent the spaces for cards to be dealt to the player (bottom half of the dial) and the dealer (top half); the spaces not in use are covered by a rectangular disc. The pusher at 9 o'clock shuffles and deals two cards to the player and one to the dealer. The user then has the choice of a 'hit' (8 o'clock) or for the dealer to draw (10 o'clock). When the dealer busts or stands, the player and dealer buttons are pressed to clear their respective hands. As with the Poker model, there is a roulette wheel on the back, but in addition the Blackjack has two windows on the caseband that reveal the cathedral 'hit' hammer (2 o'clock) and a tiny pair of free rolling dice (4 o'clock).

The Christophe Claret Baccara has a similar mechanism to the Blackjack and pits the player (6 o'clock) against the dealer (12 o'clock). The pusher at 9 o'clock shuffles and

Above: The Romain Jerome Space Invaders® watch does not have a game complication but gets special mention for its game-themed lacquer dial. Of arguably greater technical merit is the case, which connects to the lugs and strap via 4 ball-and-socket joints, allowing the watch to articulate around the wrist.

© 2016 RJ Watches S.A

Opposite: The Christophe Claret Poker. © 2016 Christophe Claret

deals. The pushers at 10 and 8 o'clock distribute the cards to the bank (2 cards) and to the player (2 cards), sounding a cathedral gong at each depression. The rules are similar to blackjack in that they attribute values to the cards, the main differences being that the goal is to achieve 9, the Ace is worth 1 and the King / Queen / Jack are worth 0, and when your hand exceeds 9 you only count the right digit. As with the Blackjack, the caseback features a roulette wheel and the hammer and dice can be viewed through the windows in the band. The dial of each model is embellished with either a dragon (luck) or a tiger (strength).

Opposite, right and below: The Christophe Claret Blackjack.
© 2016 Christophe Claret

Above: The Christophe Claret Baccara. © 2016 Christophe Claret

Opposite: The Girard-Perregaux Vintage 1945 Jackpot Tourbillon boasts a very handsome tourbillon and golden bridge, but despite this the eye is drawn to the slot-machine! This is an actual slot-machine with a crank arm on the right side, which acts as an all-or-nothing activator and mainspring charger. When the arm is pulled all of the way back the three gold rollers, each with five lacquered symbols, roll at a high speed. Then, one after the other, the rollers stop dead from left to right, each with a chime. The sequence is random and there are 124 combinations that you might have to endure before you see three liberty bells.   © 2016 Girard-Perregaux

Romance / Erotica

The erotic automaton complication has already been illustrated in the Andersen Eros, but there are two additional complications to cover, one that is romantic and the other that sits on the same bench as the Eros. First is the he-loves-me-he-loves-me-not complication, a play on the game that involves mechanically pulling petals from a daisy while alternating the saying. The Christophe Claret Margot features a 12-petal flower (useful as a backup hour marker) in a recessed dial. Two widened apertures sit at 7 and 5 o'clock, the first says (in French) 'He loves me', and the other is blank. When the pusher at 2 o'clock is pressed one or two petals are removed in an instant while a gong sounds and the aperture at 5 o'clock rotates the ending of the phrase from 'a little' to 'a lot' to 'passionately' to 'madly' but also to 'not at all'. What makes the process random is not the order of phrase but the number of leaves that are removed on each press of the button. When you have your answer, a press of the pusher at 4 o'clock will reset the mechanism. The hammer is visible through a window at 9 o'clock on the caseband and the back has a 360° floral motif with eight precious stones to denote different sentiments. Similar to the roulette wheel, the sentiment will align with a marker at 6 o'clock. The crown is concealed behind lugs at 12 o'clock.

Second is what can only be described as a mechanical adult haiku generator! The Richard Mille RM69 Erotic Tourbillon is armed with a tourbillon, power reserve indicator and an 'oracle complication', which produces a random selection of a three-part sentiment, each more naughty than the last. The pusher at 10 o'clock activates the oracle, and the button at 8 o'clock causes the hands to fly out of the way of the reading.

Left, above: The Christophe Claret Margot.
© 2016 Christophe Claret

Left, below: The Richard Mille RM69 Erotic Tourbillon.
© 2016 Richard Mille, Horometrie S.A

Opposite: The Ulysse Nardin Hourstriker Erotica Jarretiere is an hour repeater and sonnerie with automaton lovers that fall into the throws of passion when the mechanism is activated (by the button at 4 o'clock) and move to the rhythm of the chimes. The button at 2 o'clock switches the sonnerie and silence mode.
© 2016 Ulysse Nardin SA

Abandoning Time

Imagine a complication that serves to deliberately 'mess' with another one, namely the timekeeping function; or a watch that ignores its primary responsibility, which is to tell the time. That's what is to be found in this dark corner of the chapter. Whether it be a philosophical rumination about time, a statement of its relativity, or a good-humoured challenge to its importance, there do in fact exist such watches.

The Richard Mille RM 63-01 'Dizzy Hands' complication allows the wearer to temporarily suspend and reanimate time. By pressing the pusher integrated with the crown the sapphire disc carrying the hour numerals will rotate anticlockwise while the hour hand simultaneously rotates clockwise. Order is restored by pressing the crown button once more. While the complication is extremely whimsical, it is no less impressive to deliver than a more serious one, such as the chronograph. In fact, the movement uses a

similar clutch mechanism, allowing the hour hand to be dislodged while it joins the numerals in a dance.

The Hermès Le temps suspendu, as the name suggests, suspends time. When you press the pusher at 9 o'clock the hour and minute hands snap into a V-formation around the 12 o'clock numeral. The movement continues with timekeeping, the dial simply stops. By suspending time, nothing short of turning off your phone says that you are engaging with the moment and those in your company. The first iteration of this curious timepiece has a retrograde date, the second version has a 24-second anticlockwise subsidiary seconds!

Above: The Hermès Arceau Le temps suspendu. © 2016 Hermès

Opposite: The Richard Mille RM 63-01 'Dizzy Hands'.
© 2016 Richard Mille, Horometrie S.A

The Hublot MP-12 'Key of Time' looks as unusual as it functions. The hours and minutes are on a subsidiary dial at 1 o'clock, an aperture showing the passing seconds sits at 6 o'clock (on the case) and immediately beneath it (on the caseband) is a window showing the vertically mounted flying tourbillon. A reserve indicator sits at 8 o'clock. Time setting and winding take place at the 3 o'clock crown. Things get more unusual when the crown is turned at 9 o'clock: the time indication can be set to run 4x fast or 4x slow (as indicated by respective 'pistons'). The watch can do this for as long as the movement is kept powered, with the time on the dial drifting further and further from the true time like an untethered balloon. When it's time to return to Earth the crown sets the mode back to normal speed. As with the Richard Mille RM 63-01 this is chronograph technology put to poetic, rather than scientific, use.

Left: The Hermès Dressage L'heure masqueé is like a companion piece to the Arceau Le temps suspendu. In the ordinary course of business the hour hand hides behind the minute hand, and the dual time aperture simply reads 'GMT'. When the crown-integrated pusher is depressed the hour hand leaps into its correct position, as does the reference time in the aperture. The dual time is adjusted via the pusher at 9 o'clock.   © 2016 Hermès

Opposite: The Hublot MP-12 'Key of Time'.   © 2016 Hublot

Above: Both the Haldimann H3 and the H8 Flying Sculpture have no hands. They feature centrally mounted flying tourbillons, but aside from that, no visual means by which to indicate hours or minutes. The H3 is accompanied by a minute repeater, providing the whimsical dial with complex chiming functionality. The H8 has no chiming mechanism and therefor is a step further into the realm of horological art. © 2016 Haldimann Horology

Right: The Haldimann H9 Reduction features a centrally mounted flying tourbillon similar to the H1 Flying Central model. What makes the H9 particularly unusual is that the dial is concealed beneath an entirely opaque sapphire crystal. In doing so the purest and most essential element of a timepiece is exchanged for something more artistic. Whereas the H8 turns the movement into a living sculpture, the H9 is more of a piece of conceptual art, the wearer must come to terms with a beauty and mechanical precision that is not just concealed within, but is unattainable. © 2016 Haldimann Horology

Romain Jerome enjoy playing with the line between serious watchmaking and whimsy. Their products will often incorporate the 'DNA' of famous objects or places into their designs and materials. Cases made from the steel of the Apollo 11 spacecraft, dials made of sculpted lava. The Titanic DNA range incorporates steel recovered from the wreck of the Titanic into its bezel and coal (also recovered from the ship) into a portion of the dial on the Day & Night Tourbillon. But what immediately stands out is the lack of hands and numerals. The watch has two flying tourbillons, one with a carriage in the shape of the Sun (12 o'clock) and the other with a carriage in the shape of the Moon (6 o'clock).

A differential and 'switch' mechanism is held under a bridge on the left of the dial. The two tourbillons are driven in alternating 12-hour shifts, enabling the wearer to separate day from night, but nothing in between. This is a full commitment to the abandoning of time, no background timekeeping that is brought back to the dial when the wearer becomes anxious.

The Romain Jerome Titanic DNA Day & Night Tourbillon.
© 2016 RJ Watches S.A

2.11 Super-Complicated Watches

This chapter very briefly considers the 'rules' of the grand complication, the super and the ultra-complicated watch, before letting the images speak for themselves. Take some time to study them, enjoy them, and see how many complications you can spot. Some complications are so unique and unusual, such as the Hebraic calendar complications of the Vacheron Constantin 57260, that they have made it this deep into the book without being identified.

The concept of the 'grand complication' was born out of a small number of very important pocket watches created in the late 18th century. These watches were commissioned by the French monarchy as statements of both the opulence and the pioneering horological achievements of the time. Legendary watchmakers such as Jean-Antoine Lépine and Abraham-Louis Breguet produced watches that bundled a number of impressive complications into one movement and provided the foundation for the grand complications of today. It is generally accepted that a modern grand complication will combine at least one timing complication, one chiming complication, and one astronomical / calendar complication. So a minute repeating perpetual calendar with split-second chronograph earns the title.

At the beginning of this section the six core complications of 'high horology' were identified: the minute repeater, the

moon phase, the split-second chronograph, the perpetual calendar, the ultra-thin and the tourbillon. The first four overlap with the concept of the grand complication, but the last two do not. And when one considers some of the more whimsical complications, which are no less challenging to deliver, one realises that the concept of the grand complication is a traditional and purist subset of what is a much larger pool of complicated watchmaking. Consequently, what makes a super-complication or an ultra-complication is even less scientific and largely down to how much awe they can inspire by their over-delivery of the 'basic' grand complication. The matter is subjective because there is no consensus on what should constitute a complication in the final tally of a watch. What differentiates a 'super' from an 'ultra'? Again, there is no consensus, so for the purposes of this book they will be considered to be adjectives describing the same thing, the latter possessing a fraction more superlative potency.

Some of today's most prestigious manufacturers will produce a small range of grand complications in their portfolio. It is not unheard of for a smaller brand to deliver a grand complication, but the infrastructure required in terms of the facility and the expertise to deliver and maintain such a beast is a very large barrier to entry. Only the brave will venture into the super-complicated realms, producing limited pieces in celebration of a milestone or at the request of a deep-pocketed collector, or as part of an arms-race dynamic between competing brands. Sometimes they are crammed into a two-faced wristwatch, other times there is simply too much going on and the larger pocket watch format is preferred. The reasons for their existence are many, and the world of watchmaking is the richer for them.

The Breguet No.1160 'Mary Antoinette' replica

The original Breguet No.160 'Mary Antoinette' pocket watch was commissioned in 1783 by a lover of the namesake, with Abraham-Louis Breguet being given one simple mandate — to put every possible complication into a watch made with as much gold as possible; money was no object. Breguet himself called it "a monument to 18th Century horological

Left The Breguet No.1160 'Mary Antoinette' replica.
© 2015 Gary Getz

Opposite: The Patek Philippe Henry Graves Jr. Supercomplication.
© 2016 Patek Philippe SA

skills". The original watch has a troubled past; it never made it to the Queen, who lost her head before it was completed. In fact, Breguet himself died four years before its completion. In 1983 it was stolen from a museum in Israel by an infamous burglar and did not resurface until 2007, during which time the Swatch Group rebuilt the watch using the original technical drawings. The No.1160 (pictured) was completed in 2008, it has no dial so that the movement can be admired through the crystal, which is imprinted with the scales and chapter rings. The self-winding mechanism features a perpetual calendar with large retrograde date (at 2 o'clock), day (the internal ring on the sub-dial at 6 o'clock), and month (the large wheel at 8 o'clock — notice the equation of time cam). The large fan-form register at 10 o'clock gives the equation of time, the smaller one at 10:30 provides the reserve indication, and the one at 1:30 provides the temperature in °C. The central hour hand is jumping and the central seconds hand is independent and can be used as a 60-second chronograph (versus the running seconds hand in the sub-dial). The 1160 also possesses a minute repeater.

The Patek Philippe Henry Graves Jr. Supercomplication

Two hugely competitive 20th century collectors, Henry Graves Jr. and James Ward Packard, with equally deep pockets and a passion for horology engaged in what can only be described as bespoke super-complication warfare. The battleground was staged under the same factory roof of Patek Philippe and the coup de grâce was delivered in 1933 by Patek on behalf of Graves. The three-tiered movement of the Patek Philippe Henry Graves Jr. Supercomplication delivers 24 horological complications. Starting with the front, you have central hours and minutes, as well as chronograph split-seconds and (gold) alarm indicator. The 6 o'clock sub-dial features running seconds and date wheel. Three-character month and day apertures for the perpetual calendar are at 3:30 and 8:30. Power reserve indicator and chronograph minutes are on the sub-dial at 2:30, chronograph hours and reserve indicator for the striking mechanism is at 9:30. Moon phase is at 12 o'clock. On the back of the watch sits a central sidereal hours and minutes indication, sky chart calibrated to Graves' New York home, sunset and sunrise times (sub-dials at 4 and 8 o'clock), equation of time and running sidereal seconds (at 6 o'clock). The caseband features the repeater slide, chronograph pushers, and grande / petite / silent sonnerie and alarm mode settings, alarm winding slide, and date adjusters. The two mainsprings are wound, and the sidereal and mean times are adjusted, via the crown

The Patek Philippe Calibre 89

The Patek Philippe Calibre 89, produced to celebrate the 150th anniversary of the brand, took the title from the Henry Graves Jr. Supercomplication in 1989. Many of its 33 complications are indicated by one of 24 hands and made possible by a movement of 1,728 parts. The front features a four-digit year, leap year and retrograde date and crown position indication, all at 12 o'clock. Month and day apertures are at 3:30 and 8:30. The central dial displays the hours and minutes with gold Breguet-style hands, split chronograph seconds, and a blued Breguet-style hand for a second time zone. The sub-dials at 3 and 9 o'clock record the chronograph minutes and hours and indicate the reserves of the movement and sonnerie. The sub-dial at 6 o'clock is for running seconds, temperature in °C, and moon phase. The reverse dial features a sky chart with 24-hour sidereal time, sun hand to indicate the season and zodiac sign, sunrise and sunset. At 6 o'clock the equation of time is indicated around a subsidiary sidereal seconds hand. The blue scale around the top of the sky chart is a calculation for the date of Easter each year. It features a wheel geared from the sidereal movement and a snail cam to reset the scale on 1st January each year, and the lever attached to the indicator takes a reading from an unusual 30-year stepped cam to determine the new date. Note to owner: the cam will need to be replaced in 2019.

The Vacheron Constantin ref. 57260

To celebrate their 260th year, Vacheron Constantin decided to produce the most complicated watch in the world. The ref. 57260 (57 complications, 260 years) is so packed with complications and a layer-cake of a movement it is almost spherical. With so much going on, let's focus on what this watch has that the others don't. Starting with the 'front' dial (no view of tourbillon), at 1 o'clock the alarm reserve indicator and mode for normal bells or the full carillon. At 11 o'clock you can select 'night' mode for the sonnerie so

---

Left: The Patek Philippe Calibre 89.   © 2016 Patek Philippe SA

Opposite: The movement of the Vacheron Constantin 57260 is actually a series of movements comprised of: A. The front movement, B. The chronograph plate, C. Hebraic calendar and chronograph plate, D. The back movement, E. The Gregorian calendar, and F. The astronomical plate. Plate C is engraved with the Vacheron Constantin motto, a quote from an 1819 letter from François Constantin to Jacques Barthélémy Vacheron: "Do better if possible, and that is always possible." © 2015 Vacheron Constantin

you can keep it operational but to be silent between 10pm and 8am. The central hands are the running minutes and two 'detached' split second chronograph hands; all are retrograde. The chronograph hands therefore start timing the same event and one can be stopped while the other continues. The watch includes a suite of functions devoted to the Hebraic calendar (which links 235 lunar months to a 19-year window): it tracks day and month number in the apertures at 8 and 4 o'clock, a 29 / 30-day lunar month on the sub-dial at 6 o'clock, and the 4-digit Hebrew date also at 6 o'clock. In the sub-dial at 9 o'clock the alternating indicator reminds the owner that it is a 12 or 13-month year (7 years during the 19-year cycle are 13 months long). The 19-year cycle is tracked in the sub-dial at 3 o'clock. The inner chapter ring of the sub-dial at 6 o'clock tracks the month and day of

the next Yom Kippur as per the Gregorian calendar. Flip the watch over and you have a Gregorian perpetual calendar and astronomical cockpit. Notable complications include the day number in the week (square aperture at 1 o'clock), week number (sub-dial at 3 o'clock), and a length of day / night reading has been added to the usual sunrise / sunset times. The outer ring of the sub-dial at 9 o'clock is a dual time display, complete with 24 cities on a wheel behind the aperture above it (and the respective day / night above that). The case has a few tricks up its sleeve too, by twisting the bow (the loop for the chain) a crown pops out of the band at 4:30 so the alarm barrel can be wound; and at 1 o'clock on the band is a small aperture displaying the crown position (R=winding the two barrels, C=sky chart correction and alarm setting, M=time setting).

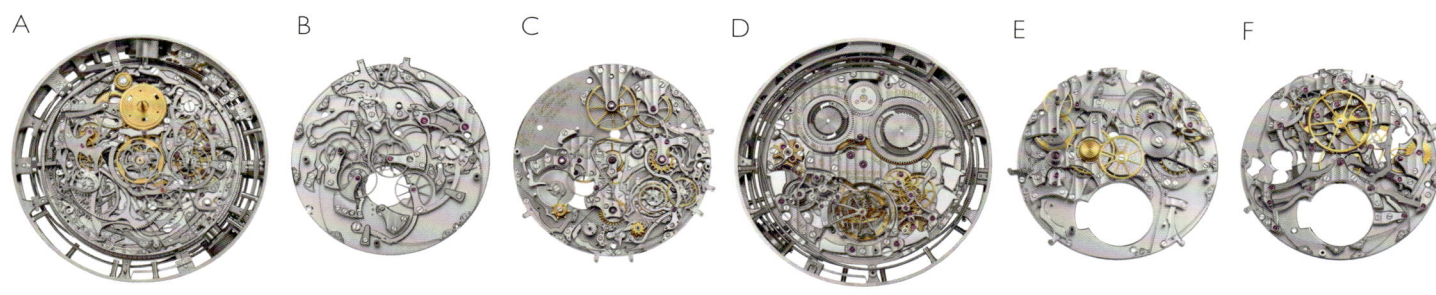

sonnerie (red hands) and the modes of the sonnerie (blue hands). The sub-dials at 3 and 9 o'clock indicate the day and month (blue hands), the chronograph minutes and equation of time (red hands). There are two additional 24-hour time zone indicators at 4:30 and 7:30, with a small leap year indicator and 24-hour reference to the running time at 4 and 8 o'clock. A 3-digit year indicator is located at 6 o'clock above the tourbillon, which functions as a subsidiary second indicator. The start / stop chronograph pusher is integrated with the crown, the pusher at 3:30 activates the flyback function. Two dual time indicators are changed by pushers at 5 and 7 o'clock, the sonnerie silence pusher is at 10 o'clock and the grand / petite mode selector is at 2 o'clock.

The Jaeger-LeCoultre Hybris Mechanica à Grande Sonnerie

Jaeger-LeCoultre's Hybris Mechanica à Grande Sonnerie is the second most complicated wristwatch in the world, with 27 complications. It is an exquisite perpetual calendar with flying tourbillon, jumping hours and minutes, and the full suite of chiming functions. The power reserve for the regular mainspring is at 12 o'clock as well as the leap year indicator. The retrograde date spans from 7 to 11 o'clock, and the retrograde month and weekday are indicated by small arrows that sweep around the dial. The four trebuchet hammers and gongs sound out the full Westminster chimes. The sonnerie mode is indicated at 6 o'clock, along with the state of its independent power reserve. A phenomenal amount of power is required to run a Westminster sonnerie; as a consequence, after six hours of grande sonnerie activity, which uses half of the full power of the mainspring, it will automatically switch to silent mode to preserve the power.

Comprising 1,406 component parts, the movement was designed to isolate the chiming mechanism from the keyless works and motion works. Aside from the integrated repeater button, the crown on the earliest versions was used solely for winding. The caseband had four pushers in two 'rows' (the two at 2 o'clock advancing the hour and minute hands, and the two at 4 o'clock regressing the minutes and alternating the sonnerie mode). The more recent models use two pushers with weekday correction at 2 o'clock and mode selection at 4 o'clock. Discreet pushers at 11 and 12 o'clock adjust the date and the month respectively. The crown is used to adjust the time when the 'M' setting is selected. Only three of these are produced a year, each by the combined efforts of six watchmakers, and the model is limited to 30.

The Franck Muller Aeternitas Mega 4

The Franck Muller Aeternitas Mega 4 possesses 36 complications and 1483 components, making it the world's most complicated wristwatch. Impressively, the watch indicates 25 of them on one dial. It features central hours, minutes and split chronograph seconds, at 12 o'clock is a date and chronograph hour indicator, both are retrograde, and a moon phase sits beneath. The fan-form registers at 2 and 10 o'clock indicate the reserve of the movement and the Westminster

Above: The Franck Muller Aeternitas Mega 4.
© 2012 Christie's Images Limited

Opposite: The Jaeger-LeCoultre Hybris Mechanica à Grande Sonnerie. © 2016 Jaeger-LeCoultre

The Patek Philippe ref. 5175 'Grandmaster Chime'

Released in celebration of the brand's 175th anniversary, the Patek Philippe ref. 5175 'Grandmaster Chime' has 20 complications and as the name suggests is a chiming juggernaut. The 18k rose gold case is hand engraved with laurel leaves and comprises 214 parts alone — arguably a complication in its own right. The two dials are reversible allowing the wearer to choose which one will face them. The main dial features central minutes and hours, with a gold second time zone indicator (with its moon-shaped day / night aperture at 2:30). The sub-dial at 12 o'clock provides a 24-hour alarm indicator and contains a bell-shaped alarm mode aperture. The sonnerie and movement reserve indicators are at 3 and 9 o'clock, and the sub-dial at 6 o'clock displays the date and moon phase. To the right of the sub-dial is a crown position indicator: R=Remontage (wind), A=Alarm, H=Hand setting. To the left is the sonnerie mode (Silent, Grande and Petite). The sonnerie has an 'isolator display', the aperture at 1:30, which turns red when the sonnerie is disengaged (due to low power or the operation of other conflicting mechanisms). The other side of the dial is dedicated to the calendar functions, indicating digital year at the centre, 24-hour running time at 12 o'clock, month at 3 o'clock, date and leap year at 6 o'clock, and weekday at 9 o'clock. Looking at the watch with the crown at 3 o'clock, the integrated pusher is a repeater button, the slide at 9 o'clock is the sonnerie mode selector, the pushers at 8 and 10 o'clock adjust the second time zone forward and backward, the pusher at 1 o'clock turns on / off the alarm, and at 4 o'clock is a rather unusual pusher — it activates a day-of-the-month repeater: double chimes for 10-day increments and single chimes for single days.

The Patek Philippe ref. 5175 'Grandmaster Chime'.

The Jaeger-LeCoultre Reverso Grande Complication à Triptyque

Being a Reverso, the watch is immediately at an advantage with its second dial. The Triptyque, as revealed by the name, uses three dials to spread its 19 complications without clutter. The front boasts a carrousel-style tourbillon, day / night 24-hour sub-dial, and a reserve indicator for the two days of power. The second dial delivers a sky chart with rotating zodiac wheel, central 24-hour sidereal hand. The sun hand indicates the equation of time and the two sub-dials indicate the sunrise and sunset times. The third dial, a perpetual calendar with moon phase, still faces the wearer and is viewed when the main dials are held in their transitional position. How does the third dial receive its power? First, it's not even a movement, it is a detached and dormant set of gears and sub-dials. At midnight, while the watch is running, a lever extends from the top of the reversible case and activates a pusher at the corresponding part of the back dial. This clicks the perpetual calendar ahead by one day. So the watch is effectively a single movement with two dials and the responsibility for managing an independent mechanical calendar.

The Jaeger-LeCoultre Reverso Grande Complication à Triptyque.
© 2016 Jaeger-LeCoultre

The Vacheron Constantin ref. 80250 'Tour de l'Ile'

Vacheron Constantin created just seven pieces of their highly complicated ref. 80250 'Tour de l'Ile', which for some might bear a passing resemblance to the equally complex Vacheron Constantin Maître Cabinotier Astronomica produced a few years later and mentioned in Chapter 2.7. Key differences on the front of the watch include the bezel-mounted repeater slide, 24-dual time dial at 11 o'clock, striking torque indicator at 1 o'clock, and the Geneva seal worn proudly on the dial at 4:30. The astronomical features on the back are similar to its younger sibling, it's the fine 'special anniversary guilloché' on the dial that stands out in comparison (all seven dials of the 80250 are different). The screw-down pusher at 8 o'clock is used in conjunction with the crown to set the sky chart.

The Patek Philippe ref. 5002 Sky Moon Tourbillon

Respect should be paid to the watch that employs a tourbillon but doesn't showcase it through an aperture, or even use a running seconds hand, as is the case with the Patek Philippe ref. 5002 Sky Moon Tourbillon. The front dial has gold central poire-shaped hour, and feuille-shaped minute hands, and a blued steel retrograde date indicator. The four sub-dials at 12, 3, 6 and 9 o'clock indicate the leap year, month, moon phase and weekday. On the back sits the 24-hour sidereal time, and the majestic sky chart / moon phase discs discussed in Chapter 2.7.

Above: The front and back dials of the Patek Philippe ref. 5002 Sky Moon Tourbillon. © 2016 Patek Philippe SA

Opposite: The Vacheron Constantin ref. 80250 'Tour de l'Ile'. © 2015 Vacheron Constantin

Bibliography

Textbooks

Daniels, George, *Watchmaking*. Philip Wilson Publishers, London, 1981.

Haldimann, Beat, *Haldimann Horology*. Haldimann Horology, Thun, 2005.

Reymondin, Charles-André, Monnier, Georges, Jeanneret, Didier and Pelaratti, Umberto, *The Theory of Horology*. The Technical College of the Vallee de Joux, Le Sentier, 1999.

Articles

De Bethune, 'De Bethune Resonique'. http://www.debethune-resonique.com/

DeCorte, Ron, 'The Urban Jürgensen P8 detent escapement', *Watch Around*, No.012, p.48, 2012.

Dje (username), 'SIHH 2007 Report: Secrets of Duometre', *WatchProSite*, April 2007. http://www.watchprosite.com/page-wf.forumpost/fi-2/pi-2217737/ti-362557/s-0/t—sihh-2007-report-secrets-of-duometre/

Doerr, Elizabeth, 'History Rebooted: The Chronograph's Inventor is...Louis Moinet!', *Forbes*, March 2013.

Doerr, Elizabeth, 'L-Evolution Tourbillon Carrousel by Blancpain: Whirlwind and Karussel Converge', *Quill & Pad*, June 2015.

Doerr, Elizabeth, 'The Harry Winston Opus Series: A Complete Overview from Opus 1 through Opus 13', *Quill & Pad*, May 2015.

Forster, Jack, 'In Plain Sight: Revealing the Secrets of F. P. Journe's Resonance Chronometer', *Revolution*, May 2014.

Forster, Jack, 'The Evolution of the Minute Repeater', *Revolution*, December 2012.

Forster, Jack, 'The MB&F Legacy Machine Perpetual Calendar, and Why it Matters to Anyone Interested in Watches', *Hodinkee: Hands-On*, November 2015.

Griffin, Shane, 'Technical Notes: Column Wheel vs Cam Actuated Chronographs', *Wound For Life,* August 2014.

International Organization for Standardization, *ISO 6425:1996, Divers' Watches*, July 1996.

Manousos, Nicholas, 'How Modern Watchmakers Are Grappling With One of Breguet's Greatest Inventions', *Hodinkee: Letters to the Editor*, July 2015.

Morrison, James, 'The Astrolabe'. www.astrolabe.org

Munchow, Joshua, 'Cartier Rotonde de Cartier Astromystérieux: An Illusion Inherited from the Father of Modern Magic', *Quill & Pad*, March 2016.

Munchow, Joshua, 'The 8 Most Accurate Moon Phase Wristwatches Today', *Quill & Pad*, July 2015.

Randall, Anthony, 'F. P. Journe's Chronomètre à Résonance', *Horological Journal*, British Horological Institute, March 2002.

Rogivue, Marc, 'Astrolabium Galileo Galilei'. Presentation based on Marcus Hanke, *The Trilogy of Time*. Ulysse Nardin SA, Le Locle, 2000.

'Ultimate Guide to the Heuer Solunar', *Calibre11*. http://www.calibre11.com/heuer-solunar/

Vacheron Constantin, 'Reference 57260'. http://reference57260.vacheron-constantin.com

General Product Reviews, Articles and Press Releases

0024 *WatchWorld Magazine*

www.ABlogToWatch.com

www.EuropaStar.com

HH Journal, Fondation del la Haute Horlogerie (FHH)

www.Hodinkee.com

www.ProfessionalWatches.com

QP Magazine

www.Quill&Pad.com

Revolution Magazine

www.WatchProSite.com

WatchTime Magazine

Visit the brand websites for technical specifications of all contemporary models.

This book is dedicated to my two sons, Seb and Wolfy

Acknowledgements

François Quentin at 4N; Frances Clift and Matt Sullivan at A. Lange & Söhne; Ariel Adams at ABlogToWatch.com; Nicolas Wiederrecht at Agenhor; Rachel Taliaferro at Ana Martins; Michael Philip Horlbeck at Andreas Strehler; Melody Bon at Angelus; Martin Braun at Antoine Martin; Nadine Rieck at Antoine Preziuso; Gaëlle Pantier at Arnold & Son; Aurelia Jouhanneau, Mark Schmid and Nour Karam at Audemars Piguet; Georgia Solomon at Bell & Ross; Stephannie Zeeck and Allison Kelso at BPCM; Lindsay Paterson at Breitling; Vincent Dupontreué at Breva; Stacey Kobelski at Bulova; Laetitia Hirschy and Pascal Brandt at Bvlgari; Carine Masson at Cabestan; Lauren Roffle at Cartier; Nikolas Parser at Cecil Purnell; Desiree Gallas and Brian Cheng at Chopard; Maria Reintjes at Christiaan van der Klaauw; Eliza Catenazzi, Vivian Chen, Cissy Ngan, Abbey Green, Charles-Henri Gounod, Amber Yu and Stephane von Bueren at Christie's; Alexandra Beurier at Christophe Claret; Nathalie Cobos at Comm' On Sàrl; Noémie Charpiot at Corum; David Deillon at Czapek & Cie; Tifanny Poupaert at De Bethune; Coco Rudolf and Vanessa Nyoundou at de Grisogono; Ron Jackson at Devon Works; Chia-Chia Thu at DeWitt; Wes Burke at Duber Time; Eva Zhang at Eterna; Brigitte Bocquet-Makhzani at F. P. Journe; Christina Hentschel at Glashütte Original; Sylva Greubel, Emmanuel Vuille and Sylvain van Muylders at Greubel Forsey; Bart and Tim Grönefeld at Grönefeld; Maria Habring at Habring²; Beat Haldimann; Caroline Buechler at Hautlence; Heather Wharton at Helvetia Time; Ben Clymer at Hodinkee; Richard Hoptroff at Hoptroff; Mike Margolis at Horology Works; Annabelle Galley and Romain Gourdain at Hublot; Paul Lerner and Kerry Aronchick at HWPR; Cloé Biessy and Bibiane Ferreira Oliveira at HYT; Jamie Williams at IWC; Cecile Tinchant at Jaeger-leCoultre; Kari Voutilainen; Jessica Gasser and Valentine Matray at Laurent Ferrier; Alysa McKenna at Longines; Aurélie Jordi at Louis Moinet; Ludovic Ballouard; Charris Yadigaroglou at MB&F; Satine Soukiassian at MCT; Iesha Reed and Sia Bondi and Montblanc; Yara Ainsworth at Moser & Cie; Jamie Hector at OMEGA; Jamie McCorry at Oris; Allison O'Brian at Panerai; Naomi Alonso at Parmigiani Fleurier; Kelley Smith and Noémie Steiner at Patek Philippe; Marie Ozaki at Perrelet; Britta Towle, Catherine Dillard and Marc Menant at Piaget; Theodore Diehl and Mikeal Lecor at Richard Mille; Erica Son at Roger Dubuis; Caroline Smith at Roger W. Smith; Steven Rogers at Romain Gauthier; Adeline Vernaz at Romain Jerome; Taisa Scors and Priscilla-Marie Ilarraza at Seiko; Natasha Berg at Shaman Abas; Tim Burlon at Sinn; Véronique Goerg at Speake-Marin; Catherine Eberle-Devaux at TAG Heuer; Lumpa Rossi at Terra Cielo Mare; Thomas Prescher; Nicole Baume and Romain Robert-Nicoud at Ulysse Nardin; Mercedes Gonzalez-Gorbena and John McBarron at Urban Jürgensen & Sønner; Marion Baudino at URWERK; Catanna Berger, Michelle Crowe and Vincent Brun at Vacheron Constantin; Meredith Keller and Kelsey Becker at Van Cleef & Arpels; Vianney Halter; Daniel Wechsler at Vulcain; Ines Berwanger at Zeitwinkel; Fabiana Chiacchio and Robert Lopes at Zenith; and to Sue Schmidt, Claire Wallace, Gary Getz, Rich Lopez, Magnus Bosse and François-Xavier Overstake.

Special thanks to Robert Dreyfuss, CEO of Eterna; John Reardon, International Head of Watches at Christie's; Elizabeth Doerr, Editor-in-Chief and co-Founder at Quill & Pad; Joshua Bale and Ryan Harrington, Certified Watchmakers at Betteridge in Greenwich CT; Catherine Pierre-Bon for French translation; Sue Bennett, James Smith and Craig Holden at ACC Art Books; and Tanya Schmidt for your constant support and belief in this project from day one.

Technical Index Page numbers in BOLD refer to images

Brands Index Page numbers in BOLD refer to images

British Library Cataloguing-in-Publication Data
A catalogue record for this book is available from the British Library

Frontispiece: The MB&F Legacy Machine Perpetual.   © 2016 MB&F

Title Page: Exploded Roger Dubuis Quatuor RD101 calibre.   © 2015 Roger Dubuis

Contents: The Angelus U20 Ultra-Skeleton and its A-250 calibre.   © 2016 Angelus

Endpaper: Calibre L001.1 of the A. Lange & Söhne Double Split.   © 2016 A. Lange & Söhne

Printed in Slovenia for ACC Art Books Ltd., Woodbridge, Suffolk, England

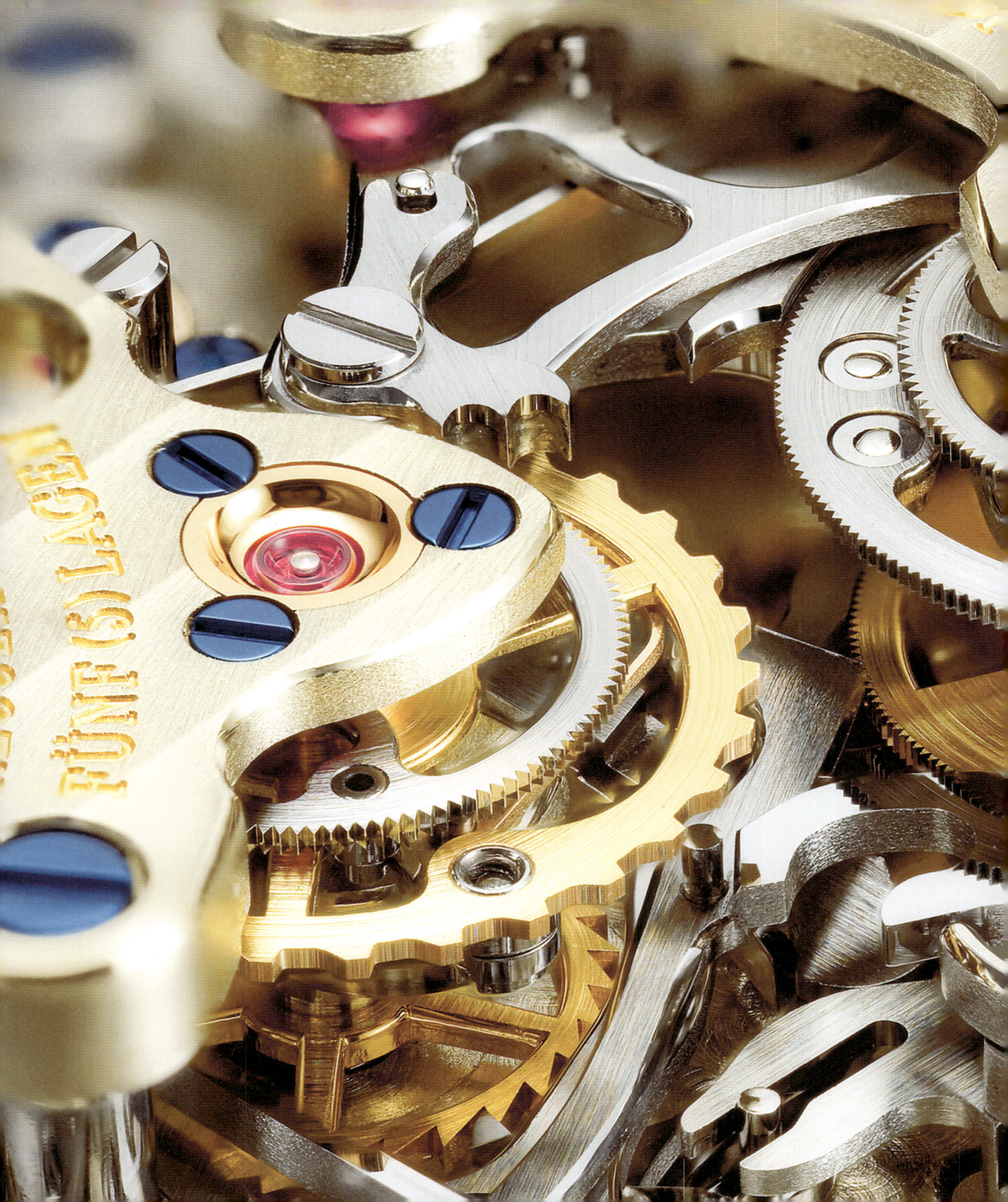